Milton and
the Book of Revelation:

The Heavenly Cycle

Austin C. Dobbins

Studies in the Humanities No.7
Literature

The University of Alabama Press
UNIVERSITY, ALABAMA

To Mama May
and
Daddy Dobbins

Copyright © 1975 by
THE UNIVERSITY OF ALABAMA PRESS
ISBN 0–8173–7320–9
Library of Congress Catalog Card Number: 73–22715
All rights reserved
Manufactured in the United States of America

CONTENTS

1. Before the Beginning   1
2. The War in Heaven   26
3. Orthodoxy and Confusion   53
4. Flight and Frustration   67
5. Sin and Death   86
6. Lust and Will   96
7. Justice and Mercy   110
   Conclusion   117
   Appendixes   121
   Notes   125
   Indexes   162

Preface

To many readers the most puzzling aspect of *Paradise Lost* is that portion of Milton's poem which is sometimes called the "heavenly" or the "celestial cycle" (P.L. I–VI, IX). In this portion of his epic Milton describes an actual war in heaven. The cause of this war Milton attributes to Lucifer's refusal to accept God's arbitrary proclamation of Christ as the future Ruler of the Angels. To this episode Milton adds a portrait of an apparently admirable villain. Cast out of heaven, in hell Lucifer (now Satan) refuses to admit defeat. Instead, joining forces with Sin and Death, his comrades-at-arms, Satan renews his rebellion against God. Having already corrupted a third of the angels, Satan proceeds to corrupt the whole of mankind.

What right had Milton to insert episodes of this nature in a poem which seeks to "justifie the wayes of God to men"? Theologically, reply a number of critics, Milton had very little right. Typical is the objection stated by James H. Sims.

> It is obvious that many of the cited passages from *Paradise Lost* ... have their roots in epic necessity and convention: the supernatural machinery of angels and demons, the scenes in Heaven and Hell, the dialogues between persons of the Godhead, the space devoted to the speeches of heroic characters (Books II, V, and VI), the long catalogue of names, the beginning *in medias res* with the later recounting of earlier events of the story, the description of mighty antagonists in single combat (Abdiel and Satan in Book VI), the maintenance of a highly dignified and serious style, and the repetition of certain epithets, phrases, and syntactical formulas.[1]

---

[1] *The Bible in Milton's Epics* (Gainesville, 1962), p. 217.

In the heavenly cycle, then, Milton's "justification" of God would seem more epic or classical than biblical: The War in Heaven is based upon four verses of Scripture (Revelation 12:4, 7–9). The remaining episodes of the heavenly cycle—in fact, the War in Heaven itself—are better explained in terms of literature, particularly epic literature, than in terms of the Bible.

This study suggests an alternate approach to *Paradise Lost*. The incidents which Milton describes in the heavenly cycle are epic and poetic. They are also, however, distinctly scriptural. Indeed, from Milton's point of view, the events of the heavenly cycle were far more scriptural than epic. The primary source of the heavenly cycle is the Bible, specifically the Book of Revelation. The incidents which have puzzled many readers—Christ's exaltation in eternity as the Son of God, the War in Heaven, the creation of Sin and Death, Satan's first flight from earth, the construction of the Bridge Across Chaos—Milton based directly upon a well-known Renaissance interpretation of the Bible.

To support this thesis, copious citations have been made from sixteenth- and seventeenth-century texts. The citations should not be regarded as "sources." An attempt has been made to refer to authors with whom Milton unquestionably was familiar (as Ames, Foxe, Junius, Pareus, Tremellius, Wollebius, and Zanchius). Other authors Milton may or may not have read. Milton's primary source was the Bible. The purpose of numerous references is to suggest the "commonplace" nature of many of the theological concepts which Milton presented in the heavenly cycle.

A word of appreciation should be expressed to the friends, critics, and students who have made this study possible. A special note of thanks is due the Directors of the Folger, the Duke, the Newberry, and the Huntington Libraries for grants in aid and for permission to study otherwise inaccessible texts. To co-workers and readers Helen Ensley, Margaret Brodnax, Jo Voce, Wilbur Helmbold, Samuel Mitchell, and others of the Samford University faculty and library staff, a warm thank you for useful counsel and advice. Without financial assistance from Samford University (Samford University Research Grant No. 37) publication of this study would have been impossible. Last but not least, to my family I should like to express heart-felt gratitude. To my wife—for her

constant encouragement and understanding, and for her willing-
ness to endure the trials of two sabbatical years—I am deeply
grateful. Without the unfailing interest and (no less important) the
scholarly advice of my parents, this study could not have been
undertaken.

AUSTIN C. DOBBINS
April 27, 1974   Samford University

CHAPTER ONE

Before the Beginning

This day I have begot whom I declare
My onely Son, and on this holy Hill
Him have anointed, whom ye now behold
At my right hand; your Head I him appoint;
And by my Self have sworn to him shall bow
All knees in Heav'n, and shall confess him Lord.
(P.L. V, 603–608)

Basic to the understanding of *Paradise Lost* is the meaning of the word "begot," a word which occurs in the initial, crucial scene of the poem. In an attempt to explain this term, scholars have turned to an apparently relevant passage in the fifth chapter of the first book of Milton's *The Christian Doctrine*. In this chapter, basing his argument upon Psalm 2, Milton maintains that the Father may be said "to have begotten the Son in a double sense, the one literal, with reference to the production of the Son, the other metaphorical, with reference to his exaltation" (C.D. V, 181, 13–16).[1] The action described in the opening scene of *Paradise Lost* scarcely would seem to be meant literally, that is, physically, in any human sense. Thus Kelley, with whom Gilbert, Rajan, Muir, Adams, Hughes, and Empson are substantially in agreement, maintains that in P.L. V, 603–608, Milton intended the word "begot" to be understood in the metaphorical sense of "exalted" or "glorified" as King of Heaven.[2]

This view of the meaning of the word "begot," unfortunately, would seem to raise as many problems as it resolves. The major objection is that, according to a second passage in *The Christian Doctrine,* the proclamation of the Son as King of Heaven in P.L. V, 603–608, cannot validly be termed metaphorical. In the fifth chapter of *The Christian Doctrine* Milton states specifically that

Christ may be considered begotten metaphorically *in two senses only:* first, with regard to his "resuscitation from the dead," and second, with regard to his "unction to the mediatorial office" (C.D. V, 183, 15–16). Neither of these conditions applies to the action which is depicted in P.L. V, 603–608. In *Paradise Lost* the proclamation of Christ as King is in no way related to Christ's (future) mediatorial activities on earth. The world has not yet been created. Thus, although in P.L. V, 603–608, the Son is "begotten," that is, "exalted" or "glorified" as King of Heaven, he is not, according to Milton's definition of the term in *The Christian Doctrine,* "begotten" (exalted) metaphorically.

The question of the proper nomenclature to be assigned to Milton's use of "begot" in P.L. V, 603–608, involves more than an academic quibbling over terms. A larger issue is at stake. If Christ's "begetting" in *Paradise Lost* has metaphorical significance, then Milton must be censured for having based the introductory scene of his epic upon art rather than upon Scripture. In P.L. V, 603–608, Milton has shifted the place and time of Christ's assumption of his mediatorial office as King from earth to heaven, from a period after the beginning of time to a period before the beginning. This shift, charge modern critics, is theologically unjustified. As the result, states Hutchinson, Milton has placed Christ's exaltation "not at the Ascension, as the New Testament writers appear to place it, but before the fall of the angels." Compounding his error, writes Kelley, "Milton has twice... presented this concept in scenes that occur long before Christ actually assumed his mediatorial duties."

"God himself is confused," states Broadbent. "It is not until after the creation of man that Christ assumes the messianic office of anointed liberator, and reigns by merit of his self-sacrifice."[3] By shifting the action of Christ's anointing from earth to heaven, Milton has turned his opening scene into a highly imaginative, dramatically plausible image of truth. Theologically, however, the interpretation upon which Milton has based his opening scene should be considered no more than "theological fiction" — "human truth," literary "embroidery" which, although poetically effective, is scripturally unsound.[4] As an expression of "poetic truth" the action in the opening scene of *Paradise Lost* has very real value. As dogmatic theology, however, the view that Christ was metaphorically "begotten" as King of Heaven before the creation of the world is distinctly questionable.

The criticism that Milton has used "fiction" to motivate the initial scene of *Paradise Lost* is, of course, not new. Using a slightly different argument, in 1698 Charles Leslie objected vigorously to Milton's "Groundless Supposition" that *"God, upon a certain Day in Heaven, before the Creation of this Lower World, did Summon All the Angels to Attend, and then Declar'd His Son to be their Lord and King."* Particularly distasteful to Leslie was Milton's use of Psalm 2:7, "Thou art my Son; this day have I begotten thee." Leslie's outraged reaction echoes across the centuries:

> To make the *Angels* Ignorant of the B. *Trinity;* And to take it ill to Acknowledge Him for their *King*, whom they had always Ador'd as their God; or as if the *Son* had not been their *King*, or had not been *Begotten* till that Day. This Scheme of the *Angels* Revolt cannot answer either to the *Eternal Generation* of the *Son*, which was before the *Angels* had a Being, or to His *Temporal Generation* of the B. *Virgin*, that being long after the *Fall* of the *Angels*.[5]

Much the same objection to Milton's use (or misuse) of Scripture was made by Daniel Defoe in 1726:

> This is, indeed, too gross; at this meeting he makes God declare the Son to be *that day begotten . . . ;* had he made him not begotten that day, but declared General that Day, it would be reconcileable with Scripture and with Sense; for either the begetting is meant of ordaining to an office, or else the eternal Generation falls to the ground; and if it was to the office (Mediator) then Mr. Milton is out in ascribing another fix'd day to the Work [P.L. III, 227–343]. But then the declaring him *that day,* is wrong chronology too, for Christ is declar'd *the Son of God with power,* only by *the Resurrection of the dead,* and this is both a declaration in Heaven and in Earth. Rom. i.4. . . . In a word, Mr. *Milton* has indeed made a fine Poem, but it is *the Devil of a History.*[6]

Since *The Christian Doctrine* was not published until 1825, Leslie and Defoe do not suggest, as do modern critics, that Milton deliberately (although artistically) founded the initial action of his epic upon unsound theology. However, turning to Psalm 2, the text which furnishes the basis for Milton's statements in *The*

Christian Doctrine, Leslie and Defoe come to much the same conclusion: The interpretation upon which Milton has based the action of P.L. V, 603–608, is theologically objectionable. It follows the explication neither of Augustine nor of Calvin, the two commentators whose interpretation of the Second Psalm seventeenth-century theologians generally regarded as "established" or "received." According to Augustine, "This day have I begotten thee" refers to Christ's eternal generation, before the creation of the angels, in the secret counsel of God.[7] According to Calvin, the passage refers to Christ's temporal generation, after the creation of the angels, in the presence both of the angels and man.[8] In *Paradise Lost* Milton has followed neither of the received interpretations. In P.L. V, 603–608, Christ's "begetting" is neither eternal (in "the secret counsel of God")[9] nor temporal (in "the church of all ages").[10] The result is (as critics from the seventeenth to the twentieth century have suggested) theological confusion. By picturing Christ as having been "begotten" in heaven in the presence of the angels, Milton apparently has confused the eternal with the temporal. (Christ's metaphorical generation has been transferred unjustifiably from earth to heaven.) This may be good poetry. It is scarcely, however, good theology.

The issue raised by the criticism that the initial episode of *Paradise Lost* is theologically questionable may be resolved, of course, by insisting that *Paradise Lost* is, after all, a poem, not a theological treatise. If the opening scene is not theologically valid, then it need not be studied as theology. As a highly imaginative passage, P.L. V, 577–802 (the larger passage), contains poetic value (skillfully designed tonal effects, masterfully contrived rhythms, harmoniously patterned images). It presents poetic truth (plausibly designed episodes, psychologically motivated characters, "epic" truth) of the highest order.

Comforting as this point of view may be—it at least justifies the reading and teaching of *Paradise Lost*—it somehow seems less than satisfactory. For much the same objection that is made against P.L. V, 603–608, may be raised against other episodes of Milton's epic. The War in Heaven, the allegory of Sin and Death, Satan's first flight from earth, the construction of the Bridge Across Chaos—each of these incidents is as invalid theologically as is P.L. V, 603–608. If the initial, crucial episode of *Paradise Lost* is based upon a scriptural misinterpretation—an interpretation which Milton himself knew was invalid—then the entire heavenly cycle of *Paradise Lost,* approximately half of the poem, must also be regarded as feigned. Christ was not exalted in heaven, Satan did not wage war against Christ, the rebel angels did not fall from heaven to hell—these and other incidents Milton deliberately contrived to support his fable. What follows? Surely, as Defoe suggested long ago (with a deliberately intended double meaning), "Mr. *Milton* has indeed made a fine Poem, but it is *the Devil of a History.*"

Perhaps an alternate suggestion is in order. This suggestion is that, regardless of assertions of critics to the contrary, Milton did not regard Christ's precreation begetting as a metaphorical and thus as a "fictional" event. Milton was a brilliant literary craftsman—surely the statement need not be argued! The action of P.L. V, 603–608, is, however, far more than a literary device which Milton utilized skillfully to provide his epic with an effective poetic beginning. To Milton, the view that Christ was exalted literally, in heaven, before the beginning of time was a serious statement of theological truth. This view, which will be discussed in some detail in the following pages, may or may not be accepted by Milton's readers. Acceptance or rejection is not the issue, however. The question under consideration is the extent to which Milton should be charged with having based a key episode of *Paradise Lost* (P.L. V, 603–608) upon a deliberate misinterpretation of Scripture and/or a consciously contrived poetic fable. The thesis of this chapter is that in his initial scene Milton did not deliberately misinterpret Scripture. To Milton, P.L. V, 603–608, represented considerably more than an artistically patterned fable. Indeed, in his epic Milton meant exactly what he wrote: Christ *was* exalted literally as the King of Heaven before the creation of the world.

To support this contention it is necessary to refer again to Milton's statements in the first book of *The Christian Doctrine*. In chapter five Milton declares that according to Scripture the Father may be said "to have begotten the Son in a double sense, the one literal, with reference to the production of the Son, the other metaphorical, with reference to his exaltation." It is generally assumed that "metaphorical" refers to Christ's "begetting," in eternity, as the King of Heaven. Since Christ's heavenly generation cannot be physical (literal), Christ's "begetting" in heaven must be metaphorical. ("Metaphorical" refers to the "exaltation" of the Son.) Need we assume, however, that Milton regarded the term "literal" as a synonym for "physical"? If the begetting of Christ in *Paradise Lost* is, as has been suggested, metaphorically intended, then the criticism that P.L. V, 603–608, is founded upon fiction must be accepted. If the begetting of Christ depicted in this scene has a literal significance other than physical or earthly, then the initial episode of Milton's poem presents a theological concept which, at least from Milton's point of view, may be defended. What does Milton mean by the terms "literal" and "metaphorical"? It would be worthwhile to examine Milton's statements in *The Christian Doctrine* in some detail.

In the fifth chapter of *The Christian Doctrine,* Milton attempts to demonstrate that Scripture does not justify the view that Christ was begotten from eternity. Romans 1:4, Colossians 1:18c, Revelation 1:4, Hebrews 1:4–5, 5:6, John 10:35–36, biblical texts which refer to Christ's generation on earth, as mediator between God and man, Milton maintains, do not prove that Christ was begotten from eternity. Moreover, Milton argues, John 1:1–3, 17:5, Colossians 1:15, 16, 18b, Revelation 3:14, I Corinthians 8:6, Ephesians 3:9, Hebrews 1:2–3, 10, passages which refer to Christ's generation in heaven, as Deity, are also used invalidly as proof of Christ's generation from eternity. According to Milton, the second group of passages prove

> the existence of the Son before the world was made, but they conclude nothing respecting his generation from all eternity. The other texts which are produced [the first group of texts cited above] relate only to his metaphorical generation, that is, to his resuscitation from the dead, or to his unction to the mediatorial office, [not to his physical generation,] according to St. Paul's own interpretation of the second Psalm: "I will declare the decree; Jehovah hath said unto me, Thou art my Son; this day have I begotten thee," which the apostle thus explains, Acts xiii. 32, 33. "God hath fulfilled the promise unto us their children, in that he hath raised up Jesus again; as it is also written in the second Psalm, Thou art my Son; this day have I begotten thee" (C.D. V, 183, 11–22).

In this passage, which in part has been quoted earlier, Milton argues that as commonly defined the terms "metaphorical" and "literal" are misapplied. According to Acts 13:32-33, Christ was begotten "metaphorically" in time as the Mediator, the Son of God, not as the Son of the Virgin. But Christ existed (was begotten) in heaven before he was begotten on earth. Thus, applied to Christ's heavenly generation, the term "literal" refers to Christ's begetting in eternity as the King of Heaven, the Son of God, not as Saviour or Redeemer. According to Psalm 2:7,

the first and most important [of God's SPECIAL DECREES] is that which regards his SON, and from which he [God] primarily derives his name of FATHER. Psal. ii. 7. "I will declare the decree: Jehovah hath said unto me, Thou art my Son, this day have I begotten thee." Heb. 1. 5: "Unto which of the angels said he at any time, Thou art my son, this day have I begotten thee?" (C. D. III, 89, 7–12; cf. V, 189, 5–9).

The decree, which was accomplished metaphorically in time, was declared in eternity. Properly interpreted, then, Psalm 2 (as well as Heb. 1:5) contains two levels of meaning. Neither level indicates that Christ was "begotten" either physically or from eternity. As the criticism by Leslie indicates, seventeenth-century theologians sometimes interpreted Psalm 2 in both senses. Milton questioned these interpretations. To Milton, whether on earth or in heaven, Christ was begotten as the Son of God. The "metaphorical" sense of Christ's begetting refers to Christ's generation on earth as Deity—as Mediator, not to Christ's incarnation. The "literal" sense of Christ's begetting refers to Christ's generation in (not from) eternity as the Son of God—as the King of Heaven, not as the Mediator.

The distinction which Milton draws here admittedly is confusing. Earth is literal, that is, real or actual. But heaven also is literal, real or actual. Depending upon one's point of view, then, the terms "literal" and "metaphorical" may be applied either to heaven or to earth. Both usages appear in Renaissance commentaries.[11] To Milton, only the first usage was legitimate. Properly interpreted, the context of John 1:1-3, Colossians 1:15, and Hebrews 1:2-3 is heaven. In these passages Christ is described *literally* as being "the Word" (John 1:1), "the image of the invisible God" (Col.

1:15) who, before the creation of the world, upheld "all things by
the word of his power" (Heb. 1:3). The context of John 10:35–36,
Acts 13:32–33, and Colossians 1:18c is earth. In these passages
Christ is described *metaphorically* as "the Son of God" (John
10:36), as the fulfillment of "the promise which was made unto the
fathers" (Acts 13:32), and as "the firstborn from the dead" (Col.
1:18c). The literal place of the Kingdom of God is heaven. In
context, then, "literal" is a term which properly applies only to
heaven. "Metaphorical" is a term which applies only to earth.
Literally, in heaven, Christ was "begotten" in eternity as the
"Head" of the angels (the angels "are not comprehended in the
covenant of reconciliation. . . . they are included under Christ as
their head, not as their Redeemer," C.D. IX, 99–101, 28–2).
Metaphorically, on earth, Christ was "begotten" in time as the
Mediator between God and man. In neither aspect of Christ's
generation was Christ "begotten" either physically or from
eternity.

   Indeed, to regard the term "physical" as a synonym for
"literal" is to charge Milton with compounding the confusion
which he himself charged against the theologians of his age. The
very basis of Milton's argument against the view that Christ was
begotten from eternity was his contention that theologians had
misapplied the biblical texts which refer to Christ's metaphorical
and literal generations. The relevant passage, again from the fifth
chapter of *The Christian Doctrine,* should be quoted in full:

> What Scripture says of the Son generally, they [theologians] apply,
> as suits their purpose, in a partial and restricted sense; at one time to
> the Son of God, at another to the Son of Man, now to the Mediator
> in his divine, now in his human capacity, and now again in his union
> of both natures. But the Son himself says expressly, "the Father
> loveth the Son, and hath given all things into his hand," John iii.
> 35.—namely, because "he loveth him," not because he hath
> begotten him—and he hath given all things to him as "the Son," not
> as Mediator only. If the words had been meant to convey the sense
> attributed to them by my opponents, it would have been more
> satisfactory and intelligible to have said, "the Father loveth
> Christ," or "the Mediator," or "the Son of Man." None of these
> modes of expression are adopted, but it is simply said, "the Father
> loveth the Son"; that is, whatever is comprehended under the name
> of the Son (C.D. V, 303–305, 23–10).

In *The Christian Doctrine* Milton objected to the use of Scripture for purposes for which (he felt) it was not designed. Some scriptural texts contain two levels of meaning. Thus Psalm 2 might be interpreted either metaphorically or literally. Other texts, such as John 1:1–3 and Hebrews 1:2–3, have but one sense, the literal. Still other texts, such as John 10:35–36 and Acts 13:32–33, are properly interpreted only on the metaphorical level. These and other passages which refer to the two aspects of Christ's generation (see above), Milton insisted, should not be combined indiscriminately. John 1:1–3 should not be used to explain the meaning of Acts 13:32–33. Hebrews 1:2–3 should not be understood in terms of the meaning of John 10:35–36. John 1:2–3 and Hebrews 1:2–3 refer to Christ's begetting in heaven as the Son of God, not to Christ's assumption of his office as mediator between God and man. John 10:35–36 and Acts 13:32–33 apply to Christ's begetting on earth as Mediator after, not before, his incarnation. None of the passages refers to Christ's generation from eternity. Nor—Milton's refusal to consider this interpretation of Christ's begetting is striking—do any of the passages refer to Christ's physical generation.

Milton's view that there are two levels of meaning which may be applied properly to Christ's "begetting" is basic in the theological assumptions which appear in *Paradise Lost*. In P.L. V, 603–608, Christ was not "begotten" in heaven in a confused metaphorical (earthly) sense as the mediator between God and man. Christ was "begotten" literally (in heaven) as the "Head" of the angels, the Son of God. As the Son of God, Christ was then exalted (not "begotten") in heaven in his "office" of mediator. To Milton, the meanings of the terms "begotten" and "office" are not the same. In the fifteenth chapter of *The Christian Doctrine* Milton defines the word "office":

> THE MEDIATORIAL OFFICE of Christ is that whereby, AT THE SPECIAL APPOINTMENT OF GOD THE FATHER, HE [the Son] VOLUNTARILY PERFORMED, AND CONTINUES TO PERFORM, ON BEHALF OF MAN, WHATEVER IS REQUISITE FOR OBTAINING RECONCILIATION WITH GOD, AND ETERNAL SALVATION (C.D. XV, 285, 3–7; cf. XVI, 303–313).

The word "office" Milton restricts to Christ's offer of himself as the means by which man might be reconciled to God. The term "begotten" refers to Christ's nature as divinity:

> . . . when the Son is said to be *the first born of every creature* [Col. 1:15], and *the beginning of the creation of God* [Rev. 3:14], nothing can be more evident than that God of his own will created, or generated, or produced the Son before all things, endowed with the divine nature, as in the fulness of time he miraculously begat [*procreavit,* brought forth] him in his human nature of the Virgin Mary (C.D. V, 193, 1–7). . . . I. Tim. ii. 5. "one mediator between God and man, the man Christ Jesus." Now he is not mediator inasmuch as he is man, but inasmuch as he is Θεάνθρωπος" [God-man] (C.D. XIV, 279, 22–24; cf. V, 303–305, 27–3, and 309, 3–5).

To Milton, Christ's mediatorial "office" was not "begotten" as a part of Christ's nature. First, in eternity, Christ was "begotten" as the Son of God. Then, in time, Christ was "begotten" as the Son of Man (Son of God and of Man). Before he was "begotten" as the Son of Man (Θεάνθρωπος), Christ was exalted (not "begotten") in his "office" as the mediator between God and man. This "office," which Christ voluntarily assumed, was not included in Christ's original "begetting." Christ first was "begotten" as the Son of God (P.L. V, 600–615). Then, freely expressing the will of the Father, before the fall of man, Christ assumed the "office" of mediator (P.L. III, 168–175, 227–322; XI, 1–44). Fulfilling his "office," both "God and Man," Christ then was "begotten" (not physically but metaphorically) on earth as Mediator (P.L. III, 313–316, 241–253; XII, 386–455).[12] Finally, in heaven, after he has fulfilled his mediatorial "office," Christ will re-ascend his throne as the Son of God (P.L. XII, 451–465).

To Milton, the view that Christ was "begotten" literally in eternity, as God rather than as God-man, was considerably more than a myth or a literary device which he might employ effectively as the basis of his epic. Such a conclusion misinterprets Milton's intention. In *Paradise Lost* Christ is first "begotten" as the Son of God. He assumes his mediatorial "office" after he has been "begotten." The two actions are not the same. First God proclaims the "begetting" of Christ as the Son of God:

> This day I have begot whom I declare
> My onely Son, and on this holy Hill
> Him have anointed, whom ye now behold.
>
> (P.L. V, 603–605)

Then God proclaims the Son's assumption of his "office" as the Son of Man:

> Because thou hast, though Thron'd in highest bliss
> Equal to God, and equally enjoying
> God-like fruition, quitted all to save
> A World from utter loss ...
> Here shalt thou sit incarnate, here shalt Reign
> Both God and Man, Son both of God and Man,
> Anointed universal King. ...
>
> (P.L. III, 305–308, 315–317)

The elevation of the Son to his universal throne does not, as has been suggested, repeat the same action twice. Nor does the scene represent a tautology which would have "disappeared in perfect revision." Nor is the Son "exalted to God's level as a reward for good behaviour, as it were."[13] Christ is already the Son of God. Christ is not "begotten" in heaven as Mediator (an Arian view). Nor is Christ "begotten" on earth physically (a Socinian view). Christ is "begotten" literally as the Son of God.

Throughout the heavenly cycle Milton's view that Christ was "begotten" as the Son of God is basic. Why did Lucifer rebel against God? Milton's answer was that Lucifer rebelled because Christ was "begotten" as the visible expression of the majesty of God. For this view Milton found considerable scriptural evidence.[14] In Psalm 2:7 God proclaims his decree: "Thou art my Son; this day have I begotten thee." In Psalm 110:1 God declares the same decree: "The Lord said unto my Lord, Sit thou at my right hand, until I make thine enemies thy footstool." In Revelation 5:5 one of the angels proclaims: "Behold, the Lion of the tribe of Juda, the Root of David, hath prevailed to open the book, and to loose the seven seals thereof." In Revelation 12:5, after the "man child" has been born, he is said to have been "caught up unto God, and to his throne." Interpreted literally, each of these four texts

reveals precisely what happened before the creation of the world:
Christ (the Son, the Lord, the Lion, the man child) was begotten
literally (not physically) as the Son of God (not as Mediator) in
eternity (not from eternity).

Modern commentators frequently suggest that in *Paradise Lost*
Milton was concerned with "matters on which the Bible is
virtually silent".... "For Milton the theologian, Scripture offered
little concrete or specific concerning Satan's early history."[15]
Milton would have disagreed. According to the four biblical texts
quoted above, the central event in eternity was the begetting of the
Son. Each of the texts presents an identical situation: The time is
eternity.[16] Rebellion is in procinct (Ps. 2:1–2, 8–9, 110:1–2; Rev.
6:1–4, 12:7). What is the cause of the rebellion? Milton's
answer—based upon four parallel texts of Scripture—is that the
rebellion could have been caused by one and only one event, the
exaltation of Christ as the Son of God.

In heaven, in the presence of the angels, the Son is "begotten"
as the King of Heaven:

> ... him who disobeyes
> Mee disobeyes, breaks union, and that day
> Cast out from God and blessed vision, falls
> Into utter darkness, deep ingulft, his place
> Ordaind without redemption, without end.
> (P.L. V, 611–615)

The occasion is clearly "nothing else but the instalment and
coronation of Jesus Christ."[17] Christ is proclaimed "victour,"
"conqueror," "King," the "Lord mightie in battaile,"[18] the
"Lion of the tribe of Juda." God necessarily speaks sternly,
dictatorially, perhaps even, as Pope has suggested, as a "school-
divine." The speech is eminently suitable. God speaks as a god of
authority and law, not as a god of mercy and love. Nor does the
Son, "the express image" of the Father, appear in his mediatorial
office. He is the Lion—the Messiah (the anointed one): To him
"shall bow All knees in Heav'n" (P.L. V, 607–608).

It is Christ's appearance as the "Lion" which provides the
impetus for Lucifer's revolt:

> Thrones, Dominations, Princedomes, Vertues, Powers,
> If these magnific Titles yet remain
> Not meerly titular, since by Decree
> Another now hath to himself ingross't
> All Power, and us eclipst under the name
> Of King anointed . . .
>
> (P.L. V, 772–777)

Lucifer complains bitterly to his as yet unfallen followers. The complaint scripturally is well founded. According to Revelation 5:3, prior to Christ's appearance God existed absolutely, solely as the Sovereign of Heaven (Rev. 4:2–3).[19] Christ, of course, existed, but he existed invisibly, unbegotten and unrevealed, the unseen glory of the Father. "Strange point and new!" says Lucifer, paraphrasing Psalm 24:8. "Who is this King of glory?"[20] (He is "The Lord strong and mighty, the Lord mighty in battle.") With the appearance of the Son, the King of Glory, Lucifer rebels and falls.

In ascribing the motivation of Lucifer's rebellion to Christ's begetting as the Son of God, Milton was well aware that he was presenting a controversial view. Virtually all seventeenth-century commentators held that Lucifer's original sin was pride (I Tim. 3:6; John 8:44; Isa. 14:13; Ezek. 28:2). The cause for Lucifer's pride was a matter of disagreement, however. Many theologians held that the Scriptures assigned no definite cause for Lucifer's fall. Speculation as to cause was, therefore, foolish, perhaps even blasphemous.[21] Other commentators felt that in his pride Lucifer fell because he had convinced himself that he was self-sufficient and needed not the assistance of God. Therefore he refused to worship the majesty of God.[22] Still other biblical scholars stated that Lucifer's pride took the form of rebellion against God's proclamation of the Son as the future mediator between God and man. Lucifer and his followers "were not contented with the truth of the Gospell Concerning Christ propounded to them at the beginning, and . . . they chose to leave their heavenly mansion, then [than] subscribe to the truth."[23]

To Milton none of these views was satisfactory. To be sure, Lucifer's original sin was pride (P.L. I, 36; V, 665; VI, 131).

Lucifer fell because he refused to accept his place as a creation of God (P.L. V, 792–793, 853–861; VI, 418–422). But what was the immediate cause, the initial incident which provoked Lucifer's pride? To Milton, the answer of the Bible was simple and clear: Christ was begotten "to rule all nations with a rod of iron" (Rev. 12:5; Ps. 2:9). Lucifer rebelled because Christ was begotten *literally* as the Son of God, not because Christ was elevated to his office or begotten as the Son of Man.

To assume otherwise would be to accept the view that Christ's begetting depended upon man's creation and fall. By no means was this the case. Christ was begotten, as Milton later makes Adam state in P.L. VIII, 419–421, of the free will of God, without reference to antecedent cause, intermediate circumstance, or future condition. "Necessitie and Chance," states God, "Approach not mee, and what I will is Fate (P.L. VII, 172–173). Theologians who maintained that the "begetting" of Christ in heaven referred to Christ's assumption of his mediatorial "office" might be willing to impose limits upon God. Milton was not. The only restriction which Milton placed upon God involved a restriction which God, according to Milton, placed upon himself by granting his creatures freedom of will. To Milton, this was an absolute gift or, to use theological terminology, an absolute decree, a decree which was unqualified by any future act of man. Thus, unless God decreed man's fall, Christ could not have been "begotten" initially in heaven as Mediator. First man must exercise freedom of choice. Until then there was no necessity that Christ mediate between God and man.

Milton's point of view may be compared profitably with the views of two of his contemporaries. "In God," wrote Wollebius, [there is but]

> one only will, which is called the will of his *good pleasure,* because out of his most free good pleasure he hath decreed what shall be done. It is called also his *antecedent* will; because it had existence before any creature, and from eternity with God it was established: It is named also *absolute,* because it depends upon Gods good pleasure, and not from the things that are done in time. Lastly, it is called *secret,* because in respect of priority it is known neither to men nor Angels.[24]

Polanus, claiming the authority of Augustine, presented much the same point of view:

> The will of God is an essential proprietie of God, by which he willeth all the things that he willeth, and that from all eternitie, of himselfe also, and that by one constant act. And this will is most free, so that God doth not any thing, or command or suffer it to be done, but freely willing [wills] it: whereupon also it is called Gods free will. . . . By this he willed to create the world: by this he gave the Messias: by this he will raise vp at the last all the dead. By this all things are done necessarily, that is to say, whatsoeuer God willeth by his absolute will, that is necessarily done: for this wil of God, is the necessitie of things. So saith Augustine lib. 6. de Genes ad litteram. cap. 15.[25]

The principal difference between Milton's view and the views quoted above appears in the definition of the word *absolute*. To Wollebius and Polanus, God was a being who from eternity, before the creation of man, willed absolutely, that is, completely, freely, and without qualification, all things that he willed. Thus, necessarily, the "begetting" of Christ as Mediator was included in God's original (and final) decree regarding man. To question this view was to challenge a basic tenet of Christianity—

> election presupposes the decree of the fall . . . , the eternal decree of God, by which he determined within himself whatever he wished to happen with regard to every man. All are not created on equal terms, but some are preordained to eternal life, others to eternal damnation. . . .[26]

To Milton, this Calvinistic interpretation of God's absolute decrees was objectionable. To be sure, God's original decree of freedom of choice was absolute—absolutely free, complete, and without condition. However, a decree which elected some to salvation and others to reprobation scarcely should be called a free decree. Less objectionable, certainly more reasonable, was the position attributed to Aquinas by Francisco Suárez, Milton's contemporary:

> . . . in accordance with the opinion which many attribute to the Divine Thomas, God predestined the Incarnation as a second plan after the sin of Lucifer . . . ; therefore the second plan could not have the Incarnation as its cause, without setting aside the predestining

power of an all-knowing God. The preceding is proven since God did not preordain the Incarnation until after Eve sinned, for originally and as it were similarly the Incarnation had been preordained as a remedy for those who sinned; thus, as the authors of this opinion contend necessarily, if Adam had not sinned the present state of the decree would not have been possible: but the sin of Eve follows the sin of the angels in the order of causation; since, inducing man to sin, the evil angel was the cause; therefore, clearly, the sin of the angel preceded the purpose of the Incarnation in the divine prevision; therefore the cause of sin could not have been the Incarnation.[27]

To Milton, God's original decree was absolutely free, complete, and unconditional, unlimited by the future activities of man. Thus, unless God restricted his decree, Lucifer's fall could not have been occasioned by God's proclamation of Christ as the future mediator between God and man. Result is not cause. It was this ringing challenge to the type of Calvinism represented by Wollebius and Polanus that underlay Milton's depiction of the literal "begetting" of Christ as the Son of God:

Seeing, then, that God has predestined from eternity all those who should believe and continue in the faith, it follows that none can be reprobated, except they do not believe or continue in the faith, and even this rather as a consequence than a decree; there can therefore be no reprobation of individuals from all eternity. For God has predestined to salvation, on the proviso of a general condition, all who enjoy freedom of will.... For otherwise one of God's decrees would be in direct opposition to another.... Whatever, therefore, was left to the free will of our first parents, could not have been decreed immutably or absolutely from all eternity (C.D. IV, 141, 19–26; III, 77, 4–5; 79, 11–13).

From a metaphorical point of view, after the creation of man, Christ's begetting might be regarded as a "necessary" act on the part of God. In heaven, however, begotten not as the Mediator but as the Son of God, Christ's generation was wholly independent of necessity.[28] Only by confusing the two senses in which Christ might be said to have been "begotten," according to Milton, was it possible to contend that Christ's begetting in heaven depended upon necessity rather than upon the free will of God.

To Milton, not only was it theologically questionable to attribute Christ's begetting to contingency but such a view contradicted the

Bible. Psalm 2, Psalm 110, Revelation 5, and Revelation 12 (with the more general statements of John 1:1–3, Col. 1:15, and Heb. 1:2–3; see above) offered clear evidence that Christ was begotten in eternity as the Son of God.[29] Revelation 5, moreover, furnished "proof positive" that Christ was begotten solely as the Son of God, as divinity, not as the divine-human redeemer of the world.

In Revelation 5:2–11, John, the human author of the Book of Revelation, hears an angel proclaiming with a loud voice:

> 2 Who is worthy to open the book, and to loose the seals thereof? 3 And no man [οὐδείς, no one] in heaven, nor in earth, neither under the earth, was able to open the book, neither to look therein. 4 And I wept much [writes John], because no man was found worthy to open and to read the book, neither to look thereon. 5 And one of the elders saith unto me, Weep not: behold, the Lion of the tribe of Juda, the Root of David, hath prevailed to open the book, and to loose the seven seals thereof. 6 And I beheld, and, lo, in the midst of the throne and of the four beasts, and in the midst of the elders, stood a Lamb as it had been slain, having seven horns and seven eyes, which are the seven Spirits of God sent forth into all the earth. 7 And he came and took the book out of the right hand of him that sat upon the throne. 8 And when he had taken the book, the four beasts and four and twenty elders fell down before the Lamb, having every one of them harps, and golden vials full of odours, which are the prayers of saints. 9 And they sung a new song, saying, Thou art worthy to take the book, and to open the seals thereof: for thou wast slain, and hast redeemed us to God by thy blood out of every kindred, and tongue, and people, and nation; 10 And hast made us unto our God kings and priests: and we shall reign on the earth. 11 And I beheld, and I heard the voice of many angels round about the throne and the beasts and the elders: and the number of them was ten thousand times ten thousand, and thousands of thousands.

The time is eternity (Rev. 5:1, 12:1; Ps. 2:7, 110:1).[30] "Round about the throne" of God (Rev. 5:11, 4:4) appear the encircling angels, "the beasts and the elders" with their "ten thousand times ten thousand" ensigns (Rev. 5:11, 4:8; Ps. 68:17):

> 2 And immediately I was in the spirit; and, behold, a throne was set in heaven, and one sat on the throne. 3 And he that sat was to look upon like a jasper and a sardine stone: and there was a rainbow round about the throne, in sight like unto an emerald. 4 And round about the throne were four and twenty seats: and upon the seats I saw four and twenty elders sitting, clothed in white raiment; and

they had on their heads crowns of gold. 5 And out of the throne
proceeded lightnings and thunderings and voices: and there were
seven lamps of fire burning before the throne, which are the seven
Spirits of God (Rev. 4:2–5).

Christ, whose presence is at first unknown to the angels (Rev. 5:3,
4:2–3; Ps. 2:7), appears "in the midst of the throne" (Rev. 5:6,
12:5; John 1:18; Col. 1:15; cf. pp. 50–52 below), at "the right hand"
of the Father (Rev. 5:7; Ps. 110:1; Heb. 1:3), to "open the book"
(Rev. 5:5, 9, 6:1; John 3:35) of the secret decrees of God.[31]

The scene unquestionably is the same as that which Milton
presents in P.L. V, 577–615:

As yet this world was not, and *Chaos* wilde
Reignd where these Heav'ns now rowl, where Earth now rests
Upon her Center pois'd, when on a day...
As Heav'ns great Year brings forth, th' Empyreal Host
Of Angels by Imperial summons call'd,
Innumerable before th' Almighties Throne
Forthwith from all the ends of Heav'n appeerd
Under thir Hierarchs in orders bright
Ten thousand thousand Ensignes high advanc'd,
Standards, and Gonfalons twixt Van and Reare
Streame in the Aire, and for distinction serve
Of Hierarchies, of Orders, and Degrees;
Or in thir glittering Tissues bear imblaz'd
Holy Memorials, acts of Zeale and Love
Recorded eminent. Thus when in Orbes
Of circuit inexpressible they stood,
Orb within Orb, the Father infinite,
By whom in bliss imbosm'd sat the Son,
Amidst as from a flaming Mount, whose top
Brightness had made invisible, thus spake.
    Hear all ye Angels, Progenie of Light,
Thrones, Dominations, Princedoms, Vertues, Powers,
Hear my Decree, which unrevok'd shall stand.
This day I have begot whom I declare
My onely Son, and on this holy Hill
Him have anointed, whom ye now behold

At my right hand; your Head I him appoint;
And by my Self have sworn to him shall bow
All knees in Heav'n, and shall confess him Lord:
Under his great Vice-gerent Reign abide
United as one individual Soule
For ever happie: him who disobeyes
Mee disobeyes, breaks union, and that day
Cast out from God and blessed vision, falls
Into utter darkness, deep ingulft, his place
Ordaind without redemption, without end.

The time is eternity (P.L. V, 577–583). Around the throne of God appear the orders of the angels (P.L. V, 587), 'Orb within Orb'' (P.L. V, 596), with "Ten thousand thousand Ensignes high advanc'd" (P.L. V, 588). Christ, of whose visible existence the angels are at first unaware (P.L. V, 603, 679–682), appears "imbosm'd" in the "midst" of the throne (P.L. V, 597, 598), at the "right hand" of God (P.L. V, 606), to publish the decrees of God (P.L. V, 605–615).

Renaissance theologians constantly cited Revelation 5 as proof that Christ was begotten initially as the Mediator ("the Lamb slain from the foundation of the world," Rev. 13:8). Milton rejected this exegesis. According to Revelation 5:5, Christ could not have appeared in heaven first in his divine-human form. In Revelation 5:5 one of the elders (one of the angels) states that Christ, "the Lion of the tribe of Juda, the Root of David, hath prevailed to open the book." But it is not as the Lion that Christ appears to open the book. He appears as the Lamb. What, then, is the function of the Lion? Renaissance theologians tended either to ignore the problem or to maintain that the two designations of Christ referred to Christ's two-fold messianic functions, first, as the conqueror of the devil, and, second, as the saviour of man. Christ, both as the Lion and as the Lamb, simultaneously triumphed over the devil and redeemed mankind in his victorious crucifixion, resurrection, and ascension to heaven. George Gyffard states the typical view:

> ...our Lord Iesus, in respect of the enemies, namely the diuell, death, and sinne, hath shewed himselfe as a mightie conquering Lion, euen that Lord mightie in battaile: for he vanquished and

spoyled them, . . . but in respect of his redeemed, he is that lambe of
God which taketh away the sinnes of the world [Matt. 22:44, Ps.
110:1, I Cor. 15:25, Ps. 68:18, Ephes. 4:8, Gen. 49:9, Ps. 24:8, Col.
2:15, John 1:29].[32]

To Milton the type of explication advanced by Gyffard was
unsatisfactory. Certainly Christ was the "lambe of God which
taketh away the sinnes of the world" (John 1:29). As the "Lamb"
Christ assumed his "office" as mediator (opened the book) in
heaven before the foundation of the world (P.L. III, 213–415). But
Christ did not appear, nor did he open the book, in heaven solely as
the Lamb. Before he was revealed as the Lamb, Christ was visible
(at least to one of the angels) as the "Lion." In heaven, Christ was
first begotten as the Lion, the Son of God ($\alpha \nu \alpha \tau \epsilon \tau \alpha \lambda \kappa \epsilon \nu$, Heb.
7:14; Ps. 110:5; Isa. 11:1–4; Zech. 3:8), without reference to the
creation of man or to the victory on the cross. It was the
appearance of Christ as the "Lion" that led directly to the
rebellion of Lucifer.

Doctrinal interpretation might present a different point of view.
Thus, for example, the Apostles Creed stated that Christ ascended
the throne of God only after he had completed his earthly ministry
as mediator between God and man. Scripture, literally interpreted, led to a different conclusion. According to Psalm 110:1
(P.L. V, 606) Christ sat at the right hand of God in heaven before
he assumed his mediatorial office.[33] Doctrinal interpretation might
maintain that the angels were not created in eternity. A literal
explication of Revelation 5, however, stated otherwise. Doctrine
might insist that Christ was initially revealed as the Redeemer.
Literally interpreted, contended Milton, the Bible stated that
Christ was first begotten as the Son of God. He was and is "the
Lion of the tribe of Juda," the "Lord mightie in battaile" (Ps.
24:8), the conqueror of "the enemies . . . the diuell, death, and
sinne" (Matt. 22:44; Ps. 110:1, 68:18; *not* I Cor. 15:25; Ephes.
4:8). The scriptural distinctions between the literal and the
metaphorical generations of Christ, declared Milton repeatedly in
The Christian Doctrine, must not be confused.

One of the most interesting aspects of Milton's concept that
Christ was begotten literally as the Son of God appears in the
changes which Milton made in the structure of Revelation 4–5 as

the result. Two shifts in structure are apparent: 1) In Revelation 4:2–5 God is pictured absolutely; Christ is not depicted until after he is described in Revelation 5:5 as the Lion of Juda. 2) In Revelation 4:8–11 the beasts and the elders (angels) sing their praise and cast their crowns before God as creator before Christ is revealed either as the Lion or as the Lamb; in Revelation 5:8–10, 12–13, the beasts and the elders sing their songs and offer their tribute to Christ as redeemer after Christ appears as the Lamb. In *Paradise Lost* Milton has combined the description and action of Revelation 4 with the description and action of Revelation 5. P.L. V, 577–627, contains details drawn from Revelation 4:2–5 and 5:5–7. P.L. III, 344–391, brings together details from Revelation 4:8–11 and 5:8–10, 12–13.

For rearranging the structure of Revelation 4–5 Milton might be criticised for altering the order of biblical incidents to suit his poetic purposes. (P.L. V, 603–608, is "theological fiction.") The criticism (again) would not be justified, however. Milton's interest in Revelation 4–5 (Rev. 4:2–5, 5:5–7, as well as 5:5–6) was more theological than poetic. The combination of Revelation 4:2–5 with Revelation 5:5–7 further emphasizes the theological concept which has been discussed throughout this chapter: Christ was begotten literally as the Son of God. In P.L. V, 577–627, Milton focuses the attention of his reader upon God the Father-SON rather than upon God the FATHER and the Son. Except in one line (P.L. V, 596), God is not pictured as existing alone or independently of the Son. In P.L. III, 344–391, the angels sing Hosannas and cast their crowns "inwove with Amarant and Gold" (P.L. III, 352) in token of their praise of Christ, the Son, whom they adore and honor as God. God is first praised as the Creator; immediately, almost simultaneously, Christ (God) is praised as the Redeemer. In both passages the Son is presented as being one with the Father, the visible expression of God.

In magnifying the position of Christ as the Son of God, Milton unquestionably altered the chronology of Revelation 4–5. Interestingly enough, however, if Milton had not followed the "fictional" order of Revelation 4–5 in his epic, to Milton's contemporaries the theology of *Paradise Lost* indeed would have been objectionable. If Milton had not combined the descriptions and actions of

Revelation 4–5, the result would have been Arianism. Christ would have been presented as a created being, a being distinctly inferior to God.

In Revelation 4:2–5, as Renaissance theologians well knew, God was depicted, solely and separately, as absolute God.[34] The angels cast their crowns and sang their praise to God as the Creator, not as the Son or as the Redeemer. Christ, the Son, was neither described nor worshipped until he appeared as the Lion-Lamb in Revelation 5:5–7. Most commentators on Revelation avoided the Arian implications of these two passages by insisting that Revelation 4:2–5 and Revelation 5:5–7 were identical in meaning. In both passages Christ was God. In Revelation 4:2–5 Christ existed either invisibly in God (John 1:18; I John 4:12), or visibly as God in the symbols of the jewels and the rainbow of God's throne (Rev. 4:3).[35] There was no need for the Son to be worshipped separately or apart from God, stated the commentators. In casting their crowns and in singing their anthems before God, truly the angels worshipped both God and Christ, Christ and God. In Revelation 4:2–5 the Son existed co-eternally with the Father. The same statement applied to Revelation 5:5–7. In his visible manifestation as the Lion and as the Lamb in Revelation 5:5–7, the Son was equally as divine as he had been in Revelation 4:2–5. In every important aspect Revelation 4:2–5 and Revelation 5:5–7 were identical.

It is foolish, maintained Bullinger, Fulke, Brightman, Pareus, Boys, à Lapide—indeed, virtually every commentator on the Book of Revelation, Protestant or Catholic, during the sixteenth and seventeenth centuries—to attempt to separate the nature of Christ and God.[36] The two are the same essence, co-equal and co-eternal. Concerning Revelation 5:6, wrote William Fulke,

> ...the lambe apeareth in the middest of the throne, that the equalyte of the diuine glorie he hath with the father might be shewed. Away therfore with the cursed impietie of the heretiques, which pratleth y[t] Christ is not equall with the father, when as S. Ihon sawe him in the middest of the throne, and of the 4. beastes and 24. elders, by which figures the greatest maiestie & glorie of the mightye God is described.... Christ therefore came out of the bosome of his father and out of the middeste of the throne, an interpreter of Gods diuine will and pleasure, and for our instruction

hath opened the booke whiche he tooke oute of the right hand of him
that sat vpō the throne.

Clearly, stated Pareus, when

> Iohn speaketh of the office of Christ, as hee is our mediator, [this]
> doth not diminish the equalitie of the son, with the father, but
> supposeth it: because so as he was meer man, or a creature of what
> power soever, he could not have performed the workes of a
> mediator.

In his human nature, concluded Renaissance theologians, Christ
was inferior to God. In his divine nature, however, Christ was
God.

To some theologians (the "heretiques" to whom Fulke referred)
this solution of the textual difficulty presented by Revelation 4:2–5
and Revelation 5:5–7 was scarcely satisfactory. Ribera and
Alcazar, two well-known "Arian" theologians, for example,
maintained that Revelation 4 and 5 were not identical in meaning.
Interpreted sequentially—that is, according to the order of their
appearance in the Bible—declared Ribera and Alcazar, Revelation 4:2–5 and 5:5–7 "proved" that Christ was not "begotten"
equal to God. Perhaps the clearer statement of this view is that of
Francisco Ribera (1602):

> In this [Rev. 5:5–7], however, because Christ is said to come to
> the Father, Christ is shown to be less than God, in so far as He is
> man, not having equal honor with the Father. For the Father is
> seated; He stands, and He comes to the Father, not the Father to
> Him. He receives the book, as if it is assigned to Him alone, that He
> may open it, that He himself who is the judge and Master of all men,
> may pronounce the penalties and order them to be inflicted.[37]

In Revelation 4:2–5 John described God as existing absolutely. In
Revelation 5:5–7 Christ appeared before "the throne" to take "the
book" from God. These were not the actions of an equal.
Literally, therefore, Christ was a created being, a being inferior to
God.

To Milton, neither of the interpretations discussed above
presented an accurate view of the nature of Christ and of God.
Milton seems to have accepted the conclusion of most theologians
that Revelation 4:2–5 and 5:5–7 were identical in meaning (struc-

ture). The distinction between Christ as the Lion (Rev. 5:5) and Christ as the Lamb (Rev. 5:6), however, Milton maintained. Initially, Milton insisted, Christ was not "begotten" with a divine-human nature. (Certainly Christ was not a created being.) Initially Christ was "begotten" as the wholly divine Son of God. Thus, in *Paradise Lost,* Christ is not represented as taking "the book out of the right hand of him that sat upon the throne" (God). Christ appears instead "in the midst of the throne" (Rev. 5:6, 4:3), that is, "in the bosom of the Father" (John 1:18; P.L. V, 597; cf. III, 169, 239). As God, Christ appears *seated* on the throne with the Father. As the Son, he appears *at the right hand of* God (Rev. 5:1, 7; P.L. V, 606, VI, 747; cf. III, 279.)[38] In his visible aspect, Christ is inferior to God. It is only in his visible aspect, however, that Christ is inferior to God. Otherwise Christ is God. God is invisible—except to his Son.

> Only when alone with him is he unshrouded; . . . in the midst of the angels, who could not have sustained his brightness, he [God] envelopes himself in a cloud, and though he suffers only the extremity of his rays to appear beneath it, all heaven is dazzled, the seraphim cover their eyes with their wings.[39]

This is the meaning of Milton's identification of Revelation 4:2–5 with Revelation 5:5–7. To the angels, God is invisible. As the visible image of God, therefore, Christ initially could not have been equal to God. Whether visible or invisible, however, Christ is God. So far as the reader of *Paradise Lost* is concerned, the Son and the Father are One. Christ is the only begotten Son of the Father, the agent by whom all things are created; he is the visible manifestation of God.[40]

For depicting Christ's begetting in heaven as the Son of God, Milton has been criticised for presenting a distorted, fictionalized view of Scripture. This was the opposite of Milton's intention. In presenting the view that Christ was begotten literally in eternity Milton sought to be theologically exact. To Milton, Christ was not God-created. Nor was Christ initially begotten as a being partly human and partly divine. To Milton, Christ was God. In *Paradise Lost* Milton might well have presented an Arian or a Socinian point of view. Christ could have been begotten as the Son of Man rather than as the Son of God. This view Milton rejected as unscriptural. In heaven, literally, Christ was begotten as the Son of God. On earth, later, in the fullness of time, Christ was begotten as the Son of Man. To Milton, the two-fold begetting of Christ represented the most important events both in eternity and in time. In heaven Christ's begetting furnished the basis for Lucifer's rebellion. On earth Christ's begetting made possible the salvation of mankind.

CHAPTER TWO

The War in Heaven

> ...now storming furie rose,
> And clamour such as heard in Heav'n till now
> Was never, Arms on Armour clashing bray'd
> Horrible discord, and the madding Wheeles
> Of brazen Chariots rag'd; dire was the noise
> Of conflict; over head the dismal hiss
> Of fiery Darts in flaming volies flew,
> And flying vaulted either Host with fire.
>   (P.L. VI, 207–214)

It is a critical commonplace to state that in *Paradise Lost,* and in particular in the episode of the War in Heaven (P.L. VI), Milton sought to imitate (emulate) the devices of epic poetry. Milton's allusions to the writings of Homer, Virgil, Hesiod, Ariosto, Tasso, Du Bartas, Spenser, and other poets of the past are deliberate. In one passage Lucifer is Achilles sulking because he has been forced to obey the authority of Agamemnon; in another passage he is Turnus fighting valiantly, albeit foolishly, against Aeneas; in still a third passage he is a Titan fighting against Zeus. Christ is an epic hero; he is also Jupiter with his awe-inspiring chariot, his "three-bolted Thunder," and his countenance "full of wrauth bent on his Enemies." In detail after detail—soliloquies and personal combats, armaments of the angels, the wounding of Lucifer, the spoiling of the landscape of heaven—Milton refers his reader to classical and poetic sources.

The reader who fails to recognize the allusive nature of Milton's poetry misses much of the grandeur of the Battle of the Angels. Books V and VI of *Paradise Lost* are a carefully designed mosaic of epic allusions and practices. To restrict one's study to this aspect of Milton's poem, however, does Milton an injustice.

Milton's literary allusions are important. They are not, however, primary. The basis for Milton's picture of the War in Heaven is the Bible, not the writings of the poets—great and near-great—of the past.

It is worthwhile to pause at this point, for if Milton's primary sources for the War in Heaven are Homer, Virgil, Ariosto, and other great *poets*, then the view that Milton's account of the War in Heaven is irreverent, even profane, would seem to have considerable validity. "Theophilus," writing in the *Gentleman's Magazine* in 1738, states the criticism clearly:

> Tho' we are taught by an inspired Apostle, that there was War in Heaven (if that Passage in the *Apocalypse* is to be understood according to the Letter); yet to me it seems, at least, unbecoming the Reverence due to Religion; if it be not very prophane, professedly to take the Advantage of Fiction in order to embellish a Poem, pretended to be built upon religious Truth, and to make so free with the Scriptures of God's Word, as to introduce so many Circumstances purely invented. But neither is this all; for had this been done any Way analogously with what is revealed, it had been pardonable; but being quite otherwise, it must argue ye Poet to have had but little Respect for those Holy Books (March, 1738, p. 124).

As a poet Milton had every right to present poetical fiction as truth. Theologically, however, according to commentators both old and new, Milton had no right to "improve" the Scriptures. Theologically, if Milton's portrayal of the War in Heaven is no more than "fiction" or an "epic device," then the account of the war is decidedly questionable, perhaps even blasphemous.[1]

It is impossible, of course, to defend Milton objectively from the charge of irreverence. Irreverence and reverence are both qualities which are incapable of objective proof. To the extent that the charge of irreverence is based upon the view that the War in Heaven is primarily an epic device, however, the charge can be challenged. The War in Heaven is far more than an epic or a literary device. The primary source for the War in Heaven is the Bible, not the writings of classical and Renaissance poets. Throughout his description of the war Milton consistently employs four biblical texts. These texts are, as has been suggested earlier, Psalm 2, Psalm 110, Revelation 5, and Revelation 12. Of particular importance are the latter two texts.

In Psalm 2:7 (Ps. 110:1; Rev. 5:5, Rev. 12:5), Christ (the Lord, the Lion of Juda, the man child) is revealed to the angels in heaven as the only begotten Son of God: "Thou art my Son; this day have I begotten [יְלִדְתִּיךָ, begotten or brought forth] thee." Immediately there is rebellion:

> 3 . . . behold a great red dragon. . . . 4 And his tail drew the third part of the stars of heaven, and did cast them to the earth: and the dragon stood before the woman which was ready to be delivered, for to devour her child as soon as it was born. 5 And she brought forth a man child, who was to rule all nations with a rod of iron: and her child was caught up unto God, and to his throne (Rev. 12:3–5).

Lucifer and his angels meet in council against the "man child" (Christ):

> 2 The kings of the earth [מַלְכֵי־אֶרֶץ, Molocs] set themselves, and the rulers take counsel together, against the Lord, and against his anointed [מָשִׁיחוֹ, Christ], saying, 3 Let us break their bands asunder, and cast away their cords from us (Ps. 2:2–3).[2]

Then Abdiel, the "Servant of God" who warns that God's anger (רֹגֶז) will rest upon "the land of the North" (Rev. 7:1–4; Zech. 6:1–8; Eccles. 10:4; Isa. 14:12–13), reports the decision of the rebel angels: Lucifer and his followers have refused the "just Decree of God" that "every Soule in Heav'n Shall bend the knee" to Christ, the "rightful King" (P.L. V, 814–818; VI, 19–21). Rebellion has broken into open war.

First, when Christ was "begotten" as the Son, there was rebellion. Then

> 7 . . . there was war in heaven: Michael and his angels fought against the dragon; and the dragon fought and his angels, 8 And prevailed not; neither was their place found any more in heaven. 9 And the great dragon was cast out, that old serpent, called the Devil, and Satan, which deceiveth the whole world: he was cast out into the earth, and his angels were cast out with him (Rev. 12:7–9).

This war John, the human author of the Revelation, also described in Revelation 6:1–8:

> 1 And I saw when the Lamb [the Lion; see Chapter 1] opened one of the seals, and I heard, as it were the noise of thunder, one of the four beasts saying, Come and see. 2 And I saw, and behold a white

horse: and he that sat on him had a bow; and a crown was given unto him: and he went forth conquering, and to conquer. 3 And when he had opened the second seal, I heard the second beast say, Come and see. 4 And there went out another horse that was red: and power was given to him that sat thereon to take peace from the earth, and that they should kill one another: and there was given unto him a great sword. 5 And when he had opened the third seal, I heard the third beast say, Come and see. And I beheld, and lo a black horse; and he that sat on him had a pair of balances in his hand. 6 And I heard a voice in the midst of the four beasts say, A measure of wheat for a penny, and three measures of barley for a penny; and see thou hurt not the oil and the wine. 7 And when he had opened the fourth seal, I heard the voice of the fourth beast say, Come and see. 8 And I looked, and behold a pale horse: and his name that sat on him was Death, and Hell followed with him. And power was given unto them over the fourth part of the earth, to kill with sword, and with hunger, and with death, and with the beasts of the earth.

These two passages furnish the major scriptural bases for Milton's account of the War in Heaven. In heaven, Christ, the mighty *Lion* of Juda, unseals the book of God's decrees (P.L. V, 600–615). When the first seal is opened, a rider appears seated upon a white horse (P.L. VI, 748–892). Christ is the rider of the white horse (or chariot) who appears when the book is opened. He is also the Lion who unseals the book. Both as the Lion and as the rider of the white horse Christ "conquers" (Rev. 6:2) "the dragon" (Lucifer) "and his angels" in heaven. The occasion of the war is the opening of the seals. When Christ appears to open the seals (is "begotten" as the Lion, the Son of God), Lucifer rebels. Michael and his angels fight unsuccessfully against the dragon. Then (Rev. 6:2, 7; 12:9–10) Christ enters the action. As the rider of the white horse, Christ conquers the dragon.

Milton's account of the War in Heaven is based upon a "literal" interpretation of Revelation 12:7–9 and Revelation 6:1–8. Initially, according to Milton, it is the Lion (not the Lamb) who opens the book of God's decrees. The result is "war in heaven." In heaven, literally, as the Lion, the rider of the white horse, Christ first defeats evil. Later, metaphorically, as the Lamb, the rider of the white horse, Christ conquers the forces of evil on earth. First, however, there is "war in heaven." In this war, after Michael and his angels prove unsuccessful in their attempts to defeat the devil,

Christ, the Lion, the rider of the white horse, conquers Lucifer and casts him from heaven.

For authority to describe Christ as the ultimate victor over Satan in heaven, Milton turned directly to the Bible (Rev. 6:2, 7, 12:9–10; Ps. 68:18, 110:5; Matt. 22:44; Col. 2:15). For authority to state that first, under the leadership of Michael, the loyal angels waged war unsuccessfully before Christ intervened, Milton also turned to the Bible. Interpreters of Revelation 12:7, wrote Milton in *The Christian Doctrine,* generally identify Michael as Christ. According to the exact wording of this text, however, declared Milton, it was Michael—not Christ—who led the army of God in the initial conflict with the devil. Christ

> vanquished the devil, and trampled him under foot singly; Michael, the leader of the angels, is introduced in the capacity of a hostile commander waging war with the prince of the devils, the armies on both sides being drawn out in battle array, and separating after a doubtful conflict (C. D. IX, 105, 20–25).[3]

Christ alone was the victor over the devil. This view Milton based upon a careful analysis of Revelation 12:5–10 and Revelation 6:2–8. According to the first passage, although exalted ("caught up unto God, and to his throne") as the Son of God in Revelation 12:5, Christ did not exert his power until he appeared in Revelation 12:10 ("Now is come salvation, and strength, and the kingdom of our God, and the power of his Christ: for the accuser of our brethren is cast down") as the conqueror of Lucifer and his angels. Similarly, in the second passage, although described as the rider of the white horse in Revelation 6:2, Christ did not intervene in the war against Satan until after he had opened the third seal of the book of God's decrees in Revelation 6:5–6. In both Revelation 12:5 and 6:2, John described Christ's actions by prolepsis, that is, before they actually occurred.[4] First Michael led the forces of God against the forces of the devil: "Michael and his angels fought against the dragon . . ." (Rev. 12:7). Then Christ trampled Satan "under foot singly." Until Christ appeared to vanquish the devil, however, the outcome of the battle was doubtful.

Indeed, as is stated in Colossians 2:15 (P.L. VI, 660–670):

> the day was lost, man with the wofull issues of the conquest, was either cast downe wallowing in bloud, or scattered with pursuing

crueltie.... Now one man commeth into the field in the right of
Millions (that could not stand in their owne quarrell) challengeth the
victors, with singular compassion calleth backe the scattered,
raiseth a mightie expectation, exposeth himselfe to the danger, with
incredible fury is encountred, one with Millions or Legions of
Deuils, of incomprehensible rage, and long beaten experience....[5]

The quotation refers to a biblical text which is generally considered to refer to Christ's victory over Satan on earth. But what is
earth if it is not "the shaddow of Heav'n, and things therein Each
to other like" (P.L. V, 575–576)? Heaven is the macrocosm of
which earth is the mirror.[6] In heaven, as on earth, "Michael and
his angels fought against the dragon." The angels "with the wofull
issues of the conquest" were "either cast downe wallowing in
bloud, or scattered with pursuing crueltie...." Then, on the third
day, Christ intervened to defeat the forces of Evil.

What right had Milton to specify that the War in Heaven
continued for two days before Christ exerted his power? Again
Milton's authority was the Bible. According to Revelation 6:3–8,
the "war in heaven" (metaphorically the earthly war of the Church
against evil) *did* continue for three "days" or "instants" or
"periods of time." In Revelation 6:3–8, when Christ, the Lamb
(the Lion), opened the second, third, and fourth seals of the book
of God's decrees, three horses and horsemen, symbols of rebellion, appeared. The three horses, according to the repeated
statements of commentators upon the Revelation, actually "unum
sunt, qui exierunt post album et contra album: et sessorem habent
diabolum, qui est mors."[7] Christ rode the white horse of Victory
(Rev. 6:2). Opposed to Christ was Lucifer, the rider of the red,
black, and pale horses of War, Famine, and Death (Rev. 6:3–8).
This exegesis, literally applied, furnished the basis for Milton's
division of the War in Heaven into three days or periods of time.
On the first day Michael led his hosts against the forces of the red
horse (Rev. 6:3–4). On the second day he led his angels against the
forces of the black horse (Rev. 6:5–6). First the loyal angels fought
indecisively; then, with the appearance of Christ, the rider of the
white horse, Lucifer and his angels were vanquished and cast out
of heaven.

The war in Revelation 6:1–6 was the same war which John
described in Revelation 12:7–10. At first, "Michael and his angels

fought [successfully] against the dragon..." (Rev. 12:7a). Then, during the second phase of the battle (the second "day" or "instant" of time), Lucifer and his followers almost overcame the loyal angels ("the dragon fought and his angels...," Rev. 12:7b). The combat, moreover, according to reputable theologians, was both individual ("Michael... and the dragon fought") and general (Michael's "angels fought" with the dragon's "angels"). In Revelation 12:7, wrote Bullinger and Gyffard, for example:

> S. Iohn... describeth the singular fight of one most excellent, to witte Michaell, which ouercame the Dragon: and describeth the general fight annexed with ye particular.... For Michael fighteth whiche is as captaine of this warre: And Michaelles Angelles fight also: which must be wel discerned, although that Michaell & his Angels make but one parte only. On the other side fighteth the dragō, as emperour of this warre, & his angels fight also.[8]

> here are named the captaines on both parts in this battell, together with their armies. Michael and his Angels on the one side for the Church, and the dragon and his Angels on the other side against the Church. Here is then the ioyning of the battell, they both fight, yea they all fight on both sides, both the captaines and their armies.[9]

The War in Heaven begins. On the first day Michael and Lucifer face each other in single combat:

>   ...likest Gods they seemd,
> Stood they or mov'd, in stature, motion, arms
> Fit to decide the Empire of great Heav'n.
> Now wav'd thir fierie Swords, and in the Aire
> Made horrid Circles; two broad Suns thir Shields
> Blaz'd opposite....
> Together both with next to Almightie Arme,
> Uplifted imminent one stroke they aim'd
> That might determine, and need not repeate,
> As not of power, at once; nor odds appeerd
> In might or swift prevention; but the sword
> Of *Michael* from the Armorie of God
> Was giv'n him temperd so, that neither keen
> Nor solid might resist that edge: it met
> The sword of *Satan* with steep force to smite
> Descending, and in half cut sheere, nor staid,

> But with swift wheele reverse, deep entring shar'd
> All his right side; then *Satan* first knew pain. . . .
> (P.L. VI, 301–306, 316–327)

The description abounds with epic allusions. The combat is classical *(Aeneid,* IX, 749–755, XII, 304–310; *Iliad,* XVI, 114–121, XXI, 173–187). Lucifer's (untarnished) shield is the shield of Achilles *(Iliad,* XIX, 373). His sword is the sword of Turnus *(Aeneid,* XII, 728–733). Like Turnus, Lucifer is overmastered and wounded. From his side forthwith

> A stream of Nectarous humour issuing flow'd
> Sanguin, such as Celestial Spirits may bleed.
> (P.L. VI, 332–333)

The allusion is clearly Homeric:

> From the clear vein a stream immortal flowed,
> Such stream as issues from a wounded god.
> *(Iliad,* V, 340ff.)

It is also biblical. Indeed, basically it is more biblical than it is Homeric. Throughout the Battle in Heaven Milton consciously has amplified his descriptions with details drawn from Homer, Virgil, and other great writers of the past. The term "amplified" is employed deliberately. The classical allusions which Milton uses in his account of the War in Heaven enlarge the meaning and expand the action of the poem. They do not provide the meaning and the action, however. The combat between Michael and Lucifer exists primarily not because it is epic but because it is scriptural. The basic frame of reference is the Bible, not the classics.

The contention between Michael and Lucifer (Abdiel and Lucifer, Gabriel and Moloc, Uriel and Adramelec) furnishes an excellent example of Milton's general practice. Details of the incident allude to the classical combat between Aeneas and Turnus *(Aeneid,* XII, 697–952). Milton's primary reference, however, is to Revelation 12:7 ("they both fight, yea they all fight on both sides, both the captaines and their armies"). The structure of the combat is scriptural. Michael takes his sword from the

"Armorie of God" (Jer. 50:25; Heb. 4:12; Rev. 1:16). His shield—as radiant as the sun—is the "shield of faith" (Eph. 6:16; I John 5:4). When Michael and Lucifer fight, necessarily Lucifer's sword must be sheared in half and Lucifer must retreat sorely wounded. Lucifer's sword (Rev. 6:4) is the sword of war and destruction. Michael's sword is the "sword of the Spirit" (Eph. 6:17) which pierces "even to the dividing asunder of soul and spirit, and of the joints and marrow" (Heb. 4:12). When Michael, "Like to God," meets Lucifer, "the Morning Star," the result of the combat is foreordained. The "sword of the Lord" is raised in heaven (Isa. 34:5–6, 14:19) and the beast, "that old serpent, called the Devil, and Satan," receives a "deadly wound" (Rev. 13:3, 12, 14; Joel 2:6–8).[10] "And I saw," wrote John, "one of his heads as it were wounded to death; and his deadly wound was healed" (Rev. 13:3). Essentially the dragon and the beast are one.[11]

> . . . then *Satan* first knew pain. . . .
> Yet soon he heal'd; for Spirits that live throughout
> Vital in every part, not as frail man
> In Entrailes, Heart or Head, Liver or Reines,
> Cannot but by annihilating die.
> (P.L. VI, 327, 344–347)

The allusions in Milton's description of Michael's combat with Lucifer are classical. The structure and the basic meaning, however, are scriptural. Indeed, the underlying structure of the entire War in Heaven is so distinctly scriptural that it is difficult to select single details for comment. Revelation 12:7 states that "Michael and his angels fought against the dragon." Thus Michael and at least one angel, Abdiel (the faithful "Servant of God"), must confront Lucifer in single combat. Michael and Lucifer, "stars" (angels) of heaven, face each other like "Two Planets rushing from aspect maligne Of fiercest opposition in mid Skie" (P.L. VI, 313–314). Lucifer, struck by Abdiel, falls like "a great mountain" (Rev. 8:8):[12] "as if on Earth Winds . . . had push't a Mountain from his seat" (P.L. VI, 195–197). The angels of God march high above the ground like "Birds in orderly array" (P.L. VI, 74; Isa. 6:2; Rev. 4:8).[13] Lucifer's army comes from the North (Isa. 14:13; Zech. 6:8; Joel 2:20). The battle begins with the sounding of "Th' Arch-Angel trumpet":

> . . . now storming furie rose,
> And clamour such as heard in Heav'n till now
> Was never, Arms on Armour clashing bray'd
> Horrible discord, and the madding Wheeles
> Of brazen Chariots rag'd; dire was the noise
> Of conflict; over head the dismal hiss
> Of fiery Darts in flaming volies flew,
> And flying vaulted either Host with fire.
> So under fierie Cope together rush'd
> Both Battels maine, with ruinous assault
> And inextinguishable rage. . . . all Air seemd then
> Conflicting Fire.
>   (P.L. VI, 203, 207–217, 244–245)

The biblical source for the trumpet and the dreadful events that follow is Revelation 8:6–8:

> 6 And the seven angels which had the seven trumpets prepared themselves to sound. 7 The first angel sounded, and there followed hail and fire mingled with blood, and they were cast upon the earth: and the third part of trees was burnt up, and all green grass was burnt up. 8 And the second angel sounded, and as it were a great mountain burning with fire was cast into the sea: and the third part of the sea became blood.

The trumpet is the trumpet of the first angel. The "storming furie," the "fiery Darts," and the "Conflicting Fire" correspond to the "hail and fire mingled with blood" which fall upon the third part of the inhabitants of heaven. Lucifer, as has been suggested, is the "great mountain" that falls. As the footnotes in the editions of Newton, Todd, and Verity demonstrate clearly, many of these details (fighting in personal combat, use of swords and darts, floating in the air like gods) are poetic in nature. They are also—and far more meaningfully—scriptural.

Milton's use of the Bible may seem "strained" (even "wildly imaginative") to modern readers. Seventeenth-century readers of Pareus, Cowper, and Mayer would have understood exactly what Milton has done in describing Lucifer's revolt. First, Milton's account of the War in Heaven is "literal." Milton's descriptions are based upon biblical texts which reputable theologians have applied literally to the Kingdom of Heaven (as distinguished from

the Kingdom on earth) from the time of, say, Origen (c. 254)[14] to
that of Pareus (1622), Milton's favorite commentator upon the
Revelation.[15] Second, in depicting the Battle in Heaven Milton
has deliberately paralleled Revelation 12 with Revelation 6 *and*
Revelation 8. This second statement should be underscored and
repeated. Milton's references to Revelation 12:4 in P.L. VI, 156,
to Revelation 8:7 in P.L. VI, 203, to Revelation 6:4 in P.L. VI,
324, are not "strained" or "wildly imaginative" allusions.[16] To
Milton, as well as to a number of his contemporaries, these
passages in Revelation were related. The Book of Revelation,
declared Pareus, Cowper, and Mayer, is composed of a series of
visions (seven) which are parallel, not successive or linear:

> ... we must remember: That howsoever the Revelation may seeme
> to be one continued *Vision:* yet indeed it is not one, neither revealed
> at one time, but are many distinct Visions, to wit, *Seven* [Preface,
> Rev. 1:1–9; (1) Rev. 1:9–3:22; (2) Rev. 4:1–7:17; (3) Rev. 8:1–11:19;
> (4) Rev. 12:1–14:20; (5) Rev. 15:1–16:21; (6) Rev. 17:1–19:21 (7)
> Rev. 20:1–22:21]. ... divers Visions by changed types do represent
> the same period of the Ecclesiasticall History.[17]

> *Sic eadem multis modis repetit Ioannes in Apocalypsi* [Augus-
> tine]. ... in this Booke the same things are many waies repeated. ...
> This is a maine point· most needefull to bee obserued for the
> vnderstanding of this Booke: the neglect, or not obseruation of it,
> hath bred vnto many Writers inextricable difficulties; which may
> bee tryed by this one Argument; that they who goe through this
> Prophecie by one continuall course of time, making alway the
> former chapter prior in time to the subsequent, when they come to
> the twelfth chapter, there they finde themselues straited, they are
> forced there to interrupt their course, and to come backe againe
> unto the dayes of Christ and state of the Church Primitiue.[18]

> ... these Trumpets [are parallel] with the Seales, at the opening
> whereof, issued first a white horse, here is fire and haile mingled
> with bloud, as the effect of the Apostles preaching amongst the
> wicked Iewes. Secondly, a red horse, here is a burning mountaine,
> hot persecution stirred vp by the Heathen Emperours to the
> destruction of many. Thirdly, a blacke horse, here a Starre falleth
> from Heauen, setting forth the Authors of bitter heresies. Fourthly,
> a pale horse, here the Sunne, Moone, and Starres are said to be
> darkned, all things growing corrupt in the Church.[19]

Underlying the statements of Pareus, Cowper, and Mayer is the
assumption that the place of the opening of the seals is earth, not

heaven: Christ was "begotten" in heaven as the Lamb, the Redeemer of the World, rather than as the Lion, the Ruler or King of Heaven. This assumption Milton rejected. Milton accepted, however, the structural aspect of the interpretations of Pareus, Cowper, Mayer—or the other commentators who expressed similar views.[20] Structurally, the Book of Revelation contains a number of visions which are parallel in time, place, and action. In each vision or groups of chapters certain ideas are repeated. Revelation 6:4, for example, contains details which also appear in Revelation 8:7–9 and Revelation 12:7. Particulars of Revelation 6:5–6 (Rev. 8:10–11, 12:7) are further explained in Revelation 6:12 (Rev. 9:17–18) and Revelation 8:12. The relationship of the groups of chapters or visions is not exact, of course. Each group of chapters presents different aspects of the preceding vision. The incidents in each vision, however, are generally parallel. In each vision the context is rebellion and war.

When was this rebellion? According to Pareus, the war referred to in Revelation 12:7 took place in time—on earth, not in heaven.

> *The place* of the war was heaven. But heaven is a place of peace, not of war: of quietnesse[,] not of dissention. It is so indeed. This is therefore to be attributed onelie to the Vision, the which I ohn saw in the heaven above.[21]

With this restricted, figurative interpretation of the Book of Revelation Milton disagreed. True, metaphorically the war against Satan was (and is) an earthly war. But earth is not "heaven." First, literally, according to Revelation 12:7, war was fought in heaven. The instigator of this war was Satan (Lucifer),

> first Gods most excellent creature, and most bounden subiect, who by rebelling agaynst the maiestie of God, of the bryghtest and most glorious angell, is become the blackest and most foule feende & deuill.[22]

This was the view of no less an authority than John Foxe, the eminent martyrologist and author of *Eicasmi Sev Meditationes, In Sacram Apocalypsin* (1587):

> Well, and at what time will [does] this fall of the Dragon occur? After the woman's giving birth or before [Rev. 12:1–7]? If after the birth, what shall we reply then to those who argue from the passage

in Jude, the brother of James, from Isaiah, and from the opinion of
the ancient theologians, concerning the fall of Lucifer and the ruin of
the angels, who, they assert, not observing his origin, had fallen
from their heavenly home long before the birth of Christ? [Marginal
Gloss: Solution. Two-fold Lucifer fallen from heaven.] Let me
answer this objection: We may not deny this, that Lucifer was
driven from heaven with his angels before the coming of Christ to
earth. But nothing hinders, however, that it also may be true that
this passage refers to both times of Lucifer's ruin, as well as to
others also.[23]

Foxe's view that Revelation 12:7 contained two levels of
interpretation found support not only in the Anglican Book of
Homilies (quoted above) but also in the writings of Thomas
Tymme (1605) and Thomas Manton (1658) as well as in the
writings of many of the Fathers of the Church.[24] Wrote Manton:

That Scripture I confess is mystical, and speaketh of the overcum-
ming of Sathan in this present world, and casting him out of the
Church, which is there expressed by *Heaven,* as the *World* by
Earth ... but however there is a plain allusion to Sathans first fall
from Heaven, as the ground of these expressions, and therefore I
may use that place as a proof in this matter. . . .

First, in eternity, there was a "war in heaven"; later, in time, this
war was continued on earth. In heaven, frustrated in his rebellion
against God, Satan was unable to "throwe down all the starres, but
onely a third part, so as two third parts remain still in their orbes &
shining" (Rev. 8:7–12, 12:1–7).[25] Instead, conquered by Christ,
Satan himself was cast from heaven: "Here in the beginning of the
Battell he [Christ] appeares riding on a white Horse, and there
again neere the end of the Battel, he appeares with his Warriours
riding on a white Horse [as] mighty Conqueror" (Rev. 6:2, 8,
12:1–7).[26]

The view that the Book of Revelation contains literal and
metaphorical meanings as well as parallel passages (as Rev.
8:7–12, 12:1–7, 6:2, 8) has direct relevance to Milton's account of
the War in Heaven. On the first day of the war, Michael and his
angels overcome the forces of Lucifer, the rider of the red horse, in
personal combat. The details of the combat (swords engaging
swords, darts hissing through the air, the heavens turning lurid
with fire) Milton found in the parallel accounts of Revelation 12:7,

6:4, and 8:7–9. A similar statement applies to Milton's description of the second day of the War in Heaven. On the second day of the conflict, the fighting becomes general and the hosts of Lucifer, the rider of the black horse, overpower the forces of God with artillery:

> ...chaind Thunderbolts and Hail
> Of Iron Globes, which on the Victor Host
> Level'd, with such impetuous furie smote,
> That whom they hit, none on thir feet might stand,
> Though standing else as Rocks, but down they fell
> By thousands, Angel on Arch-Angel rowl'd.
>   (P.L. VI, 589–594)

Michael and his angels retaliate by picking up the hills of heaven and casting them at their foes:

> ...terrour seis'd the rebel Host,
> When coming towards them so dread they saw
> The bottom of the Mountains upward turn'd....
> [They] in imitation to like Armes
> Betook them, and the neighbouring Hills uptore;
> So Hills amid the Air encounterd Hills
> Hurl'd to and fro with jaculation dire,
> That under ground, they fought in dismal shade;
> Infernal noise; Warr seem'd a civil Game
> To this uproar; horrid confusion heapt
> Upon confusion rose: and now all Heav'n
> Had gon to wrack, with ruin overspred,
> Had not th' Almightie Father [intervened].
>   (P.L. VI, 647–649, 662–671)

The basis for Milton's account of these two incidents again is the Bible, specifically Revelation 12:7, 6:5–6, and 8:10–11 (9:17–18).

The origin of Milton's concept of Lucifer's use of artillery in heaven (a concept "which has always been a scandal to all true believers")[27] is generally traced to Ariosto, *Orlando Furioso* (1532), IX, 9; Spenser, *Faerie Queene* (1590), I, vii, 13; or Valvasone, *L'Angeleida* (1590), II, 20. The source of Milton's description of the near destruction of heaven ("a Thing not only

ridiculous but profane'')[28] is usually ascribed to Hesiod,
Theogony, 665–712; Homer, *Iliad*, VIII, 130; or Ovid, *Metamorphoses*, I, 152–158. That Milton was thoroughly familiar with
the writings of these poets, with the possible exception of
Valvasone, scarcely needs to be demonstrated. Even a casual
reading of the passages listed above reveals Milton's indebtedness. The source for Milton's account of these two actions is not,
however, *primarily* literary. Milton's primary source is the Bible,
specifically three parallel passages in the Book of Revelation.

According to Revelation 12:7b, the first of the parallel passages,
after ''Michael and his angels'' triumph over the dragon and his
hosts (Rev. 12:7a), ''the dragon ... and his angels'' overcome the
forces of God. Revelation 6:5–6, the second of the parallel
passages, explains the nature of Lucifer's ''victory.'' In Revelation 6:5–6, when Christ opens the third seal of the book of God's
decrees, there appears a black horse with a rider who has a pair of
balances in his hand. With the appearance of the black horse, a
voice is heard saying: ''A measure of wheat for a penny [a day's
wages], and three measures of barley for a penny; and see thou
hurt not the oil and the wine.'' Literally (not metaphorically) the
rider of the black horse is the devil and devil-inspired heresy. The
blackness of the horse and the scarcity of the wheat and the barley
symbolize famine, spiritual rather than physical, of the word of
God (Amos 8:11–12; Lam. 4:8–9). The pair of balances ($\zeta\nu\gamma\grave{o}\nu$, a
yoke) represent the impending justice of God. The voice from
heaven signifies the protection of the faithful (the oil and the wine)
from the wiles of the devil.

On the second day of the War in Heaven, Lucifer, the rider of
the *black* horse, appears to torment the faithful angels of God
(Rev. 6:5, 12:7b) with the darkness of heresy and spiritual famine.
Famine, black and noisome, spreads across the heavens. With
false (black) thunder Lucifer challenges the power of God.
''Honour, Dominion, Glorie'' (P.L. VI, 422), declares Lucifer,
belong not to God but to the rebel angels. God is mutable and
weak, a pretender to powers which he does not actually possess
(P.L. VI, 418–445; see C.D. II, 41–61, 16–26). So strong shall be
our attack, Lucifer boasts, that the loyal angels ''shall fear we have
disarmd The Thunderer of his only dreaded bolt'' (P.L. VI,

490–491). Lucifer no longer is satisfied to claim equality with the begotten Son (P.L. V, 864–866). He now defies the power of God himself (Isa. 14:13–14; Ezek. 28:6; II Thess. 2:4). Truly here is black "famine," "wofull scarcitie," and dearth of "the bread of life, which is the pure Word of God."[29] Christ stands aloof. Without the aid of Christ, necessarily the loyal angels fall before the forces of darkness. Michael and his angels cannot be conquered (Rev. 6:6b; see C. D. IX, 99, 22–24). Nor can they defeat the devil (P.L. VI, 689–694). They can, however, be afflicted and oppressed.

Afflicted by the blackness of heresy and spiritual famine, Michael and his angels fall before the forces of evil. Milton's picture is graphic: The rebel angels not only utter heresy but they enforce their statements with the power of cannon. The origin of this "scandalous" concept appears in Revelation 8:10–11 (9:17–18), the third passage which, according to Pareus and other commentators, explains the meaning of Revelation 12:7 and Revelation 6:5–6.[30] In Revelation 8:10–11, when the third angel sounds his trumpet, immediately, according to John,

> 10 . . . there fell a great star fom heaven, burning as it were a lamp, and it fell upon the third part of the rivers, and upon the fountains of waters; 11 . . . and the third part of the waters became wormwood; and many men died of the waters, because they were made bitter.

Lucifer, the "great star" that falls from heaven, poisons (blackens) the waters. The reference to the men who "died of the waters" parallels the reference to "the third part of men [who were] killed by the fire, and by the smoke, and by the brimstone" in Revelation 9:17–18. "Thus I saw," writes John, returning to his earlier symbolism,

> 17 . . . the horses in the vision, and them that sat on them, having breastplates of fire, and of jacinth, and brimstone: and the heads of the horses were as the heads of lions; and out of their mouths issued fire and smoke and brimstone. 18 By these three was *the third part of men killed* [italics inserted], by the fire, and by the smoke, and by the brimstone, which issued out of their mouths (Rev. 9:17–18).

The "horses" and their riders (the "great star" of Rev. 8:10, the "black horse" of Rev. 6:5) are symbols of Lucifer and his hosts of evil. The "men" who are "killed" by the power of the devil are the same "men" (angels, beasts, elders; see Rev. 5:3–5, 11) who "died" when the "third part of the waters" was poisoned in Revelation 8:11 (6:5, 12:7). The action is described in Revelation 9:17–18. The time of the action, however, is that of Revelation 8:10–11. What is the significance of the "fire," the " smoke," and the "brimstone" which issue from the mouths of the "horses" of Revelation 9:17–18? Thomas Brightman, one of the most frequently quoted Protestant theologians of the seventeenth century, furnishes the answer:

> That which commeth out of their movth is of three sorts, *fire*[,] *smoke,* & *brimston,* which thre seme to note out one thing, namely their *warlike gunnes,* & *peeces of ordinance,* the original where of was not much later then the *offspring of the Turkes,* & which the *Turkes* do vse in a more outragious desire to worke mischiefe, then any other kinde of men. The greatnes of that *Gunne* was almost incredible which *Mahnmet* vsed in beseeging Cōstantinople, for the *drawing where of there were seauenty yokes of oxen & two thousand men were vsed as Laonicus Chalcocondular reporteth, in the eigt Booke of his Turkish Histories* [1556]. And those twelue thousand *Ianizers,* which are the ordinary gard of his body, are al Gunners. Now se if any thing could be spoken more fitly to declare the nature of Gunnes. First here is mention made of fire, but least it should be thought to be vulgar, there is a double difference added of *smoke* and *brimstone.* For the *fire* that commeth from *Gunnes,* is notably known from ordinary fire by an abūdant *smoke,* which ariseth out of the sodain inflamming and extinguishing there of, as is vsually seen in descharging of ordinance. Where the fire continueth burning and flamming out brightly, there is least smoke of all, as which the flame doth wholy almost cōsume. Besides this fire is of brimstone, is not gun powder made of saltpeter, cole, and brimstone? The *Holy Ghost* therefore describes this enemy vnto vs by those warlike instruments, which should take their beginning almost with this tyranny.[31]

The "fire," "smoke," and "brimstone" of Revelation 9:18 are saltpeter and sulphur ("Sulphurous and Nitrous Foame," P.L. VI, 512), the ingredients of gunpowder. According to Brightman, Bernard, Pareus, Cowper, Mede, Hammond, and Trapp,[32] seven quite prominent, presumably sincere Renaissance Protestant divines, in Revelation 9:17–18 John prophesied the coming of the Turks with their destructive artillery and pieces of ordinance. This exposition, which assumes a metaphorical (earthly) interpretation of the Revelation, may seem "scandalous" to modern readers. The interpretation remained almost unchallenged, however, during the seventeenth century. Only George Hakewill, author of *An Apologie or Declaration Of The Power And Providence Of God in the Gouernment of the World* (1630; 1st ed., 1627), seems to have questioned the validity of the interpretation:

> *Brightman* in his exposition on the *Revelation* of S. *Iohn*, tels vs that by the *fire*, and *smoake*, and *brimstone* which in that place are said to haue issued out of the mouth of the horses, are to be vnderstood our *powder* and *gunnes* now in vse, and that of them S. *Iohn* prophesied, but how these can be said to issue out of the *mouthes* of horses, he doth not well expresse, nor I thinke well vnderstand (p. 280).

Other writers found Brightman's exposition to be scholarly and in accord with the facts: Some fourteen hundred years before the event occurred, John foretold the use of gunpowder (fire, smoke, and brimstone) by the Turks (the devil).

The connection between the exposition advanced by Brightman and Milton's account of Lucifer's activities should be obvious. Milton's description of Lucifer's use of artillery in heaven follows a well known seventeenth-century interpretation of the meaning of Revelation 9:17–18 (Rev. 8:10–11). Milton's immediate source probably was Pareus. Whether Milton had read Pareus, Brightman, Mede, or some other commentator, however, is relatively unimportant. The fact that reputable theological authority underlies Milton's account of Lucifer's activities is important. It is difficult to charge Milton with a lack of reverence for Scripture when one realizes that Milton's account, here as elsewhere in the heavenly cycle, is based on the Bible. Milton's picture of the devil's invention and use of artillery in heaven is not primarily literary or poetic. Allusions to Ariosto, Spenser, and other great writers exist in *Paradise Lost* for the reader to consider and to enjoy. The factor which combines these allusions, however, is Milton's *literal* interpretation of the Bible.

In presenting his picture of Lucifer's "hallow Engins" Milton was completely serious. According to eminent biblical authority, the devil *did* invent artillery. To Milton, however, the original place of the invention was heaven, not earth. Metaphorically, Milton agreed, the ectypes—the human representatives—of Lucifer were the Turks.[33] Literally, however, Lucifer was the "great Sultan" to whose "uplifted Spear" the devils rallied in their rebellion against God (P.L. I, 347–348; cf. X, 455–459). Lucifer was the heavenly archetype of the "horses" and the "horsemen" of Revelation 9:17–18. Milton thus minimized the historical, earthly aspects of the exposition of Pareus (Brightman, and the other commentators who stated similar views). With the structural aspects of this exposition, however, Milton agreed. Revelation 12, 6, and 8 are parallel visions. Each vision refers in general to the same time, action, and place: "there was war in heaven."

The view that the Book of Revelation is composed of a series of related visions supplies the reason for the appearance of cannon in heaven. It also in large part supplies the basis for Milton's description of the "earthquake" which follows (P.L. VI, 634–669): Lucifer's deadly engine belches thunder. "Fire and smoke and brimstone," the sulphur and nitre which the rebellious angels mine from the celestial soil (P.L. VI, 509–515), strike the Hosts of God with "devilish glut" and "impetuous furie" (P.L. VI, 589, 591). Seeking to defend themselves, with righteous indignation the loyal angels pluck up the hills and cast them at their foes. The result is a cataclysm which almost destroys the foundations of heaven. Indeed, says Raphael, heaven would have been destroyed if God had not intervened.

Milton's account of the cataclysm, or the "Battle of the Titans" as it is generally termed, is drawn from Revelation 12:7b, 6:5–6 (6:12), and 8:10–11. On the second day of the Battle of the Angels, according to Revelation 12:7b, Lucifer and his hosts "conquer" the forces of God. According to Revelation 6:5–6 and 8:10–11, Lucifer's instruments of victory are black, corrupting heresy and spiritual famine. Lucifer is black. His means of warfare likewise are black. (On the first day of the war, Lucifer appears as the rider of the red horse. The heavens turn red with fire, flame, and fury. On the second day, Lucifer appears as the rider of the black horse. The heavens turn black with thick, obscuring smoke). An alternate explanation of Lucifer's "blackness" Renaissance commentators found in the reference to the "great earthquake" which John describes in Revelation 6:12–13:

> 12 And I beheld when he had opened the sixth seal, and, lo, there
> was a great earthquake; and the sun became black as sackcloth of
> hair, and the moon became as blood; 13 And the stars of heaven fell
> unto the earth, even as a fig tree casteth her untimely figs, when she
> is shaken of a mighty wind.

This earthquake must have occurred before the time of the sixth
seal, for in the third trumpet (Rev. 8:10), in the passage which is
parallel to the third seal (Rev. 6:5–6), Lucifer, the "great star" of
heaven, has already fallen. In the sixth seal, the "stars of heaven,"
including Lucifer, again are said to fall. Lucifer could not have
fallen twice. The time of the fall, or at least the time of the
beginning of the fall, must have occurred during the period of time
covered by the third trumpet (Rev. 8:10 and 6:5–6), not during the
period covered by the sixth seal.[34] Here, as was true of the incident
described in Revelation 9:17–18, the event which is described in
one seal actually occurs earlier. The time of the earthquake
described in Revelation 6:12 actually is that of Revelation 6:5–6
(Rev. 8:10–11).

This relatively simple explanation of the source of Milton's
description of the earthquake in heaven may not be as aesthetically
pleasing as the view which restricts Milton's account to the epic or
classical "Battle of the Titans" of Hesiod, Homer, and Ovid. It
does, however, remove the imputation of irreverence. It emphasizes, moreover, the basic scriptural nature of Milton's account. In the second, necessarily concluding phase of the War in
Heaven, according to Joel 2:10, Psalm 68:16, and Isaiah 14:16,
texts which commentators used as cross references for Revelation
6:5–6 (6:12), the heavens and the earth tremble, the hills leap,
"confusion" is "heapt Upon confusion" (P.L. VI, 668–669). The
Hosts of God lie crushed under the weight of famine, "the heaviest
[judgment] that can befall a people on this side Hell" (Lam. 1:4,
4:6).[35] But the power of the devil is limited. With the opening of the
third seal, when Lucifer appears as the rider of the black horse
(Rev. 6:5–6), a voice speaks from heaven:

> ... two dayes are past,
> Two dayes, as we compute the dayes of Heav'n,
> Since *Michael* and his Powers went forth to tame
> These disobedient.... the third is thine;

For thee I have ordain'd it, and thus farr
Have sufferd, that the Glorie may be thine
Of ending this great Warr, since none but Thou
Can end it.

(P.L. VI, 684–687, 699–703)

In the midst of the earthquake, when the Saints of God (angels, P.L. VI, 742, 801; קְדוֹשִׁים, Ps. 89:7; ἅγιος, Matt. 25:31; compare Dan. 8:13, Zech. 14:5, Job 15:15; Joel 2:19–20; Jude 14; Rev. 14:10) lie stricken by those who have "horribly mingled the truth of pure white and lightsome doctrine, with blacke darknesse of heresies and errours,"[36] Christ, the rider of the white horse, the conquering Lion of Juda, the mighty Son of God, appears to claim his own:

And the third sacred Morn began to shine
Dawning through Heav'n: forth rush'd with whirlwind sound
The Chariot of Paternal Deitie,
Flashing thick flames, Wheele within Wheele undrawn,
It self instinct with Spirit, but convoyd
By four Cherubic shapes, four Faces each
Had wondrous, as with Starrs thir bodies all
And Wings were set with Eyes, with Eyes the wheels
Of Beril, and careering Fires between;
Over thir heads a chrystal Firmament,
Whereon a Saphir Throne, inlaid with pure
Amber, and colours of the showrie Arch.

            . . . into terrour [the Son] chang'd
His count'nance too severe to be beheld
And full of wrauth bent on his Enemies.
At once the Four spred out thir Starrie wings
With dreadful shade contiguous, and the Orbes
Of his fierce Chariot rowld, as with the sound
Of torrent Floods, or of a numerous Host.
Hee on his impious Foes right onward drove,
Gloomie as Night; under his burning Wheeles
The stedfast Empyrean shook throughout,
All but the Throne it self of God. Full soon
Among them he arriv'd; in his right hand

Grasping ten thousand Thunders, which he sent
Before him, such as in thir Soules infix'd
Plagues; they astonisht all resistance lost,
All courage; down thir idle weapons drop'd;
O're Shields and Helmes, and helmed heads he rode
Of Thrones and mighty Seraphim prostrate,
That wisht the Mountains now might be again
Thrown on them as a shelter from his ire.
Nor less on either side tempestuous fell
His arrows, from the fourfold-visag'd Foure,
Distinct with eyes, and from the living Wheels,
Distinct alike with multitude of eyes,
One Spirit in them rul'd, and every eye
Glar'd lightning, and shot forth pernicious fire
Among th' accurst, that witherd all thir strength,
And of thir wonted vigour left them draind,
Exhausted, spiritless, afflicted, fall'n.

(P.L. VI, 748–759, 824–852)

The appearance of the Son brings to a focus each of the major texts upon which Milton has based his account of the War in Heaven. In sound, imagery, and meaning the passage reaches a tremendous climax. The day of wrath (Rev. 6:17; Isa. 34:8, 13:9; Ps. 110:5) has come! Christ, the Lion of Juda, the Son of God, appears to claim his inheritance and to rule the nations with a rod of iron (Ps. 2:8–9; Isa. 5:14–26, 30:26–33; Joel 2:20; Rev. 6:2, 12:9–10). Before him goes "pestilence" (Hab. 3:5); from his chariot flash arrows of fire (Ezek. 1:13; Isa. 66:15; Ps. 45:4–6). In his hand he carries thunder, the Power of God (Rev. 4:5; Job 26:14). Now are the enemies of the Lord vexed and overthrown (Ps. 2:5, 110:6). With the opening of the fourth seal, Christ overcomes Death, the rider of the pale horse, and Lucifer, the old serpent called the Devil and Satan, is driven from heaven (Rev. 6:6–8, 12:9; Isa. 14:15; Ezek. 28:14–19):

13 And the stars of heaven fell unto the earth, even as a fig tree casteth her untimely figs, when she is shaken of a mighty wind. 14 And the heaven departed as a scroll when it is rolled together; and every mountain and island were moved out of their places. 15 And

the kings of the earth, and the great men, and the rich men, and the chief captains, and the mighty men, and every bondman, and every free man, hid themselves in the dens and in the rocks of the mountains; 16 And said to the mountains and rocks, Fall on us, and hide us from the face of him that sitteth on the throne, and from the wrath of the Lamb [Lion]: 17 For the great day of his wrath is come; and who shall be able to stand? (Rev. 6:13–17)

Like a herd of goats (עֲתוּדֵי אָרֶץ . .;[37] the image comes from Isa. 14:9, Lev. 17:7, and Matt. 25:32–33) the rebel angels are driven to the bounds of heaven. Thunderstruck they see the "Chrystal wall of Heav'n" roll inward and "a spacious Gap disclos'd Into the wastful Deep":

>   the monstrous sight
> Strook them with horror backward, but far worse
> Urg'd them behind; headlong themselves they threw
> Down from the verge of Heav'n, Eternal wrauth
> Burnt after them to the bottomless pit.
>   Hell heard th' unsufferable noise, Hell saw
> Heav'n ruining from Heav'n. . . . Hell at last
> Yawning receavd them whole, and on them clos'd. . . .
>   (P.L. VI, 856–868, 874–875)

Milton's use of Revelation 6:13–17 as the basis for his description of Lucifer's expulsion from heaven is deliberate. Christ, the rider of the white horse, appears to open the fourth seal. Lucifer (Famine and Death-to-be), the rider of the black horse, falls immediately (Rev. 6:2, 7–8). (Actually there is no third day of battle. Death, the rider of the fourth horse, cannot appear in heaven; see Chapter 5.) With Lucifer's expulsion, the "Chrystal wall of Heav'n" rolls inward (departs "as a scroll"). This is no convulsion of nature ($\sigma\epsilon\iota\sigma\mu\acuteο s$) such as the angels, with their limited power, were able to produce on the second day of the War in Heaven. This is a $\sigma\epsilon\iota\sigma\mu o s$ $\bar{\rho}\bar{o}\pi\omega\iota\tau o s$, "a concussion of the Vniverse, or whole fabrick of the world."[38] This "earthquake," wrote Thomas Goodwin, Milton's friend and fellow committeeman in Parliament, cannot be explained simply in terms which refer

to the earth, (in English we have no word large enough,) for it imports the concussion or throwing down by a commotion of that heathenish world, the heavens and earth, and all of that religion, even of all that had a station in that accursed frame. . . . the throwing down [of] Satan and his devils from being worshipped any longer under the names of the host of heaven, and those appellatives given the stars, and titles to men departed, whereof he received all the real honour, may fitly be here understood to be the darkening [of] the sun and moon [Rev. 6:12], and the falling of these stars from heaven . . . from Constantine's time downward, during the space of one hundred years. . . . As Christ is the sun in his heaven, so Satan, the prince of devils, the prince of this host of heaven, as Daniel's phrase is, was the sun in this firmament. And the lesser devils, with him worshipped under the title of the lesser gods, and of the stars, are the *stars* here which fall from heaven [Compare Dan. 8:10; Deut. 17:3; Ps. 96:5 and 82:6–7].[39]

Lucifer, who is identified in Isaiah 14:16 as a "man," is also described in Isaiah 14:12 as a "star" of heaven. In context, then, as in Ezekiel 28:2, II Thessalonians 2:3–4, and Revelation 6:15, the "kings of the earth" and the other six types of "men" who seek shelter from the "earthquake" of Revelation 6:15 are either actual devils or demonic forces which masquerade in the forms of men.

To Goodwin, the "stars" of Revelation 6:13 are devils, Lucifer and the fallen angels. The "men" of Revelation 6:15 are pagan gods ("men departed") who, as the result of the "establishment" of the Church in 313 A.D. (the "earthquake"), have lost their power to corrupt mankind. To Milton, whose interpretation is literal rather than metaphorical, in Revelation 6:13 and Revelation 6:15 both the "stars" and the "men" are devils (literally, devils), Lucifer and his legions, whom Christ, the creator of the "earthquake," cast from heaven to hell prior to the creation of the world.

Basically, although differing in time and place, the interpretations of Goodwin and Milton are similar. To both Goodwin and Milton the σεισμος ρ̄οπωιτος of Revelation 6:14 is a cataclysmic event, separate from the earthquake of Revelation 6:12, which is properly interpreted only in terms of Lucifer's fall from heaven. First the sun turns "black as sackcloth of hair" and the moon becomes "as blood." Then the heaven closes as does "a scroll when it is rolled together." Only Christ (God) can create an earthquake of this nature. Lucifer and his angels understandably wish that the "Mountains now might be *again* [italics inserted]

Thrown on them." The wrath of the loyal angels cannot be compared to that of Christ, the Son of God. With the coming of Christ, Death and Hell (Rev. 6:8) cannot stand. Heaven itself casts them forth.

Interwoven in Milton's account of Christ's triumph are allusions to poetic episodes which appear in the writings of Hesiod, Homer, Ovid, Ariosto, Spenser, and perhaps Valvasone. Milton's allusions to the events described by these poets are, however, no more than allusions. Allusions should not be equated with structure and primary emphasis. (Poetic "ore" is not the mine itself.) The structure of the War in Heaven Milton derives from the Bible, specifically the Book of Revelation. The major emphasis in the War in Heaven Milton places upon Christ as the Son of God, the conqueror of the devil—to Milton, a very real being. Christ is not Jupiter or Zeus. Nor is Satan primarily a Titan. Christ does not intervene in an action (the earthquake) which to Milton had no scriptural basis. Nor is Christ the conqueror of thinly disguised pagan or poetic beings. The War in Heaven reaches its climax when the Son, the divinely appointed, visible Power of God, appears to defeat Lucifer, evil incarnate.

Point by point Milton's outline for the War in Heaven is based upon the Scripture. Christ is "begotten" as the Son of God (Ps. 2:7, 110:1; Rev. 5:5, 12:5). Lucifer wages war against the Son (Rev. 6:1–6, 8:6–11, 12:7–9). Christ conquers and Lucifer falls (Rev. 6:7–8, 8:12, 12:9–10). To Milton, these events are considerably more than poetic myth. "Measuring things in Heav'n by things on Earth" (P.L. VI, 893), Milton uses poetic myth (classical insights, philosophical concepts, scientific discoveries, political theories). The myth, however, is not primary. Primary is Milton's depiction of Christ as the Son of God. In his hand he carries thunderbolts, the Power of God. His chariot is the Throne of God himself (Rev. 4:2–8; Ezek. 1:4–28, 10:1–22; Isa. 6:1–5, 11:4–5; Ps. 18:10–15, 45:6; Heb. 1:8; cf. C.D. X, 141–142, 22–2). Christ's throne is God's throne. Christ is the visible expression of God.

Encircling the Throne of Divinity are the "elders" and the "beasts" who sing choral odes and cast their crowns before God (See Chapter 1). The elders, who are permitted to sit in the presence of God, presumably are superior in rank to the beasts, who appear "in the midst of " and "round about" the throne (Rev. 4:6). The beasts, the cherubim (חַיּﬞוֹת, "living creatures") and seraphim of Ezekiel 1:4–28 (10:1–22) and Isaiah 6:1–5, bear up and draw the throne of God:

> These four Beasts do signifie the Angels of heauen, the inuisible and elect Angels of heauen, as it is expounded, Ezeck. 10, verse 20. where the Prophet in a vision seeth foure beastes, as it were bearing vp and drawing Gods Chariot of triumph.[40]

God's "Chariot of triumph," the "Chariot of Paternal Deitie" (P.L. VI, 750), rests upon the "chrystal Firmament" (P.L. VI, 757), the "sea of glass like unto crystal" (Rev. 4:6), the "colour of the terrible crystal" (Ezek. 1:22). Under the firmament appear the angels of God's wrath: The sound of their coming is the sound of "torrent Floods" (P.L. VI, 830). Their appearance is as fire. From their eyes dart arrows of lightning (P.L. VI, 849):

> 13 As for the likeness of the living creatures, their appearance was like burning coals of fire, and like the appearance of lamps: it went up and down among the living creatures; and the fire was bright, and out of the fire went forth lightning. 14 And the living creatures ran and returned as the appearance of a flash of lightning (Ezek. 1:13–14). 9 And when I looked, behold the four wheels by the cherubims, one wheel by one cherub, and another wheel by another cherub: and the appearance of the wheels was as the colour of a beryl stone. 10 And as for their appearances, they four had one likeness, as if a wheel had been in the midst of a wheel. 12 And their whole body, and their backs, and their hands, and their wings, and the wheels, were full of eyes round about, even the wheels that they four had (Ezek. 10:9–10, 12).

Below the firmament, bearing the throne, appear the angels of Ezekiel (and Isaiah), the "chiefe and principall Ministers" of God's power.[41] Above the firmament, seated on the throne, appears the likeness of God himself: "And he that sat was to look upon like a jasper and a sardine stone: and there was a rainbow round about the throne, in sight like unto an emerald" (Rev. 4:3). The description is repeated in Ezekiel 1:26–28: "And above the firmament that was over their heads was the likeness of a throne," in appearance as "a sapphire stone," with "the colour of amber," and "of the bow that is in the cloud in the day of rain." But God is invisible. It is thus God's throne that Milton pictures as sparkling

with the brilliance of precious stones and of the rainbow. Christ is
seated on this throne. What higher tribute could Milton pay to
Christ? Christ is the visible image of God, the "Assessor"
(co-sitter; P.L. VI, 679) of God's throne. God and Christ are
one.[42]

From the throne of God proceed "thunderings and voices"
(Rev. 4:5, 8:5), symbols, by common theological agreement, of
God's judgments and decrees. God proclaims his original decree:
Christ is the Son of God (Ps. 2:7). From the "midst of the throne"
Christ appears to open the seals of the book of God's decrees
(Rev. 5:5–6, 6:1–17). War ensues. God then restates his decree:

> Two dayes are therefore past, the third is thine;
> For thee I have ordain'd it, and thus farr
> Have sufferd, that the Glorie may be thine
> Of ending this great Warr, since none but Thou
> Can end it.
>
> (P.L. VI, 699–703)

Christ ascends the Chariot of God's Judgment. Lucifer and his
angels fall. (Christ rides again in the Chariot of God's Judgment.
The world is created, P.L. VII, 192–588.)

Christ is not Zeus described as God. Christ is the rider of the
white horse (the "Chariot of Paternal Deitie"), the Lion of Juda,
the only begotten Son of God, the visible image of the Father. The
concept is more than epic or poetic.

CHAPTER THREE

Orthodoxy and Confusion

> Others apart sat on a Hill retir'd,
> In thoughts more elevate, and reason'd high
> Of Providence, Foreknowledge, Will and Fate,
> Fixt Fate, free will, foreknowledg absolute,
> And found no end, in wandring mazes lost.
>
> (P.L. II, 557-561)

To some critics, particularly those to whom reference has been made in Chapters 1 and 2, Milton's account of the second phase of the heavenly cycle (P.L. I–IV, IX) is as objectionable as is his account of the first phase of the events in heaven. Milton's picture of hell, states Defoe, "is so contrary to the nature of the thing, and so great an absurdity," that not even "Poetic License can account for it."[1] Milton's description of Sin and Death, according to Routh, de Magny, de Lille, and other critics, is a perversion of the Scriptures.[2] Indeed, according to "Theophilus," "Whether he [Milton] was a Christian or no, could scarce be determined (I believe) by any thing that occurs in his Poem."[3]

Other writers express the opposite opinion. The common eighteenth-century view, states James Thorpe, was that *Paradise Lost* had "contributed more to support the orthodox creed than all the books of divinity that were ever written."[4] Parallel to this view is the conclusion reached by a number of modern critics: "Except for a few isolated passages" the theology of *Paradise Lost* "is not even specifically Protestant or Puritan." It follows "the great central tradition" of Christianity and extends an invitation "which all Christendom in all lands or ages can accept."[5]

Which of these contradictory views is the reader to follow? Is Milton's use of the Bible heterodox or orthodox, in agreement or in disagreement with "the great central tradition" of Christianity?

The question is difficult to answer, for doctrines which are regarded as "orthodox" in the twentieth century need not have been (and frequently were not) regarded as "orthodox" in the sixteenth and seventeenth centuries. Moreover, the assumption upon which the question is based, the view that in the seventeenth century Milton's theological concepts necessarily were *either* orthodox *or* heterodox, is in itself questionable. Renaissance Protestant theologians consistently defended certain fundamental doctrines (as, for example, the tenet that the basis of doctrine is Scripture rather than Authority) as "orthodox" Christian truth. Use of the Scripture to "prove" the existence of purgatory, the efficacy of prayer to the saints, or the validity of the doctrine of transubstantiation was, of course, "unorthodox." Within the framework of established doctrine, Protestant theologians interpreted the Bible narrowly. Outside of this framework, in what may be called a "neutral" area, Protestant theologians interpreted the Bible with considerable latitude. The meaning of certain texts (as Psalm 2, 110; Isaiah 14; Ezekiel 28; Revelation 4–5, 8–9, 12, texts upon which Milton based his account of the heavenly cycle) was not established. These texts might be interpreted either literally or metaphorically. Both interpretations were "orthodox."

To William Ames, John Boys, and Richard Clerke, for example, Psalm 2 furnished proof that Christ was "begotten" literally from (not in) eternity. To Théodore Bèza, John Calvin, and Immanuel Tremellius, however, Psalm 2 was better interpreted metaphorically as evidence of God's promise to mankind of Christ's coming as mediator on earth.[6] Depending upon the exposition favored by a particular commentator, of course, one of these interpretations was preferred. The variant interpretation, however, was not regarded necessarily as being "heterodox." There was good reason for this attitude. It was difficult for Protestants to denounce the interpretations of Psalm 2 by such prominent *Protestants* as Ames, Bèza, Boys, Calvin, Clerke, and Tremellius. Moreover, historically, as Milton's contemporaries well knew, theologians had disagreed consistently regarding the meaning of Psalm 2. Augustine interpreted Psalm 2 literally. Hilary, Eusebius, and Ambrose, however, preferred the metaphorical interpretation. So far as "the great central tradition" of Christianity was concerned, there was no "orthodox" interpretation of Psalm 2.

Many Protestant divines, of course, condemned *any* interpretation with which they disagreed. As Milton's prose pamphlets demonstrate clearly, sixteenth- and seventeenth-century theological controversy was scarcely a matter of "sweetness and light."[7] The fact remains, however, that in their explications of *certain* texts Renaissance Protestant theologians frequently recognized two levels of "orthodox" biblical interpretation. Thus, for example, according to some Protestant commentators, Psalm 110 described Christ's "appointment" (exaltation) both as the King of Heaven and of Earth before the creation of the world.[8] Preferring a metaphorical level of interpretation, other, no less "orthodox," commentators explained Psalm 110 as a prophecy of Christ's future exaltation to his kingly office following the completion of his mediatorial role upon the earth.[9] Again, in Isaiah 14 (Ezek. 28), declared a number of Protestant writers, the reference to Lucifer should be understood literally as a reference to the devil, not simply to a human being.[10] Equally "orthodox" Protestant writers insisted that the allusion to Lucifer in Isaiah 14 (Ezek. 28) was improperly explained as a reference to the devil. Lucifer, the King of Babylon (the Prince of Tyrus), was a man, not a devil.[11]

The existence of two levels of scriptural interpretation may be seen even more clearly in the Renaissance Protestant commentaries on the Book of Revelation. Many Protestant commentators explained Revelation 4–5 literally in terms of events which occurred before the beginning of time: In Revelation 4–5 the heavens opened and to John there appeared a vision of God enthroned in his majesty and glory.[12] No less "orthodox," however, was the view that the place of John's vision could not possibly have been heaven. The picture of God's throne in Revelation 4–5 actually (metaphorically) was a picture of the Church on earth, not in heaven.[13] Many (indeed, most) Protestant theologians maintained that Revelation 12 was improperly explicated as a reference to an actual or literal "war in heaven." The "war in heaven" occurred, and continues to occur, but the place of the warfare was and is the Kingdom of God on earth.[14] As "orthodox," however, was the opposite view: The Kingdom of God was and is in heaven, not on earth.[15] Finally, stated a number of Protestant commentators, the dread events of Revelation 8–9 were better explicated as references to spiritual torments and plagues than to earthly (metaphorical) or physical punishments.[16] Equally "orthodox," however, was the view that Revelation 8–9 referred to events which were earthly and historical: the coming of the Antichrist and/or the Goths, the Huns, and the Turks.[17]

The difficulty with labeling Milton's thought as "orthodox" or "heterodox" is that the label presumes that Renaissance Protestant theologians were agreed upon the meaning of the major texts upon which Milton based his description of heaven. Sixteenth- and seventeenth-century Protestant commentators did not agree—indeed, they consistently disagreed in their interpretations of the texts upon which Milton based his account of the heavenly cycle in *Paradise Lost*. Particularly is this statement true of the commentaries upon the Book of Revelation. The Book of Revelation is an allegory (Apocalypse, book of hidden meanings). How should an allegory be interpreted? Should it be understood literally or figuratively? Is the time scheme of an allegory past, present, future, or a combination of the three? Is its structure repetitive or continuous? What referents should be used to explain its hidden meanings? Sixteenth- and seventeenth-century Protestant theologians did not—perhaps could not—agree upon satisfactory answers to these questions. (Modern interpreters of the Book of Revelation likewise disagree.)

Theoretically, as Protestant theologians were well aware, an allegory should be interpreted literally. The Bible, wrote Tyndale, stating a view which appears repeatedly in the commentaries:

> hath but one sense w^c is the literall sence. And that litteral sence is ye rote & grounde of all / & the ancre that neuer faileth / wher vnto if thou cleue thou cāst neuer erre or goo out of the waye. And if thou leve ye litterall sence: thou canst not but goo out of the waye. Neuer the lates the scripture vseth prouerbes / similitudes redels or allegories as all other speaches doo / but that w^c the prouerbe / similitude / redel or allegory signifieth is euer the literall sence / which thou must seke out diligently. . . . The Apocalipse or reuelacions of Iohn are able allegories whose litteral sence is herde to finde in many places.[18]

Although admirable in theory, in practice, declared a number of Protestant theologians, this principle could not always be followed.[19] Applied rigidly it would prevent the reading of secondary meanings into such texts as Psalm 2:7 and Genesis 3:15 (to cite but two passages). Thus, wrote Jeremy Taylor,

> ... although there be but one principal literal sense [in the interpretation of Scripture], yet others that are subordinate may be intended subordinately; and others that are true by proportion.... Thus when it is said, *Thou art my Son, this day have I begotten thee;* the Psalmist means it of the eternal generation of Christ; others seem to apply it to his birth of the Blessed Virgin *Mary;* and *S. Paul* expounds it *Heb*. 1. of the Resurrection of Christ: This is all true; and yet but one literal sense primely ment....[20]

Again, according to William Whitaker,

> We affirm that there is but one true, proper, and genuine sense of scripture, arising from the words rightly understood, which we call the literal: and we contend that allegories, tropologies, and anagoges are not various senses, but various collections from one sense, or various applications and accomodations of that one meaning. The literal sense, then, is not that which the words immediately suggest ... but rather that which arises from the words themselves, whether they be taken strictly or figuratively.... For example, the literal sense of these words, "The seed of the woman shall crush the serpent's head," is this, that Christ shall beat down Satan, and break and crush all his force and power; although the devil neither is a serpent, nor hath a head.[21]

The Bible should be interpreted literally, yet proper attention must be paid to the requirements of Christian faith (generally termed the "Analogy of Faith"). Thus certain passages (as Ps. 2:7) contain subordinate or secondary meanings. And other passages (as Gen. 3:15) contain meanings which primarily are figurative. Depending upon context (etymology, parallel passages, the requirements of the Christian faith), then, to a number of Renaissance theologians both types of meanings were literal: "The literal sense ... is not that which the words immediately suggest ... but rather that which arises from the words themselves, whether they be taken strictly or figuratively."

Literally, then, in the Book of Revelation, what was the meaning of such terms as "heaven," the "throne of God," "beasts,"

"stars," "earth," "locusts," and "pit"? Literally, that is, in
context, maintained a number of commentators, "heaven" and
the "throne of God" are symbols which refer to the Church (the
Kingdom of God) on earth.[22] The "beasts" are men, perhaps the
four evangelists.[23] The "stars" are pastors and teachers ("great"
men, both good and evil) whom God has appointed to lead the
Church.[24] The "locusts" (grasshoppers, crickets) are armies of
the Huns and Goths, of the Turks, and/or of the Antichrist.[25] The
"pit" represents the Kingdom of the Devil which the "locusts"
have established on the earth.[26] Literally, then, the place of
Revelation 4:1–9, 9:1–13, and 12:4–9 is earth, not heaven.

Certainly, agreed other Protestant commentators, the Church is
the Kingdom of God on earth. Yet the Kingdom of God is not
primarily earthly. Literally, according to the Bible, John saw a
"door . . . opened in heaven" (Rev. 4:1). Heaven is heaven, not
earth. The literal referent of the "throne of God" (to the extent
that the throne of God can be described in human terms) is none
other than that of the "throne of God." In this context the
"beasts" are angels.[27] The "locusts" and the "stars" are spiritual
beings, devils and angels.[28] The "pit" is a symbol for hell itself.[29]
The place of Revelation 4:1–9, 9:1–13, and 12:4–9, literally, is
heaven (or hell), not earth.

Neither of these interpretations is valid, insisted still other
commentators. The literal context of Revelation 4, the place of the
"throne of God" and of the "beasts," is heaven. In Revelation 12,
however, "heaven," the place of the "throne of God" and of the
"stars," cannot represent heaven. In Revelation 12 "heaven"
signifies "earth."[30] The "pit" which John described in Revelation
20, stated many Protestant theologians, is a symbol for hell, the
place of confinement of the devil. Yet John's reference to the "pit"
in Revelation 9 should not be connected with hell. In Revelation 9,
by "pit" John clearly meant "earth."[31]

Consistency, rather obviously, was not a virtue in sixteenth- and
seventeenth-century commentaries on the Book of Revelation.
Theoretically, declared most commentators, the Bible, including
the Book of Revelation, should be interpreted literally (in context,
in accordance with the meaning of the text). But what was the
meaning of the text? According to Revelation 9:7–10, after the

"pit" had been opened by the "star" which fell from "heaven," there appeared "locusts" which

> were like unto horses prepared unto battle; and on their heads were as it were crowns like gold, and their faces were as the faces of men. 8 And they had hair as the hair of women, and their teeth were as the teeth of lions. 9 And they had breastplates, as it were breastplates of iron; and the sound of their wings was as the sound of chariots of many horses running to battle. 10 And they had tails like unto scorpions, and there were stings in their tails: and their power was to hurt men five months.

Surely hideous apparitions such as these do not actually exist! Yet what were these "scorpiolocustes"? And who and what were the "stars" that fall, and fall, and fall again in the Book of Revelation? What was the literal referent for "beasts"—men, devils, or angels? When (where) was (is) there a "war in heaven"? Questions such as these are difficult to answer. It is not surprising, therefore, that Samuel Hartlib, the scholar to whom Milton dedicated *Of Education* (1644), complained that "the more one doth read the Expositors, the more one is confounded."[32] Indeed, in Renaissance Protestant commentaries on the Book of Revelation there were no "orthodox" or established interpretations. Few commentators agreed as to the meaning of individual symbols or texts. Commentators consistently disagreed as to whether the events and visions of Revelation should be ordered successively (chronologically, or event by event) or repetitively (in parallel groups of chapters). No commentator consistently interpreted the place of Revelation as being heaven, hell, or earth. For pious, sincere Protestant scholars the attempt to interpret the Book of Revelation produced controversy, disagreement, and, apparently, a considerable degree of frustration.

The discussion of Renaissance Protestant commentaries presented above admittedly is incomplete. It should be complete enough, however, to serve as the basis for two conclusions:

> First, the theological background of Milton's use of the Scripture in *Paradise Lost* is one of controversy and disagreement. Among Milton's contemporaries the meaning of the major scriptural texts which furnish the basis for Milton's account of the "begetting" of the Son, the War in Heaven, Lucifer's fall to Hell, was not a settled issue.

Second, applied to the Scriptures upon which Milton based his account of the heavenly cycle, the words ''orthodox'' and ''heterodox'' would seem to have little meaning. On the one hand it is possible to cite the statements of a number of reputable sixteenth- and seventeenth-century Protestant theologians to prove that virtually every aspect of the events which Milton describes in the heavenly cycle is theologically objectionable (Christ was ''begotten'' as the Lamb, there *was* no war in heaven, Lucifer was not the name of the devil, the Kingdom of God described in the Revelation is on earth, not in heaven, etc.). On the other hand, with one major exception (the ''begetting'' of Christ as the Lion), it is possible to cite the statements of equally reputable Renaissance Protestant authorities whose interpretations are in distinct agreement with those of Milton. This procedure, applied to the writings of such eminent Protestant theologians as Bèza, Foxe, Grotius, Junius, Pareus, Tremellius, and Zanchius, produces a singular conclusion: *Most* Renaissance Protestant theologians were ''heterodox.''

If one rejects this position, then the context in which Milton's use of the Bible in *Paradise Lost* may most profitably be examined is that of sixteenth- and seventeenth-century theological controversy and disagreement (not of ''heterodoxy'' and ''orthodoxy''). In *Paradise Lost* Milton sought to resolve controversy (and confusion) by interpreting the statements of the Bible consistently, regardless of the effect this interpretation might have upon dogma. This statement is important. To Milton, the commonly advanced explanations of the Book of Revelation were unsatisfactory. Yet there was a satisfactory explanation—provided one interpreted the Book of Revelation *consistently, in context,* and *in accordance with a single level of meaning.*

These three principles of biblical interpretation require at least brief comment. Milton sought to interpret the Book of Revelation:

1. *Consistently:* To Milton, explication of biblical texts based on figurative or secondary meanings was not objectionable *per se*.[33] Milton objected, however, to combining texts which were connotative (figurative or secondary in meaning) with texts which were denotative (restricted to exact meanings). Commentators tended to explain Revelation 5:5 in terms of Revelation 5:6–7. Milton questioned this type of explication, for, according to Milton, actions which are separate should not be combined (See pp. 20–24 above). First, in Revelation 5:5 Christ opened the book of God's decrees as the Lion, the King of Heaven. Then, in

Revelation 5:6–7, Christ opened the book of God's decrees as the Lamb, the Mediator between God and man. To Milton, the combination of passages containing such distinctly different levels of action so blurred the distinctions between literal and figurative meanings that the terms lost significance. According to Revelation 5:5, Christ was exalted to the Throne of God in heaven. Figuratively (not literally) the Throne of God in heaven symbolizes the Church of God on earth. Literally, however, heaven is more than a symbol. Heaven is heaven, the Empyrean, the Abiding Place of God himself. Thus, while "heaven" figuratively (or better, Milton's term, metaphorically) might designate "earth," "heaven" should not be interpreted as "earth" in one passage (Rev. 12) and "heaven" in another (Rev. 4). The symbols which John employed in Revelation—"heaven," "throne of God," "beasts," "stars," "earth," "locusts," and "pit"—might be interpreted either metaphorically or literally. They should not be applied, however, inconsistently to the Church of God on earth in one passage and to the Church of God in heaven in another.

2. *In context:* To Milton, the context of the Book of Revelation was, first, the Book of Revelation itself. According to Milton's contemporaries, the Book of Revelation was composed of seven parallel visions. In these visions no verse might be interpreted properly unless it was related to its similitude. The context of Revelation 5:5, the exaltation of Christ, was Revelation 12:5. The context of Revelation 12:4, the War in Heaven, was Revelation 6:1–8 and Revelation 8:6–12. The context of Revelation 6:12–17, the defeat and fall of Satan, was Revelation 7:2–17, 8:10, 9:1, and 12:5, 9. The elaborate series of parallels involved in this type of explication may be indicated by presenting a simplified version of Pareus' analysis of the structure of Revelation:

Revelation

Revelation 6:1–17 is parallel to Revelation 8:7–13, 9:1–21. Revelation 16:1–16, however, is related only to Revelation 6:9–17 and Revelation 8:12–13, 9:1–12. Revelation 20:1–22:6 recapitulates all visions, particularly the fifth and sixth visions, Revelation 15:1–16:21 and 17:1–19:21.

To Milton the context of the Book of Revelation was, second, the Bible as a whole. *Paradise Lost* is frequently described as an expansion of the Book of Genesis. This view is only partially justified. Actually the structure of *Paradise Lost* Milton derived from the Book of Revelation. Revelation is the whole of which Genesis and other books of the Bible are but parts. In Genesis 3:1–6 Adam and Eve are tempted by the serpent. The context of Genesis 3:1–6 is Revelation 12:6–17.[34] Isaiah 14:12–15, Ezekiel 28:1–9, Psalm 2:1–9, and Psalm 110:1–2 suggest reasons for Satan's presence in the Garden. These reasons are clarified in Revelation 12:5 and Revelation 5:5. Genesis 2:17 indicates that Adam and Eve were warned against improperly using freedom of choice. The content and context of this warning appear in Revelation 7:1–4 and Revelation 8:1–5. In Genesis 3:23–24, Adam and Eve are driven from the Garden. The history of their wanderings, the story of Satan's attacks upon mankind from the time of the fall of Adam and Eve to the end of time, appears in the parallel visions of the Book of Revelation. To Milton, properly interpreted, the Book of Revelation explained the Bible. Renaissance biblical scholarship justified the view: The Book of Revelation contains the story of "a battle that began at [the] beginning of [the] world, and shall holde on vnto the ende of the world: like as the Lorde foretold when he said to the serpent, I will set enmitie betwixt thee and the woman" (Gen. 3:15, the protevangelium; Rev. 12:7–10). It presents the story of the Church, of Adam and Eve, of "rightuous Abell, . . . Seth, Enos, Enoche, Noe, Sem, Thare, Melchisedech, Abraham, and Loth," laboring "With all hye strength . . . that the promised seede may encrease in the faith of all men."[35] With these conclusions of Renaissance scholarship Milton agreed—provided proper care was taken to distinguish between literal and metaphorical explications of Scripture.

3. *In accordance with a single level of meaning:* Texts which are literal and texts which are metaphorical should be interpreted

consistently, in context, and in accordance with a single level of meaning. In heaven, literally, Christ was "begotten" as the Son of God. Christ's appearance as the Son caused rebellion and war. After two "days," when the battle seemed lost, Christ exerted his power: Immediately Lucifer and his angels were routed and fell, ingloriously, to the depths of hell. Metaphorically, according to the Bible, the same pattern was repeated on earth. On earth, wrote Milton in *The Reason Of Church-governement Urg'd against Prelaty* (1641–42),

> the Gospell being the hidden might of Christ, as hath been heard, hath ever a victorious power joyn'd with it, like him in the Revelation that went forth on the white Horse with his bow and his crown conquering, and to conquer (RCG, III, 269, 14–18).

In heaven, as the rider of the white horse, Christ conquered Lucifer and his angels. On earth, as ("like") the rider of the white horse, Christ also conquered Lucifer and his angels. To Milton, these were two distinctly different events—events which should neither be intermingled nor combined. The War in Heaven was not the War on Earth. In heaven, literally, Christ triumphed as the Lion. On earth, metaphorically, Christ was victorious as the Lamb.

On earth, as the Lamb, Christ opened the seals of the book of God's decrees (Rev. 5:6–11, 6:1–2). Metaphorically, when the second seal is opened, Lucifer appears as the rider of the red horse (the symbol of war). Surrounded by the lurid, flickering flames of hell (P.L. I, 228–237; II, 512), Lucifer prepares to continue the War against Heaven (now the War against Earth):

Well have ye judg'd, well ended long debate,
Synod of Gods, and like to what ye are,
Great things resolv'd; which from the lowest deep
Will once more lift us up, in spight of Fate,
Neerer our ancient Seat; perhaps in view
Of those bright confines, whence with neighbouring Arms
And opportune excursion we may chance
Re-enter Heav'n; or else in some milde Zone
Dwell not unvisited of Heav'ns fair Light

Secure, and at the brightning Orient beam
Purge off this gloom.

(P.L. II, 390–400)

Somehow, someway, the war against God will be continued!

On earth the pattern of the events in heaven is repeated. On the first "day" of the War on Earth, Gabriel and the hosts of God are victorious (P.L. IV, 788–819, 977–1015; Rev. 6:3–4, 12:7a). Lucifer, defeated, again retreats ingloriously. On the second "day" of the War on Earth, Lucifer appears as the rider of the black horse. (For seven nights Lucifer circles the earth under cover of darkness, P.L. IX, 63–64. Then, with black, diabolical design, he re-enters the Garden of Eden at midnight, P.L. IX, 58. Enclosed in a "black mist" he searches for a means by which he can destroy God's new creation, man, P.L. IX, 180.) Afflicted with the black, crushing weight of heresy and spiritual famine, Eve, then Adam, is tempted and falls (P.L. IX, 655–732, 780–835, 856–885; Rev. 6:5–6, 12–13; 12:7b). The earth trembles and groans:

> Earth trembl'd from her entrails, as again
> In pangs, and Nature gave a second groan,
> Skie lowr'd, and muttering Thunder, som sad drops
> Wept at compleating of the mortal Sin
> Original.

(P.L. IX, 1000–1004)

> ...high Winds worse within
> Began to rise, high Passions, Anger, Hate,
> Mistrust, Suspicion, Discord, and shook sore
> Thir inward State of Mind, calm Region once
> And full of Peace, now tost and turbulent:
> For Understanding rul'd not, and the Will
> Heard not her lore, both in subjection now
> To sensual Appetite, who from beneathe
> Usurping over sovran Reason claimd
> Superior sway.

(P.L. IX, 1122–1131)

On the second "day" of the War on Earth, Lucifer is victorious.

On the third "day," in the midst of the "earthquake," Death, the rider of the pale horse, enters the world (P.L. IX, 792, 954; X, 588–590). Earth lies crushed under the weight of pestilence (death), spiritual famine, and war (P.L. XI, 477–493, 555–627, 637–711; Rev. 6:8). When the battle seems lost, however, Christ appears to save mankind (Rev. 6:1–2, 7–8; 8:3–5; 12:10). As the rider of the white horse, fulfilling his "office" as Mediator, Christ overcomes the power of evil (Death and Sin). Defeated, Satan again retreats to hell.

As on earth, so in heaven. Heaven, however, is not earth. Thus, although some biblical texts may contain two levels of meaning, all texts are not of this nature. This basic principle of biblical exegesis must be considered carefully if Milton's use of the Bible in *Paradise Lost* is to be understood. Whether or not Milton's interpretation of Scripture is consistently literal or metaphorical or even valid the reader alone must decide. Before passing judgment four factors should be considered, however: 1) Milton's interpretation of the Book of Revelation was based upon the view that Revelation is composed of a series of successive or parallel visions. 2) Milton's explication of Scripture was neither literal nor metaphorical in the sense in which these terms are defined in modern dictionaries. 3) The background of Milton's use of the Bible in *Paradise Lost* is seventeenth-century theological disagreement and controversy (not heterodoxy or orthodoxy). 4) "The requisites for the public interpretation of Scripture," wrote Milton,

> . . . consist in knowledge of languages; inspection of the originals; examination of the context; care in distinguishing between literal and figurative expressions; consideration of cause and circumstance; of antecedents and consequents; mutual comparison of texts; and regard to the analogy of faith. Attention must also be paid to the frequent anomalies of syntax; . . . Lastly, no inferences from the text are to be admitted, but such as follow necessarily and plainly from the words themselves; lest we should be constrained to receive what is not written for what is written, the shadow for the substance, the fallacies of human reason for the doctrines of God . . . (C. D. XXX, 263, 26–265, 1–7, 16–21).

After these conditions have been met (a requirement that certainly cannot be fulfilled by the author of this study), then perhaps questions concerning the consistency and validity of Milton's interpretation of the Bible may be answered. To interpret Milton's theology in the light of twentieth-century theology is dangerous. A tremendous amount of sifting through Renaissance commentaries remains to be done.

CHAPTER FOUR

Flight and Frustration

> A Dungeon horrible, on all sides round
> As one great Furnace flam'd, yet from those flames
> No light, but rather darkness visible
> Serv'd onely to discover sights of woe,
> Regions of sorrow, doleful shades, where peace
> And rest can never dwell, hope never comes
> That comes to all; but torture without end
> Still urges. . . .
>
> (P.L. I, 61–68)

What was God doing before he created the world? Augustine's reply (repeated by Calvin) was that this was a question to which no answer is possible.[1] Questions regarding the nature of God are unanswerable. This is "forbidden knowledge." Yet both Augustine and Calvin based much of their writings on questions which involved this type of knowledge. The entire twelfth book of the *City of God,* for example, is devoted to a discussion of the eternal acts of God. Indeed, without assuming that the original, eternal decree of God was one of election and reprobation, Calvin could not have written the *Institutes of the Christian Religion.* It is doubtful whether any serious study of Christianity may be undertaken if the acts of God are restricted to events which transpire after the beginning of time.

What happened to Lucifer, then, in the timeless eternity which existed after he was expelled from heaven? This question, which is basic in any study of man's place on earth, Renaissance Protestant theologians virtually were forced to consider in their commentaries. According to II Peter 2:4 (Jude 6), "God spared not the angels that sinned, but cast them down to hell [ταρταρώσας], and delivered them into chains of darkness, to be reserved unto judgment." Where was the hell into which the "angels that sinned" (Lucifer and his angels) were cast? What was the meaning of the "chains of darkness" ("everlasting chains under darkness," Jude 6) with which Satan was bound? If Satan was bound, when was he loosed? To these and other questions regarding the devil, Renaissance theologians (at least from Milton's point of view) produced answers which were both contradictory and confusing.

Where was the place of Lucifer's confinement? The Protestant answer to this question tended to be stumbling and uncertain. Many commentators, although convinced that hell existed, nevertheless refused to assign any definite place for its location.[2] (Thus in 1631 Catholic Bishop Richard Smith was enabled to charge Protestants with restricting hell to "nothing but a wicked conscience.")[3] Other Protestant commentators were more positive in their statements. Where was hell? Hell was located "somewhere" above the surface of the earth ("betwixt the upper region of the ayre and the globe of the sun" or the moon, Isa. 30:33; Eph. 2:2, 6:12),[4] under the surface of the earth (in the sea, Matt. 8:28–32; Luke 8:30–33; Rom. 10:7; Rev. 13:1;[5] in the center of the earth, Ps. 71:20; Isa. 30:33; Rev. 9:1, 20:1, 15),[6] or at the extreme edge of the cosmos (Gen. 1:2; Isa. 30:33; Matt. 8:12; Luke 8:30–33; Rom. 10:7; Rev. 9:1, 20:1, 15).[7]

Still more controversial, perhaps, was the meaning of the "chains of darkness" with which Lucifer was bound after his expulsion from heaven. Most theologians agreed that the chains represented some form of limitation of Lucifer's power to commit evil. The degree to which Lucifer's power had been limited, however, was thoroughly disputed. Some writers explained Lucifer's chains as a figure of speech, as a symbol of the agonizing, soul-searing pangs of conscience and remorse which the devil and his followers (superhuman as well as human) must endure for eternity.[8] Other writers regarded Lucifer's chains as more than a figure of speech. Lucifer was bound with literal chains, chains of actual pain and punishment.[9]

When was Lucifer bound in his chains? To some theologians, the initial binding of Satan described in II Peter and Jude was the same "binding" of Satan (the destruction of Satan's power by Christ) which was described in Revelation 9 and Revelation 20.[10] To other theologians, this interpretation "was not right." First, immediately after his expulsion from heaven (the Empyrean), Satan was bound with the chains referred to in II Peter and Jude. Then, cast out of "heaven" (the Church) by Christ's (or Constantine's) victory on earth, Satan was bound a second time in Revelation 12:9.[11] The third and final binding of Satan had not yet been accomplished. Nor would it be accomplished until the time of Revelation 20:2, in the future, on the day of final judgment. None of these interpretations were scripturally valid, insisted still other theologians. Although restricted, actually Satan had never been bound. Nor would he be bound until the time of the Millennium when the Saints would reign on earth for a thousand years.[12]

If, as many theologians believed, Satan had been bound in the past, then obviously he had broken his fetters. When was Satan loosed from his chains? According to Revelation 20:2, Satan was to be bound for a thousand years. When would these thousand years expire? To this question commentators gave three distinctly different answers: Some writers regarded the thousand years as no more than a past but indefinite figure.[13] Other writers related the loosing of the devil specifically to the coming of the Antichrist in the fourteenth or the fifteenth century (a thousand years after the binding of the devil by Constantine).[14] The third view (that Satan had not yet been bound) particularly interested seventeenth-century theologians. Most commentators agreed that the duration of the world was 6000 years. The conventionally accepted dates for the creation of the world ranged from 4004 to 3928 B.C.[15] To these dates, some Protestant theologians added 200 to 400 years.[16] Thus, it was argued, if creation occurred before 4300 B.C., the time of Satan's binding would occur before 1700. Similarly anticipating the Millennium, other theologians preferred to base their calculations upon a conflation of Revelation 11:1–14, 12:3–14, 13:1–18, 20:1–4, with Daniel 2:31–45, 7:23–25, 12:7–13.[17] Both groups came to much the same conclusion. First, between 1650 and 1700, Antichrist would be overthrown and/or the Jews would be converted. Then, before 1700, the Saints would begin their reign. Christ would return either visibly or invisibly to establish his kingdom on earth.

The Millennium—the thousand years of Satan's binding—was at hand! This was the view of such writers as Foster, Hartlib, More, Rogers, and Napier. Christ would return in 1650–1651

(Foster), 1655 (Hartlib), 1660 (More), 1666 (Rogers), or 1688–1700 (Napier).[18] In 1641 Milton expressed a similar view:

> ... thy Kingdome is now at hand, and thou standing at the dore. Come forth out of thy Royall Chambers, O Prince of all the Kings of the earth, put on the visible roabes of thy imperiall Majesty, take up that unlimited Scepter which thy Almighty Father hath bequeath'd thee; for now the voice of thy Bride calls thee, and all creatures sigh to bee renew'd. *(Animadversions Upon The Remonstrants Defence*, III, 148, 19–25)[19]

In *Paradise Lost,* a poem written some ten to twenty years after the *Animadversions,* chastened and wiser, Milton rejected the millennial position.[20] After 1655–1660, Milton no longer anticipated an imminent, earthly *regnum Christi.* In *Paradise Lost* the throne which Christ ascends is a spiritual throne. The ultimate binding of Satan Milton reserves to the Day of Judgment (P.L. XII, 451–463; cf. C. D. XXXIII, 359, 9–367, 13) when, metaphorically as well as literally, the cycle of Christ's victory over evil will be completed. To Milton, after 1655–1660, interpretation of the Books of Revelation and of Daniel as a history of the Antichrist, use of the Bible to predict earthly events and to establish the date of the Parousia, represented a perversion of Scripture. Instead, interpreted properly, the Book of Revelation related the story of the acts of God—of God, not of man, literally in heaven and metaphorically on earth. What happened to Lucifer after he had been expelled from heaven? To Milton, the writer of *Paradise Lost*, the simple, plain, and literal answer of the Bible was that Lucifer fell immediately into the hell of the "bottomless pit" of Revelation 9:1 and 20:1. Here for a "thousand years" (literally but not metaphorically) he was bound with the "chains of darkness" of II Peter 2:4, Jude 6, Revelation 9:1 and 20:1.

Where was this "bottomless pit"? "It does not seem probable," wrote Milton in *The Christian Doctrine,*

> that hell should have been prepared within the limits of this world, in the bowels of the earth, on which the curse had not as yet passed. This is said to have been the opinion of Chrysostom, as likewise of Luther and some later divines. Besides, if, as has been shown from various passages of the New Testament, the whole world is to be finally consumed by fire, it follows that hell, being situated in the

center of the earth, must share the fate of the surrounding universe, and perish likewise; a consummation more to be desired than expected by the souls in perdition (C. D. XXXIII, 375, 2–11).

Hell, then, could not be located within the confines of the earth. To Milton, this was the plain statement of the Bible. The word which is translated as "pit" ($\overset{\text{α}}{\alpha}\beta\upsilon\sigma\sigma\grave{o}\varsigma$) in Revelation 9:1 (King James Version) is the same word which is translated as "the deep" (תְּהוֹם) in Luke 8:31 and Genesis 1:2. The two terms (pit or abyss, without bottom; deep, sea, chaos, the "disordered forme at the first creation") are synonyms. After their defeat in heaven, therefore, Lucifer and his angels did not fall into the "sea" or into the "air" of the earth. According to the Bible, Lucifer and his followers fell into and through the chaos, the earth "without form, and void" (Gen. 1:2), the "sea" and the "air" of the bottomless pit. By this pit, wrote Pareus and Hayne, is not meant

the whole gulfe, but as it were the deepest and narrowest receptacle & filthy sinck of hell. . . . It is called in Gr. $\overset{\text{α}}{\alpha}\beta\upsilon\sigma\sigma\grave{o}\varsigma$ beeing derived from α & $\beta\upsilon\Theta\grave{o}\varsigma$, or $\beta\acute{\upsilon}\sigma\sigma o\varsigma$, which signifies *a bottom*, as it were without bottom: or from α and $\beta\acute{\upsilon}\omega$ *to cover,* for the deep is covered with waters. The word in scripture is used, *first* for the Chaos or disordered forme at the first creation, *darknesse beeing upon the face of the deep,* Gen. 1.2. *Secondly* for the depth of the sea or waters. Gen. 7.11. *And the fountains of the great deep were opened.* Psal. 42.7. *deep calleth unto deep at the noyse of thy water spouts. Thirdly* for hell, as Luk. 8.31. where the devils beseech Christ, *that he would not command them to goe out into the deep.* & Rom. 10.7. *Who shall descend into the deep?* so here and in many other places of this booke.[21]

That which in *Rev.* 20. is termed *the bottomlesse pit,* is in other notions cald *Earth and Sea, Rev.* 12.12. and *aire or darknesse; Ephes.* 2.2. *The aire,* saith Philo Jud. *is black and dark of its own nature, and is cald* $\sigma\kappa\acute{o}\tau\iota\alpha$ *darknesse.* Hence the devill is stiled the Prince of the ayre and of darknesse. The Sea and Earth also have no light of themselves, but from above. When therefore it is said, the devill hath power in the ayre, earth, or sea, by these are meant men of dark, earthly, and unquiet minds. In which sense it is said, Rev. 12.12. *Woe bee to the inhabitants of the earth and Sea,* for Satan being by Christ cast out of the heaven of the Church, hee came amongst the inhabitants of the Ayre, Sea, and Earth, that is, men who were not heavenly minded. The affinitie of these terms appears, first, because the *Beast which* Apoc. 13.1. *is said to rise out of the Sea, is spoken of* Apoc. 9.7 [17.8.] *as ascending out of the bottomlesse pit:* And secondly, there is a *Tehom*, an Abysse or bottomlesse pit, *Psal. 71.20. ascribed to the Earth,* as elswhere to the Sea.[22]

In hell (the "bottomless pit") Lucifer was bound with "chains of darkness" (II Peter, Jude, Revelation). These chains, declared a number of Protestant divines, were a symbol of spiritual anguish and suffering. Milton qualified this view. Certainly Lucifer was bound with spiritual chains, chains which condemned him to endure increasingly severe pangs of conscience and remorse. Throughout *Paradise Lost* Lucifer suffers constantly from the "hell" within himself (P.L. I, 252–255; IV, 18–23). To Milton, however, hell was considerably more than a state of mind.[23] It was more than a figurative hell, with figurative chains, figurative fire and brimstone (images of the spiritual sufferings of the creature who is "estranged from the fellowshippe of God"),[24] into which Lucifer fell. Lucifer's chains—the fires and the other torments of hell—were real, agonizingly real, and ever present. Milton's view was expressed graphically by two of his contemporaries:

> Thinke of a gloomy, hideous, and deepe Lake, full of pestilent dampes and rotten vapours, as thicke as cloudes of pitch, more palpable than the fogs of Egipt; that the eye of the Sunne is too dull to peirce them, and his heate too weake to dissolue them. Adde hereunto a fire flashing in the reprobates face; which shall yeeld no more light then with a glimpse to shew him the torments of others, and others the torments of himselfe; yet withall, of so violent a burning that should it glow on mountaines of steele, it would melt them like mountaines of Snow.[25]

> May be you will object, if there be *fire*, there is assuredly light; nay, (without question) this *fire* hath *heat*, no *light*; it is a dark smoaky flame, that burns dimm to the eye, yet sharp to the sence: or it may be, (as some do imagine) this *fire* affords a little Sulphureous or obscure light, but how? not for comfort, but confusion. Conceive it thus, he that in twilight sees deformed Images, or in the night beholds shapes of Ghosts, and spirits, by a dimm dark light, why better he saw nothing, then such terrible visions; such fears, nay a thousand times worse are presented to the eyes of Reprobates, they may discern through darkness, the ugly faces of fiends, the foul visages of Reprobates, the furious torments of their friends, or parents, while all lye together in the same condemnation.[26]

Whether or not Milton had read these particular descriptions of hell by Adams and Ambrose is relatively unimportant. Considerably more significant is the fact that Milton's view of the place and nature of hell was, as indicated by the selections presented above, based upon a literal reading of Scripture. To a number of Milton's contemporaries, hell and hell-fire were figures of speech. To Milton, as well as to other theologians, this view was invalid. According to the Bible, hell was an actual place, with literal chains of torment, both physical and spiritual. It was into this hell that Lucifer fell following his expulsion from heaven. First, declared Milton, Lucifer was cast into the hell of the bottomless pit. Later, after the "air" and the "sea" (the earth) were created, after Adam and Eve were tempted and sinned, Lucifer became "the prince of the power of the air" (Eph. 2:2). In the beginning, however, hell was unrelated to the earth. It was not until Sin and Death invaded the world that the earth became a part of the empire of the devil (P.L. X, 403–409).

In the beginning, before the world was created, Lucifer and his angels were cast into the "pit" of hell, an actual place, distinct from chaos, located at the edge of the cosmos. This was the statement of Revelation 6:8, 9:1, 12:12, and 20:1 (as well as Gen. 1:2, Isa. 30:33, Luke 8:31, and other passages), four passages in Revelation which Milton regarded as being complementary in time, place, and action. The view that three of these passages are parallel has been discussed in Chapter 2. Milton's use of Revelation 20 as an additional parallel follows the same line of thought:

1 And I saw an angel come down from heaven, having the key of the bottomless pit and a great chain in his hand. 2 And he laid hold on the dragon, that old serpent, which is the Devil, and Satan, and bound him a thousand years. 3 And cast him into the bottomless pit, and shut him up, and set a seal upon him, that he should deceive the nations no more, till the thousand years should be fulfilled: and after that he must be loosed a little season (Rev. 20:1–3).

"What is this," asked Pareus, "but the casting out of the Dragon, and his Angels into the earth by Michael, as in Chap. 12.9?[27] A similar view appeared in the commentaries written by Erasmus, Bullinger, Marlorat, Tremellius, Foxe, Napier, Junius, and Gyffard.[28] Indeed, the view that Revelation 20:1–3 and Revelation 12:9 were parallel was perhaps the one structural aspect of the Book of Revelation upon which most sixteenth- and seventeenth-century commentators were agreed. According to Gyffard, for example,

> [The binding of Satan] doth not set foorth Satans finall destruction, but is Auncient matter, how hee was bound and chained vp in old time. . . . This Angel is our Lord Iesus, the great chaine wherewith he doth bind him, is the holy and pure doctrine of the gospell, the time that he was then taken and bound with it, was when first Christ preached it, and then his Apostles vnto all nations. . . . we must not take it that Satan is shut vp in hell for this time in such sort as that he should do nothing in the world: but he is said to bee chaind vp in the bottomlesse pit, to signifie that hee could not now generally seduce as he had done. He wrought now in the wicked mightily, and with so great rage and wrath, that it is sayd Chap. 12. Woe be to the inhabitants of the earth, and of the sea: for behold, the deuil is come downe vnto you, full of wrath, knowing that he hath but a short time. Then make this account that Satan, in these thousand yeares, was bound one way, but another way he was loose. He was bound for seducing (as S. Iohn expresseth it) but he was not bound from other mischiefes which he wrought in great plentie. After the thousand yeares expired, S. Iohn saith, he must be let loose againe, for a little season. This little time, in which the deuill was let loose, is the time in which the great Antichrist did beare swaye.

Metaphorically, according to the view presented above, Satan was cast into the pit of hell and bound by Christ's victory on the cross. Milton accepted this view only in part. On earth, Milton agreed, Satan was bound by Christ's victory on the cross. Milton's statement is specific. In the fullness of time, Michael tells Adam, Christ will appear to destroy the power of Sin and Death, the "two maine armes" of Satan. Then, having fulfilled his mediatorial office, Christ will ascend

> With victory, triumphing through the aire
> Over his foes and thine; there shall surprise
> The Serpent, Prince of aire, and drag in Chaines
> Through all his Realme, and there confounded leave;
> Then enter into glory, and resume

His Seat at Gods right hand, exalted high
Above all names in Heav'n.
                    (P.L. XII, 452–458; cf. III, 250–257)

On earth Satan will be (has been) bound with the "great chaine" of
the "holy and pure doctrine of the gospell" (P.L. XII, 386–410).
This view of the commentators Milton accepted without question.
The concomitants of this view, the assumptions, first, that Satan
was not punished for his rebellion against God until Christ
appeared upon earth, and second, that Satan had complete
freedom to tempt mankind until Christ appeared on earth, long
after Satan's original expulsion from heaven, Milton rejected as
unsound doctrine. From the very beginning, Milton insisted,
Satan was bound with "chains of darkness." His powers were
restricted. "Is there no place Left for Repentance, none for
Pardon left?" asks Lucifer (P.L. IV, 79–80). Milton's answer was
a resounding "no!" In hell, damned, doomed to endure physical
pain and spiritual anguish, condemned to a future of unending and
increasing frustration, deterioration, degeneration, and despair,
from the beginning Lucifer was bound in chains—chains which
were unrelated to Christ's appearance as the Lamb or as the
Mediator on earth (see Chapter 1).

Lucifer falls from heaven to hell. There, amid "Regions of
sorrow, doleful shades, where peace And rest can never dwell"
(P.L. I, 65–66), he attempts to re-establish his kingdom. Erasmus,
commenting upon Revelation 9, suggests the type of explanation
which furnished the basis for the action that follows:

> . . . the deuyll, whiche is a counterfetter of gods workes, imageneth
> by all meanes that he can, to set vp and stablyshe all maner of
> intollerable errours, and to augment his kyngdome: And goeth
> about to make him selfe a god, and to fyght and stryue againste the
> gospell, and against all godlynes. But thorowe the iudgement of god,
> he is fallen downe from heauen, vnto the earthe, and hath receyued
> thorowe the iudgement of god, and thorowe his permission, the key
> of hell and of the botomles pyt of all wykednesse, euen lyke as
> Christ is ascended and gone vp and thorow his merites and
> rightuousnes, hath opened the heauen, and hath receyued the
> kyngdome of god, for all the faithfull electe. And out of this hellyshe
> botomles pyt, arose a smoke of worldly wysdome, & of fleshly

lustes, by the whiche, al godlynes planted of Christ and of the apostles, thorow the preachyng of the gospel, is obscured and darckened.[29]

One significant difference exists between Erasmus' and Milton's interpretation of Revelation 9. To Milton, of course, it was not to earth that Satan originally fell. Otherwise Erasmus' interpretation of this passage was similar to Milton's. Interpreted literally, Revelation 9 depicted Satan's attempt, after his defeat in heaven, to establish his kingdom in hell. This was the statement of Revelation 9:11:

And they had a king over them, which is the angel of the bottomless pit, whose name in the Hebrew tongue is Abaddon, but in the Greek tongue hath his name Apollyon.

In hell, permitted by God to break his chains (which nevertheless remain unbroken), Satan rises from the Lake of Fire. Around him, in the sulphurous, burning stink of hell, he sees "His Legions, Angel Forms, who lay intrans't Thick as Autumnal Leaves that strow the Brooks In *Vallombrosa*" (P.L. I, 301–303). The epic simile is striking. The plumes of Lucifer's warriors are gay, bedecked with the colors of Autumn. Swords glitter, shields flash, banners wave on high. Yet the grandeur of Lucifer's legions is only semblance. Cut off from the tree of life, the rebel angels are "like the chaff which the wind driveth away" (Ps. 1:4, 2:2; Isa. 17:13, 64:6; Jude 12).[30] They have the appearance of life. Actually, however, they already are brittle and sterile, spiritually "dead."

Heaping upon themselves chains of damnation (P.L. I, 215), the hosts of Satan rise like "the smoke of a great furnace" (Rev. 9:2). Like locusts (Milton follows the biblical change in figures of speech), Lucifer's legions swarm through the "air" to obey the commands of their King.

> As when the potent Rod
> Of *Amrams* Son in *Egypts* evill day
> Wav'd round the Coast, up call'd a pitchy cloud
> Of *Locusts,* warping on the Eastern Wind
> That ore the Realm of impious *Pharaoh* hung
> Like Night, and darken'd all the Land of *Nile:*
> So numberless were those bad Angels seen

> Hovering on wing under the Cope of Hell
> 'Twixt upper, nether, and surrounding Fires.
>
> (P.L. I, 338–346)

The locusts, the horsemen of Revelation 6:3–8, are the hosts of Satan which are described in Revelation 9:2–10, 15–21.[31]

Milton now reverses the picture which he has drawn of the "Synod" of God in heaven (P.L. V, 586–599; XI, 67). In hell, surrounded by his satellites (the fallen stars of heaven), Lucifer sits exalted

> High on a Throne of Royal State, which far
> Outshon the wealth of *Ormus* and of *Ind,*
> Or where the gorgeous East with richest hand
> Showrs on her Kings *Barbaric* Pearl and Gold.
>
> (P.L. II, 1–4)

Lucifer's throne (Θρόνος, Rev. 2:13) is resplendent, glittering, outwardly a glorious work of art. Appearance again is deceptive, however. Lucifer's throne, unlike God's throne (Θρόνος, Rev. 4:2–3), is heavy and ornate. Weighed down with barbaric trappings of gold, diamonds, and pearls, actually it is no more than a monstrous lie. Next to Lucifer sits Beelzebub, the Lord of the Dung Hill, the Prince of Hell (Matt. 12:24–27; Mark 3:22; Luke 11:18–19). Around the thrones of Lucifer and Beelzebub are placed the thrones of Moloc (II Kings 23:10; Ps. 2:2; Isa. 30:33; John 8:44), Belial (Ps. 2:1, 18:4; Nah. 1:9–11, 14–15; John 8:44; II Cor. 6:15), and Mammon (Matt. 6:24; Luke 16:9–13; I Tim. 6:10), Lucifer's "loyal" chieftains. Beyond Moloc, Belial, and Mammon sit the "four and twenty elders" (Rev. 4:4), the "thousand Demy-Gods" (P.L. I, 796) of hell. "Round about the throne" appear "four beasts full of eyes before and behind" (Rev. 4:6): Beelzebub, Satan's *alter ego;* Moloc, who was "a murderer from the beginning"; Belial, who "abode not in the truth, because there is no truth in him"; and Mammon, whose "love of money" (materialism) "is the root of all evil," are the infernal representatives of the four beasts of heaven. The scene of Satan's coronation is the reverse of Christ's coronation in Revelation 5:5 and 12:5.

In the midst of murders, liars, and materialists, as the King of Tophet, the garbage heap of chaos, Lucifer sits "exalted," by "merit" raised to "eminence." Who is this King of glory? He is the Ape of God, the "man of sin," "the son of perdition," the Antichrist "Who opposeth and exalteth himself above all that is called God, or that is worshipped; so that he as God sitteth in the temple of God, shewing himself that he is God" (II Thess. 2:3–4; Isa. 14:13; I John 2:22–23; Rev. 9:11). To English Protestants of the seventeenth century perhaps no more horrifying picture of the devil could have been drawn. Lucifer is the Antichrist, metaphorically the Pope of Rome. This typically Protestant view—which will not be established by quotation—Milton unquestionably accepted. Metaphorically, to Milton, Lucifer was the Pope (P.L. I, 710–730; III, 474–496; X, 312–313).[32] By referring to the earthly agents of Lucifer, Milton intensified his picture of evil. The ectype of Satan was any force which rebelled against God—Egyptian, Turk, Hun, Jew, Syrian, or Englishman (P.L. I, 338–346, 347–348, 351–355, 381–391, 446–457, 500–502). Initially, however, it was the devil, not the Pope, who had confounded the peace of heaven, corrupted the Church, and perverted the truths of religion. To Milton, who insisted upon distinguishing between texts which were metaphorical and texts which were literal, literally Lucifer was Lucifer, the "son of perdition," the ruler of the devils in hell.

As the Antichrist seated upon his throne of pride, Lucifer represents the epitome of evil. To his followers, Lucifer boasts of the advantages of hell. Hell is a republic (Job 1:6, 2:1, I Kings 22:19).[33] Here decrees are not issued by fiat from the throne (Rev. 5:1; P.L. V, 600–615). The laws of hell are established by the common consent of all:

> Whether of open Warr or covert guile,
> We now debate ...
>
>   (P.L. II, 41–42)

> Well have ye judg'd, well ended long debate,
> Synod of Gods ...
>
>   (P.L. II, 390–391)

>   ... whom shall we send
> In search of this new world, whom shall we find
> Sufficient?
>
>   (P.L. II, 402–404)

Lucifer's claim of freedom, of course, is as vast a mockery as is the pretended glory of his throne. The issue which the fallen angels debate already has been decided. Before the beginning of the Great Consult, Lucifer already has determined his plan of attack:

> I give not Heav'n for lost . . .
>
> > (P.L. II, 14)

> > To bow and sue for grace
> With suppliant knee, and deifie his power,
> Who from the terrour of this Arm so late
> Doubted his Empire, that were low indeed . . .
>
> > (P.L. I, 111–114)

> > . . . our better part remains
> To work in close design, by fraud or guile
> What force effected not . . .
>
> > (P.L. I, 645–647)

> > . . . this Infernal Pit shall never hold
> Caelestial Spirits in Bondage . . .
>
> > (P.L. I, 657–658)

> > . . . [then] *Beelzebub*
> Pleaded his devilish Counsel, first devis'd
> By *Satan,* and in part propos'd . . .
>
> > (P.L. II, 378–380)

> > Thus saying rose
> The Monarch, and prevented all reply. . . .
>
> > (P.L. II, 466–467)

In hell there is no freedom of choice.

Moloc, Belial, and Mammon may debate alternate plans of action. Only the proposal advanced by Beelzebub, Lucifer's second in command, actually will be considered, however. "The fixt Laws of Heav'n Did first create [me] your Leader, next free choice" (P.L. II, 18–19), Lucifer proclaims. The statement is a lie. Possibly, at least according to Thomas Carleton, after their fall the devils

> by common consent agreed on the election of Lucifer and placed him over themselves, first because he was by nature the most

outstanding, then out of hatred of God, inasmuch as he had offended Him more than the rest, and induced the others to offend Him; then also out of malevolence and hatred toward men, the inhabitants of the lower world hoped that certainly by his industry and wiles, both through himself and through the agents established by him, to be able to draw men into the gravest sins against God and finally into eternal torments.

Yet Hell is scarcely a republic:

> On the contrary, heaven, an inanimate thing, exercises its influence in descending steps upon man, the lion, and the rest of the animals, nay, even on the plants and trees; moreover, this holds true even among those lower down. Thus at random any Angel might be set lower than a more perfect Angel, and thus the lowest Angel would have as many masters as there were Angels more perfect than he.[34]

The concept (basically that of the Chain of Being) was expressed earlier and more exactly by Sir John Fortesque in the fifteenth century:

> Hell alone, inhabited by none but sinners, asserts its claim to escape the embraces of this order. . . . [Yet] from the highest angel down to the lowest of his kind there is absolutely not found an angel that has not a superior and inferior; nor from man down to the meanest worm is there any creature which is not in some respect superior to one creature and inferior to another.[35]

Lucifer's position in no way depends upon the choice of his subjects. As an angel, though fallen, Lucifer derives his power from heaven, not hell.

"Whether of open Warr or covert guile, We now debate," declares Lucifer magnanimously. The debate is a fraud. "Whom shall we send . . .?" Lucifer asks his council. The question is meaningless. Lucifer already has determined to send himself. The utter selfishness of Lucifer's motives is clearly revealed in Lucifer's speech to Gabriel:

> Lives ther who loves his pain?
> Who would not, finding way, break loose from Hell,
> Though thither doomd? Thou wouldst thy self, no doubt,
> And boldly venture to whatever place
> Farthest from pain, where thou mightest hope to change
> Torment with ease, and soonest recompence

> Dole with delight, which in this place I sought;
> To thee no reason; who knowst only good,
> But evil hast not tri'd: and wilt object
> His will who bound us? let him surer barr
> His Iron Gates, if he intends our stay
> In that dark durance.

>   (P.L. IV, 888–899)

Lucifer, as Gabriel points out, is no bold and courageous hero. He is, rather, a selfish, frustrated, malignant spirit who constantly asks himself a single question: How can *I* escape the tortures of hell?

To Lucifer, God is a god of vengeance. Lucifer is right. God is a god of vengeance (P.L. VI, 808–812). But Lucifer is damned. For the fallen angels there can be neither mercy nor hope:

> First, The wicked in hell, they have this loss; they are deprived of, and banished from the favourable presence of God....
> Secondly, They lose not only God and Christ, but they lose the company of Saints and Angels for ever....
> Thirdly, You lose Heaven, the place of blessedness....
> Fourthly, You lose not only God, and Christ, and Angels, but (which is not the least of your misery) you lose all pitie from God, and Christ, and all the Saints of God. It is some comfort in misery, to be pitied by a friend, but in hell you shall lose all kind of pitie. God shall not pitie you; *he shall laugh at your destruction, and mock you when your fear comes* [Ps. 2:4, 37:13, 52:6; Prov. 1:26; Rev. 14:10]. The godly shall not pitie you, they shall rejoyce to see Gods power, and Gods glory in your damnation. It is the speech of *Austine,* Neither Creator, nor creature shall be affected with any sympathy towards the damned in all their torments: When thou art scorching in thy flames, when thou art howling in thy torments, then God shall laugh at thy destruction....[36]

The passage quoted above is scarcely enjoyable. It provides, however, an excellent illustration of the attitude with which Milton intended his readers to regard Lucifer and the fallen angels. In *Paradise Lost* God shows no pity for Lucifer. Indeed, following Lucifer's revolt, God even laughs at Lucifer's "vain designes and tumults vain" (P.L. V, 735–737, 718). To Lucifer, God is merciless and cruel. But Lucifer is weighed down with chains of damnation. *For the damned* there exist only hopelessness and agony of spirit. *This* was the decree of God:

> ...him who disobeyes
> Mee disobeyes, breaks union, and that day
> Cast out from God and blessed vision, falls
> Into utter darkness, deep ingulft, his place
> Ordaind without redemption, without end.
>
> (P.L. V, 611–615)

Having broken union, Lucifer no longer can expect mercy or pity from God (Man "shall find grace, The other none," P.L. III, 131–132). The way of the transgressor is hard.

Damned, desperate, degenerating both in body and in spirit, Lucifer's only recourse is to clutch at a straw:

> There went a fame in Heav'n that he [God] ere long
> Intended to create, and therein plant
> A generation, whom his choice regard
> Should favour equal to the Sons of Heaven:
> Thither, if but to pry, shall be perhaps
> Our first eruption, thither or elsewhere.
>
> (P.L. I, 651–656)

A rumor, forsooth! It was upon a rumor ("a fame") that Lucifer based his "study of revenge, immortal hate, And courage never to submit or yield" (P.L. I, 107–108)? A rumor provided a better means of striking back at God than the plans proposed by Moloc, Belial, and Mammon? To be sure, by an "Oath That shook Heav'ns whol circumference" (P.L. II, 352–353), God has sworn to create man. To Lucifer, however, both the meaning and the time of implementation of God's oath are uncertain. God's decree is no more than a rumor. Lucifer's decision to act upon future possibility, therefore, is an act of desperation. Lucifer has fallen indeed!

> ...whatsoeuer is bright and shining in Heauen and in earth, it borroweth his brightnesse from another: but Christ is light of him selfe, and shining by him selfe, and lightening with his brightnesse the whole worlde: insomuche that there is no other cause or Originall of brightnesse, but hee.... without Christ there is not one sparke of true light. There maye appeare some shewe of bryght-

nesse, but it is lyke to a sodayne flashe, which doeth nothing else
but dasell the eyes.[37]

The devil still retains an outward "shewe of bryghtnesse"; both
externally and internally, however, his brilliance has begun to
fade. Lucifer is a creature—he is not God. Only Christ is God.

The Lord Jesus is light by nature, creatures by borrowing of an
other: he giueth light, creatures receiue light. They neede lyght
because they haue none by nature. . . .[38]

As a creature, separated from the "true Light" (John 1:9),
necessarily Lucifer must degenerate. To Lucifer, light has become
"darkness visible" (P.L. I, 63). His plan for renewing the war
against God is pitiful. It may even be described as insane! Yet he
has no better plan (Ps. 28:5). In agony, as Satan, he cries:

> Ay me, they [Satan's subjects] little know
> How dearly I abide that boast so vaine,
> Under what torments inwardly I groane;
> While they adore me on the Throne of Hell,
> With Diadem and Scepter high advanc'd
> The lower still I fall, onely Supream
> In miserie. . . .

>   (P.L. IV, 86–92)

Lucifer has been bound with chains of damnation. He may break
his chains—his chains, nevertheless, remain unbroken.

God rules! "Heaven . . . exercises its influence in descending
steps" upon devils as well as upon angels and man. Satan may
loose his chains, but he cannot escape the fetters imposed upon
him by God. To Milton, Satan was a being to be feared, a
treacherous, malignant opponent of God. Yet Satan's power was
limited. In heaven, in establishing his original kingdom, Satan
could only parody God (P.L. V, 755–766). In hell Satan's power
was even more restricted. Freed, Satan was but bound the more.
In hell Satan might build a throne "like" God's throne (Isa. 14:14);
he might be worshipped as God (P.L. II, 475–479; Rev. 13:4); he
might even repeat Christ's offer to cross the raging chaos to bring
salvation to mankind:

> But first whom shall we send
> In search of this new world, whom shall we find
> Sufficient? who shall tempt with wandring feet
> The dark unbottom'd infinite Abyss
> And through the palpable obscure find out
> His uncouth way . . .?
> This said, he sat; and expectation held
> His look suspence, awaiting who appeer'd
> To second, or oppose, or undertake
> The perilous attempt: but all sat mute
> Pondering the danger with deep thoughts; and each
> In others count'nance read his own dismay
> Astonisht. . . .
>
> (P.L. II, 402–407, 417–423)

The silence which greets Satan's proposal is the silence of heaven:

> Say Heav'nly powers, where shall we find such love,
> Which of ye will be mortal to redeem
> Mans mortal crime, and just th' unjust to save,
> Dwels in all Heaven charitie so deare?
> He [God] ask'd, but all the Heav'nly Quire stood mute,
> And silence was in Heav'n: on mans behalf
> Patron or Intercessor none appeerd,
> Much less that durst upon his own head draw
> The deadly forfeiture, and ransom set.
>
> (P.L. III, 213–221; Rev. 8:1–3)

In heaven, however, to Christ's proposal that He be sent, the angels react with shouts of adoration and praise. In hell, after Satan appoints himself his own emissary, the devils shrink back less in adoration than in fear. Satan may imitate God. But only Christ is God. The parallels which Milton draws here are deliberate. Satan is the *Simia Dei*. His powers are restricted both by and to the pattern set by God.

Examined in context, the picture which Milton draws of Satan is horrible. In hell Satan is a degenerate, degenerating, frustrated being. He is the "pale horse," the "King" of the locusts, the "dragon" and the "serpent," the "beast" of the pit, the "whore" of Babylon—each of the hideous apparitions of the Book of Revelation.[39] In hell, literally, Satan's sole glory is that he is the Ape of God.

CHAPTER FIVE

Sin and Death

> Before the Gates there sat
> On either side a formidable shape;
> The one seem'd Woman to the waste, and fair,
> But ended foul in many a scaly fould
> Voluminous and vast, a Serpent arm'd
> With mortal sting: around her middle round
> A cry of Hell Hounds never ceasing bark'd
> With wide *Cerberian* mouths full loud, and rung
> A hideous Peal: yet, when they list, would creep,
> If aught disturb'd thir noyse, into her woomb,
> And kennel there, yet there still bark'd and howl'd
> Within unseen.
>
> The other shape,
> If shape it might be call'd that shape had none
> Distinguishable in member, joynt, or limb,
> Or substance might be call'd that shadow seem'd,
> For each seem'd either; black it stood as Night,
> Fierce as ten Furies, terrible as Hell,
> And shook a dreadful Dart; what seem'd his head
> The likeness of a Kingly Crown had on.
>
> (P.L. II, 648–659, 666–673)

Satan leaves his throne of glory to attack man, the possibly present, possibly future creation of God. As the pale horse, the King of the locusts, the dragon and the serpent of Revelation 6, 9, 12, and 20, Satan first wages war against heaven. As the sea-beast, the land-beast, and the whore of Revelation 11, 13, and 17, Satan continues the war against earth.

3 . . . behold a great red dragon, having seven heads and ten horns, and seven crowns upon his heads (Rev. 12:3). 1 And I [(John); or he (the dragon), Vulgate, King James gloss] stood upon the sand of the sea, and saw a beast rise up out of the sea, having seven heads and ten horns, and upon his horns ten crowns, and upon his heads the name of blasphemy. 2 And the beast which I saw was like unto a leopard, and his feet were as the feet of a bear, and his mouth as the mouth of a lion: and the dragon gave him his power, and his seat, and great authority. 11 And I beheld another beast coming up out of the earth; and he had two horns like a lamb, and he spake as a dragon. 12 And he exerciseth all the power of the first beast before him, and causeth the earth and them which dwell therein to worship the first beast, whose deadly wound was healed (Rev. 13:1–2, 11–12).

By self-propagation and incest, the dragon and the beasts are one.

From Pandaemonium to the Gates of Hell ("the sand of the sea," chaos), Satan rises to recognize his holy spirit, Death, and to anoint his messiah, Sin. As a modern commentator suggests, the sea-beast "bears the likeness of the Dragon whose wish for a living replica of itself to dwell on earth and serve as its Messiah has evidently brought forth this Beast from the depths."[1] The Renaissance interpretation of Revelation 13:1 (Rev. 11:7) was similar:

This beast (that is to wit Antichrist) is sayd to come vp out of the bottomlesse pit, bicause that beeing ingendred of the diuell, and starting euen out of the innermost dungeon of hell, he is mounted vp so high in pride, that lyke as the Gyants went about in olde tyme to driue their Iupiter out of heauen, as the fables reporte: euen so seemeth hee too bee desirous too thrust Christ the king of all kings from his kingdome, folowing the footesteppes of his father Satan, who hathe beene a murtherer from the beginning, and abode not in the truth.[2]

. . . this beast here dyscribed [is] the pale horse in the forth age, the cruell multitude of locustes in the fyft age, and the horses of incomparable wodenesse for the syxt. . . . lyke as Christ oure Lord sytteth in the trone of God reginge with his eternall father in mekenesse, so sytteth he [Antichrist; Sin] in the trone of sathan with hys father the deuyll in all pryde & blasphemye. As touching the poure, lyke as Christe had his poure of God, so hath he his poure of the deuyll. Lyke as Christ is full of grace and verite, and of his fulnesse all they haue receiued that trulye haue beleued in him, so is this antichrist full of hate, falshede, and al other iniquitie, of whose errours and lies the vnbeleuers have tasted. Lyke as the holye sprete of Christe hath wrought in his louers the misterie of treuth and goodnesse, so hath the erroniouse and vncleane sprete of thys antichriste wrought the misterie of his wickednesse in Christes enemies, sens his deathe and ascencion.[3]

To the sea-beast, Sin, Satan gives "his power, and his seat [throne], and great authority." To the land-beast, Death, Satan gives authority to cause "the earth and them which dwell therein to worship the first beast" (Sin), whose power over Death is unquestioned ("whose deadly wound was healed").

> My Substitutes I send ye, and Create
> Plenipotent on Earth, of matchless might
> Issuing from mee: on your joynt vigor now
> My hold of this new Kingdom all depends. . . .
>   (P.L. X, 403–406)

Having succeeded in hell in counterfeiting the power of God, Satan now proposes to make a hell out of earth. Grotesquely, point by point, he imitates the structure of the Kingdom of God.

By what authority did Milton place Sin and Death at the Portals of Hell? Again Milton turned to the Book of Revelation, specifically to Revelation 6:8 and 9:1 (Rev. 13:1–12). According to Revelation 6:8, after his defeat in heaven as the rider of the red, black, and pale horses of war, spiritual famine, and death, Satan was cast into the pit of hell. Prior to Satan's fall, stated John,

> 8 . . . behold [there appeared] a pale horse: and his name that sat on him was Death, and Hell followed with him. And power was given unto them over the fourth part of the earth, to kill with sword, and with hunger, and with death, and with the beasts of the earth.

The Greek for "followed," $\overset{\backprime}{\alpha}\kappa o\lambda o\upsilon\Theta\epsilon\overline{\iota}$, may also be translated "begotten." (For the further significance of this reading, see the conclusion of this chapter.) Death could not have been begotten in heaven (Luke 20:36, 38; cf. Wisdom 1:13, 2:24).[4] Thus Satan must have fallen from heaven before the rider of the pale horse, Death, was conceived. Death cannot appear in hell. Spirits, though corrupt and evil, cannot die (P.L. I, 116–117; Isa. 14:19–20). The place of Death, therefore, must be Chaos or, better, the Gates of Hell.

Where is the place of Sin? In Revelation 9:1, a passage which Milton regarded as being parallel in meaning to Revelation 6:7–8,

12:12, and 20:3, John stated that he saw "a star fall from heaven
[ἀστέρα ἐκ τοῦ οὐρανοῦ πεπτωκότα, a star fallen out of heaven]
unto the earth: and to him was given the key of the bottomless pit."
Since Lucifer had already fallen (Rev. 8:10), and since John
specifically named Abaddon or Apollyon (Lucifer, Rev. 9:11) as
the "king" of the bottomless pit, Lucifer could not have been the
"fallen star" of Revelation 9:1. Who or what was this "star"?
Milton's answer, based upon an attempt to explain the symbols of
Revelation consistently, was that the evil (fallen) star of Revelation 9:1 was Sin, the "hell" which was begotten by Death, the
future rider of the pale horse, in Revelation 6:8. It was this "star"
that stood with Death as the guardian of the bottomless pit.
Quotation would seem appropriate:

> Sin let in death. It opened the door. Death is no creature of God's
> making. Satan brought in sin, and sin brought in death. . . . The
> weapon that death fights with, and causeth great terror, it is sin. The
> cause is armed with the power of the wrath of God for sin, the fear of
> hell, and damnation. So that wrath, and hell, and damnation, arming
> sin, it bringeth a sting of itself, and puts a venom into death. All
> cares, and fears, and sorrows, and sicknesses, are less and petty
> deaths, harbingers to death itself; but the attendants that follow this
> great king are worst of all, as Rev. vi. 8, "I saw a pale horse, and
> death upon it, and after him comes hell." What were death, if it were
> not for the pit, and dungeon that followeth it? So that death is
> attended with hell, and hell with eternity.[5]

> this Rider on the Pale Horse, named *Death,* hath a Page following
> him, called *Hell.* The word *Hades* in the Greek, and *Sheol* in the
> Hebrew, signifies somtime the Graue, and somtime the place of the
> damned, where there is *vtter darknesse,* and no light at all. The
> learned Interpreter *Beza* retaineth the word *Infernus,* or *Hell;* it
> followes Death, said *Victorine,* waiting for the deuouring of many
> soules. For if in this place the word should onely signifie the Graue,
> the iudgement were not great, sith the Graue followes the death
> both of good men and euill: And sure, it is nothing commen to them;
> both can bee called the proper punishment of sinne. Heere then is
> the greatnesse of this Plague, that the contemners of the Gospell
> shall bee punished with such a *Death,* as hath *Hell* following it.[6]

> Death and hell seem to be brought in the Apocalypse through
> prosopopoeia as if they are two persons in a comedy which threaten
> death and destruction to the Church and Christians. For Death is
> brought in as if seen first, and in the act of killing; in truth hell follows
> and devours those whom death kills: whence death is brought in as if

brandishing arrows, hell as if stretching out its opening jaws, and devouring those who have been slain. For he holds the bodies of those in the graves, their spirits bound in the lowest bowels of the earth. Hence the Wise Man affirms in Proverbs 1:12, "Let us swallow him up," as hell. And Isaiah, chapter 5:14, "Hell has enlarged herself," like a three-headed dog stretching out his three jaws and three throats. For this is the Pluto of the Gentiles, the devourer of the dead.[7]

In his portrait of Death, Milton has transferred characteristics usually applied to Hell (Rev. 6:8) from Hell to Death.[8] Sin, with her feminine appearance and serpentine shape, is both a locust and a beast (Rev. 9:8a, 10, 19; 13:1). Death, with its devouring jaws and its Kingly Crown, is (meaningfully) a triune being: locust, beast, and dragon (Rev. 9:7, 8b, 19; 13:1, 11; 12:3). Otherwise Milton's portraits of Death and Sin follow the *literal* interpretations of Revelation 6:8 advanced by the commentators of his day.[9] Sin, a creature of contradictions, is both fair and foul. She carries a deadly sting, yet she must suffer constantly from the Hounds of Hell (Rev. 6:8: *"Bestiia terrae, id est, canibus"*)[10] which infest her womb. She is the creator of Death, yet Death is her enemy. Death stands ready with "Rav'nous Maw," hideously grinning, waiting to devour the souls of men (Isa. 5:14; P.L. X, 990–991; II, 845–848; X, 264–281). Death will be destroyed when Sin is destroyed. Yet Death is eager to destroy the body of Sin (Gen. 4:7; Job 10:21–22; Prov. 27:20; Isa. 66:24; I Cor. 15:55–56; James 1:15).

Who is the creator of these monsters? Lucifer (or better, Satan) learns with dismay that he is the father of Sin. Sin is Satan's only "begotten" son (daughter). Death, the third member of the Infernal Trinity, is Satan's grandson. At first even Satan is appalled at the thought that he is related to Sin and Death. "I know thee not, nor ever saw till now Sight more detestable than him and thee" (P.L. II, 744–745), Satan declares to Sin, his daughter and his wife. Lucifer, the light-bearer, the champion of freedom, could never have stooped so low as to dally with Sin. Now Satan must face the truth. He is Sin and Death. The three are one, yet three.

The reason for the "harshness" of Satan's condemnation now becomes unmistakably clear. Satan has not been bound in chains of damnation because he has lost the War in Heaven (P.L. I, 95, 143, 169). Nor is Satan undergoing punishment because he has dared to rebel against God. Satan stands condemned because, out of himself, he has created a new thing, Sin, the outward, visible expression of his own perversion. Sin and Death, next to Satan himself, are the most odious of all beings, the "beasts," the "locusts," and the "scorpions" of hell. Into the cosmos Satan has released all the destructive forces of pride, heresy, hate, perversion, passion, selfish desires, murder, war—all of the forces of evil which are the antitheses of the goodness of God. Of necessity, if God is good, Satan must be condemned and cast into hell. Only if evil is redefined as good, pride is preferable to humility, heresy is superior to truth, hate is greater than love, could God have permitted Satan to remain in heaven.

The picture which Milton presents of Satan's relationship to Sin and Death is instructive. At first, dismayed, Satan rejects the image of himself that he sees in Sin and Death. Then, no longer shocked, he accepts his identity with Evil. Sin ("dear pledge Of dalliance") again seems attractive. Death ("fair Son") Satan welcomes as his companion-at-arms. This is the picture, according to Milton's interpretation of the Bible, of all Evil. By creating Sin, Satan has set up a pattern which he must repeat throughout eternity. Sin, at first, is hideous. Then it becomes attractive. The Hell Hounds of conscience creep into the soul. Then Sin becomes repulsive. Satan, however, cannot resist Sin. He is Sin (and Death). Only by constantly re-creating and releasing the powers of Sin and Death can Satan relieve his suffering and his pain. By releasing Sin and Death, of course, Satan only intensifies his suffering (P.L. IV, 18–26, 73–79). But this is the nature of Sin (Satan). Throughout eternity Satan must repeat this pattern. For Satan there is no hope except the "hope" of final judgment.

Milton's picture of the self-renewing, increasingly destructive nature of Sin is based upon many biblical texts (as Ps. 7:14–16, Prov. 27:20, Isa. 66:24). The primary texts, however, are James 1:14–15, Revelation 6:7–8, and Revelation 9:1. According to James 1:14–15,

14 . . . every man [or angel] is tempted, when he is drawn away of his own lust, and enticed. 15 Then when lust hath conceived, it bringeth forth sin: and sin, when it is finished, bringeth forth death.

In heaven originally evil was non-existent. Then, "drawn away" by his own lust, Satan began to question the law of God (P.L. V,

617). Satan's reaction was not in itself Sin. It was only after the motions of lust or concupiscence (appetite, desire, inclination) had been acted upon by Satan's will that Sin sprang into existence. First Sin was conceived by Satan's will. Then, after it had been "finished" or "perfected," Sin brought forth Death. This was the pattern which Satan initiated when he rebelled against God (Christ). At first lust was hidden in the recesses of Satan's mind (P.L. V, 617–672). Then, acted upon by Satan's thoughts and actions, lust conceived to become Sin; thus Sin appeared visibly when Satan defied God openly with acts of rebellion (P.L. II, 749–767; V, 772–871), war (Rev. 6:3–4), and heresy (Rev. 6:5–6), each succeeding action being worse than the preceding (Lam. 4:9, James 1:15).

Milton's picture of the actual "begetting" of Sin is unforgettable. Am I now so repulsive? Sin asks Satan, her husband-father:

> ...do I seem
> Now in thine eyes so foul, once deemd so fair
> In Heav'n, when at th' Assembly, and in sight
> Of all the Seraphim with thee combin'd
> In bold conspiracy against Heav'ns King,
> All of a sudden miserable pain
> Surpris'd thee, dim thine eyes, and dizzie swumm
> In darkness, while thy head flames thick and fast
> Threw forth, till on the left side op'ning wide,
> Likest to thee in shape and count'nance bright,
> Then shining heav'nly fair, a Goddess arm'd
> Out of thy head I sprung: amazement seis'd
> All th' Host of Heav'n; back they recoild affraid
> At first, and call'd me *Sin,* and for a Sign
> Portentous held me; but familiar grown,
> I pleas'd, and with attractive graces won
> The most adverse, thee chiefly, who full oft
> Thy self in me thy perfect image viewing
> Becam'st enamour'd, and such joy thou took'st
> With me in secret, that my womb conceiv'd
> A growing burden [Death].
>
> (P.L. II, 747–767)

Milton's account of the conception of Sin repeats almost word for word the statements of the literal commentators upon James 1:14–15:

> *Concupiscence* [lust] *when it hath conceiued bringeth forth sinne, &c.*] The degrees of temptation are here noted out; first, there is delight alluring; second, consent conceiuing; thirdly, worke performing; fourthly, custome perfecting. Lust conceiueth by the deuill, who is (as it were) the father, and lust the mother; this conception is by the consent of the will, or by delight. *Bringeth forth sinne,* that is, into act, *Psal.* 7. It is perfected by custome, and then death commeth, that is, it becommeth guilty of eternall damnation, *for the wages of sin is death* [Rom. 6:23].[11]

The view that Sin and Death were devil-begotten was a concept which was expressed frequently by Renaissance commentators.[12]

Sin, "shining heav'nly fair, a Goddess arm'd," springs from the head of Satan. Sin must issue from Satan's head, for, physiologically, the source of Sin is the will. Sin is conceived when the will, acting upon discordant motions of lust, entertains "delights" which arise "in the soul towards sinfull objects, which do antecede all deliberation and consultation."[13] Accepted by the will, expressed in thought and action, Sin then issues from the mind, the "womb" ($\dot{\epsilon}\pi\iota\Theta\upsilon\mu\iota\alpha$ $\sigma\upsilon\lambda\lambda\alpha\beta\sigma\bar{\upsilon}\sigma\alpha$, James 1:15) "wherein all wickedness is first conceived," to become Actual or Visible Sin (C.D. XI, 193–201, 20–22).[14] "Familiar grown," Sin pleases. The conception of Death, the completion or perfection of Sin, immediately follows.

Death, accompanied by Sin, now prepares to invade the earth:

> Strange alteration! Sin and Death amain
> Following his [Satan's] track, such was the will of Heav'n,
> Pav'd after him a broad and beat'n way
> Over the dark Abyss, whose boiling Gulf
> Tamely endur'd a Bridge of wondrous length
> From Hell continu'd reaching th' utmost Orbe
> Of this frail World....
>
> (P.L. II, 1024–1030)

This action, which critics have found not only strange but unnecessary, is based upon two passages of Scripture, Revelation

18:5 (Isa. 14:14; Matt. 7:13; Rev. 9:1–2, 13:1–2, 11, 16:14, 17:5–8)
and James 1:15, each of which are related in meaning. According
to Revelation 18:5, after her initial alliance with Satan, Sin
produced progeny so numerous that ultimately they "reached unto
Heaven." As the marginal gloss of the Geneva version of the Bible
(1560) expresses the concept, the progeny of sin (Sin) "followe one
another, and so rise one after another, that they growe to suche an
heape, y^t at length they touche ye verie heauen." Further,
according to Pareus, ἀκολουΘεῖ ("come vp vnto," Geneva
version; "reached," King James version) means that

> *they* [the offspring of Sin] *followed each other,* one begetting
> another, so that like chaines fastned together with many rings they
> reached as it were up to Heaven. *Andreas* and *Montanus* have it
> ἐκολλήΘησαν *glued together,* or as it were with lime or mortar
> raised up to so great a heape, as it reached even to heaven.[15]

According to James 1:15, "When lust hath conceived, it
bringeth forth sin: and sin, when it is finished, bringeth forth
death." Sin is "finished" when by continuance (Calvin[16]) of her
relationship with Satan she brings forth, Death, yes, but in
addition, further sin, hell hounds, and other imps of hell. Thus Sin
"finished . . . reached to heaven." This is the origin of the "Bridge
of wondrous length" that, according to Milton, links hell to earth.

On the outskirts of heaven, at the "three sev'ral wayes" (P.L.
X, 323) of heaven, earth, and hell, Sin and Death bind earth to hell
with a monstrous chain,

> . . . a Bridge
> Of length prodigious joyning to the Wall
> Immovable of this now fenceless world
> Forfeit to Death; from hence a passage broad
> Smooth, easie, inoffensive down to Hell.
> (P.L. X, 301–305)

By linking earth to hell, apparently Satan has successfully opposed
the will of God. Actually Satan has but contrived the means of his
own damnation. It is the "will of Heav'n" (P.L. II, 1025), not the
will of Satan, which has permitted the bridge to be built. By linking
hell to earth Satan has re-imposed the chains with which he

formerly was bound. Hell has been linked to earth; but earth ("fast by hanging in a golden Chain") also is linked to heaven (P.L. II, 1051):

> The stairs were such as whereon *Jacob* saw
> Angels ascending and descending, bands
> Of Guardians bright, when he from *Esau* fled
> To *Padan-Aram* in the field of *Luz,*
> Dreaming by night under the open Skie,
> And waking cri'd, *This is the Gate of Heav'n.*
>
> (P.L. III, 510–515)

By bridging Chaos, Satan physically has linked heaven to hell. He has re-established the order of God. Thus Satan has doomed himself. The Chain of Being has been restored. Sin may abandon her post as Portress of Hell. Death may cause "the earth and them that dwell therein to worship" the beast (Sin). Ultimately, however,

> Both *Sin,* and *Death,* and yawning *Grave* at last
> Through *Chaos* hurld, [will] obstruct the mouth of Hell....
>
> (P.L. X, 635–636)

The will of God cannot be denied. Satan may break his chains. Yet they remain.

> ... stretcht out huge in length the Arch-fiend lay
> Chain'd on the burning Lake, nor ever thence
> Had ris'n or heav'd his head, but that the will
> And high permission of all-ruling Heaven
> Left him at large to his own dark designs,
> That with reiterated crimes he might
> Heap on himself damnation, while he sought
> Evil to others, and enrag'd might see
> How all his malice serv'd but to bring forth
> Infinite goodness, grace, and mercy shewn
> On Man by him seduc't, but on himself
> Treble confusion, wrath and vengeance pour'd.
>
> (P.L. I, 209–220)

CHAPTER SIX

Lust and Will

O For that warning voice, which he who saw
Th' *Apocalyps,* heard cry in Heaven aloud,
Then when the Dragon, put to second rout,
Came furious down to be reveng'd on men,
Wo to the inhabitants on Earth! that now,
While time was, our first-Parents had bin warnd
The coming of thir secret foe, and scap'd
Haply so scap'd his mortal snare; for now
Satan, now first inflam'd with rage, came down,
The Tempter ere th' Accuser of man-kind....
                              (P.L. IV, 1–10)

Milton's picture of the origin of Sin raises many questions. What was the cause of the discordant motions of lust (the "delights" which arise "in the soul towards sinfull objects") from which Satan created original sin? Sin, according to James 1:15, is said to have been conceived by lust. What, then, is lust? Is sin the cause or the effect? These questions, which were discussed repeatedly in the commentaries, cannot be answered conclusively. Of this fact Milton was fully well aware. So far as the first question is concerned, Milton made no attempt to furnish a conclusive answer. Satan sinned. The cause of his sin, according to Milton, was his rejection of the law of God. This was and is the definition of sin: "SIN, as defined by the apostle, is $\dot{\alpha}\nu o\mu\acute{\iota}\alpha$, or 'the transgression of the law,' 1 John iii.4" (C. D. XI, 179, 20–21). By rejecting the initial decree of God, the decree that Christ was the "begotten Son," Lucifer brought Sin into existence.

Underlying Lucifer's rejection of God's decree was a desire which in itself was not evil. Lucifer desired to be like God and

Christ (P.L. V, 658–665). In itself this desire (lust) was not wrong. Indeed, to the contrary, to seek to imitate God is a virtue. As Aquinas wrote long ago:

> To desire to be as God according to likeness can happen in two ways. In one way, as to that likeness whereby everything is made to be likened unto God. And so, if anyone desire in this way to be Godlike, he commits no sin; provided he desires such likeness in proper order, that is to say, that he may obtain it of God. But he would sin were he to desire to be like unto God even in the right way, as of his own, and not of God's power. In another way one may desire to be like unto God in some respect which is not natural to one; as if one were to desire to create heaven and earth, which is proper to God; in which desire there would be sin. It was in this way that the devil desired to be as God.[1]

To seek to "exalt [one's] throne above the stars of God" (Isa. 14:13) is evil. Only God (Christ) is equal to God. Seeking to be like God, Lucifer perverted an initially good desire into evil. How? By what means? What caused Lucifer, a being perfectly good, to entertain motions in improper order "as of his own, and not of God's power"? These questions Milton does not answer. Nor does the Bible. Revelation 5:5–6 indicates that Christ, the "Lion of the tribe of Juda," initiated the action in heaven by opening the book of God's decrees. Psalm 2:7 states God's original decree: "Thou art my son; this day have I begotten thee." Psalm 110:1–2 presents Christ as God's Vicegerent:

> 1 The Lord said unto my Lord, Sit thou at my right hand, until I make thine enemies thy footstool. 2 The Lord shall send the rod of thy strength out of Zion: rule thou in the midst of thine enemies.

Revelation 12:7 describes the result: "And there was war in heaven." Each of the four proof texts which depict the "begetting" of Christ in heaven begins *in medias res*. Prior to his begetting, of course, Christ existed as "the Word" (John 1:1), the means by which the "mighty Father made All things" (P.L. V, 836–837). The nature of Christ's eternal existence, however, the Bible does not explain. Nor does Milton. The Bible states only that Satan "abode not in the truth" (John 8:44). By seeking to "exalt [his] throne above the stars of God," Satan perverted good into evil. This was Satan's act, not God's.

The original decree of God was a decree of absolute freedom. No tyrant, God permitted the angels either to accept or to reject his Vicegerent. By rejecting the Son, Satan sinned. This was as much as man could know. To Milton, further inquiry into the question of the origin of evil was "forbidden knowledge." Man may seek to understand the nature of God. Ultimate causes, however, man can not determine. A finite mind cannot answer the question of how "a natural being that is good though changeable, before he comes to have an evil will, [can] create something that is evil," i.e., the evil will itself.[2]

Man cannot determine ultimate causes. The *means* by which good becomes evil (perfection becomes imperfection), however, may be determined. Satan was created a perfect being. In what did this perfection consist? Was Satan's original nature one of undisturbed harmony between lust and will or one of change (mutability) wherein motions of lust (concupiscence, desire, impulses of nature) might conflict with volitional control? It is this second view which appears in *Paradise Lost*.

Prior to Satan's fall, in the fifty-two lines which depict the conception of Sin (P.L. V, 617, 657–696; II, 747–758), Milton describes Satan as undergoing numerous emotional disturbances. The list includes envy, pride, malice, contempt, doubt, fear, pleasure, and pain. These are motions of lust. Are they products of sin? Surely not, for sin (Sin) has not yet been conceived. Sin did not beget itself (The child was not the parent). Nor did Sin (Satan's messiah) exist as sin prior to its conception. Sin originated when Satan's will (the father), acting upon lust (the mother), conceived a being equal to itself. Prior to her (its) begetting, Sin "existed" potentially, not actually, until it had been begotten by the will of Satan. Similarly, prior to his begetting, Christ "existed" potentially, that is, invisibly rather than visibly, until he was "begotten" by the will of God. The analogy should not be taken to extremes. Sin was not the agent by whom Satan's followers, the disloyal angels, were created. Christ is divine. Sin is a creature. The analogy has value, however, in that it emphasizes Milton's consistent refusal to discuss ultimate causes.

Satan sinned. Lust was not the cause of his sin. Satan was not created weak and imperfect, with a defective will. Nor was Satan reprobated before his creation. God did not withdraw his power so that, unable by his own strength to stand, Satan rebelled against God. Each of these speculative solutions to the problem of evil Milton dealt with specifically in P.L. III, 97–117. What caused Satan to sin? "Whose fault?" God asks:

> Whose but his own? ingrate, he had of mee
> All he could have; I made him just and right,
> Sufficient to have stood, though free to fall.
> Such I created all th' Ethereal Powers
> And Spirits, both them who stood and them who faild;
> Freely they stood who stood, and fell who fell.
> Not free, what proof could they have givn sincere
> Of true allegiance, constant Faith or Love,
> Where onely what they needs must do, appeard,
> Not what they would? what praise could they receive?
> What pleasure I from such obedience paid,
> When Will and Reason (Reason also is choice)
> Useless and vain, of freedom both despoild,
> Made passive both, had servd necessitie,
> Not mee. They therefore as to right belongd,
> So were created, nor can justly accuse
> Thir maker, or thir making, or thir Fate,
> As if predestination over-rul'd
> Thir will, dispos'd by absolute Decree
> Or high foreknowledge; they themselves decreed
> Thir own revolt, not I. . . .

Satan was created perfect in all respects—in his nature (lust), in his mental abilities (reason), and in his ability to choose between good and evil (will). Why then did he sin? The *immediate* cause of Satan's sin was a deliberate act of the will. Satan rebelled because he chose to rebel—not because his reason was overcome by his passion. Before Sin was conceived, Abdiel also was moved with impulses of lust (zeal, fervor, boldness, even scorn). Was Abdiel tainted with evil? No, for although potentially evil, motions of lust originally were not evil. By his will Satan might have prevented his lust from becoming evil. Instead Satan chose to embrace lust—to create his own messiah instead of accepting the only begotten Son of God. Then lust conceived to bring forth Sin: and Sin, when it was finished, brought forth Death (James 1:15).

The point of view expressed in the text above should be emphasized, for it provides an answer to the growing number of critics who suggest that Milton, largely defeating his own purpose in writing *Paradise Lost,* depicted Adam and Eve as being victims of lust (and thus of being evil) before they actually sinned.[3] On earth, repeating the pattern initiated by Satan, Adam and Eve, beings who were created "in the image of God" (Gen. 1:27), sought to be like God ("as God," Gen. 3:5, King James text and gloss). To be like God is not evil. Yet Adam and Eve sinned. How? Adam and Eve were perfect beings. In what, then, did their perfection consist? Were Adam and Eve created with a nature in which perfect harmony existed between lust and will, or was the original nature of man one of possible change (mutability) wherein motions of lust might clash with volitional control? The first of these views was advocated by Augustine in *The City of God:*

When the first human beings began to be evil, they did so in secret, and this enabled them to fall into open disobedience. For the evil act could not have been arrived at if an evil will had not gone before. Further, what but pride [lust] can have been the start of an evil will? ... Moreover, what is pride but a craving for perverse elevation? For it is perverse elevation to forsake the ground in which the mind ought to be rooted, and to become and be, in a sense, grounded in oneself. This happens when a man is too well pleased with himself, and such a one is thus pleased when he falls away from that unchangeable good with which he ought rather to have been pleased than with himself. Now this falling away is voluntary, for if the will had remained steadfast in love of the higher unchangeable good that provided it with light to see and kindled it with fire to love, it would not have been diverted from this love to follow its own pleasure. Nor would the will in consequence have grown so dark and cold as to allow either the first woman to believe that the serpent had spoken the truth or the first man to place his wife's will before God's injunction and to think that his transgression of the command could be pardoned if he did not forsake the partner of his life even when partnership in sin was involved.

Accordingly, the evil act, that is, the transgression that involved their eating of forbidden food, was committed only by those who were already evil. For only a bad tree could have produced that evil fruit. Moreover, the badness of the tree was an event contrary to nature, because, except for a defect of will, which is contrary to nature, it surely could not have come to pass. . . . It is indeed a good thing to have an aspiring mind, yet aspiring not to oneself, which belongs to pride, but to God, which belongs to obedience, and obedience can belong only to the humble.[4]

Variations of Augustine's view appear in the writings of Ames, Mayer, Pemble, Reynolds, Wollebius, as well as other Renaissance Protestant theologians.[5] According to Ames (1642), for example,

The committing of [Eve's] transgression was accomplished in the eating of the forbidden Fruit, which was called the Tree of the knowledge of *Good* and *Evill:* but the first motion or degree of this disobedience, did necessarily goe before that outward act of eating, so that it may be truly said that Man was a sinner, before he had finished that outward act of eating. Whence it is that the very desire which *Eve* was caried with toward the forbidden Fruit, doth seeme to be noted, as some degree of her sin. *Gen.* 3.6. When the Woman saw, that the Fruit of the Tree was good for Meate, and most delightfull to the Eyes, and the Fruit of the Tree to be desired to get knowledge she tooke and eat.

The statement by Wollebius (1650) is even stronger:

There be certain degrees of that sin, by which *Adam* fell from God, not at once, but by little & little; to wit, 1. Incogitancie and curiosity of *Evahs* talking with the Serpent, her husband being absent. 2. Incredulity, by which she began by degrees to distrust God, and to give assent to Satans lies, who called in question Gods good-will towards man. 3. An inordinate desire to the forbidden fruit, and an affectation of divine glory. 4. The Fact itself. 5. The seducing of *Adam,* and an inordinate affectation raised in him also.

If, as the proponents of the Augustinian view maintained, man's *justitia originalis* was one of perfect harmony, then, of course, any discordant motion of lust experienced by Adam and Eve before they fell must have been contrary to nature and therefore evil. In *Paradise Lost* Adam and Eve certainly experienced motions of lust (as vanity, curiosity, pride, gluttony, irritation) before they partook of the forbidden fruit. Evidently, then, Adam and Eve committed evil before they sinned.

The conclusion is logical yet invalid. Unquestionably many Renaissance Protestants adopted the Augustinian concept of man's original nature:

Concupiscence is . . . either that natural faculty of desire which was
in man even before his fall, or that corruption which naturally
adheres to it, as it is in it, in the first act, and as it inclines man onely
to evil.[6]

Augustine's designation of lust as evil desire or sin offered
Protestant theologians an excellent opportunity, by opposing
Church Father to Church Father, to demonstrate the falsity of a
Catholic position. According to a decree of the Council of Trent
(1546), lust in itself was not evil: *"This concupiscence which
sometime the Apostle called sinne, the holy Synode declares that
the Catholike Church did neuer understand it to be called
sinne...."*[7] Thus a valid distinction might be drawn between
venial and mortal sin. (The traditional Protestant position, of
course, is that sin is sin. Degrees of sin do not exist.) Unfortunately the doctrine that lust is sin also might be used to support the
Arminian (Socinian and/or Pelagian) position that in Adam there
existed an "inclination to sinne . . . before his fall, *Licet non ita
vehemens & inordinata ut nuns* est, although not so vehement and
inordinate as now it is."[8] Created with a nature that was "weak
and imperfect," necessarily, then, Adam was unable "to attaine
that supernaturall end, for which he was made, and which he was
commanded to seeke."[9] But if Adam was created with a defective
nature, then God, man's creator, was responsible for man's fall. If
lust, acting without the consent of the will, was able to propagate
sin, moreover, then Adam and Eve originally either were unable to
control their own actions or they lacked true freedom of will.

These concepts, understandably, Protestant apologists found
even more disturbing than the Catholic doctrine of venial and
mortal sin. God was not the author of evil! Moreover, before they
fell Adam and Eve were perfect beings. One solution to the
difficulties inherent in the Augustinian view involved a reconsid-
eration of the nature of evil. According to James 1:15, ". . . when
lust hath conceived, it bringeth forth sin. . . ." As was suggested by
John Noble, conception could not have been accomplished

by one Agent alone, but necessarily includes the acts of two. . . .
where then shall we find a fit companion for her [lust]? What can we
think bad enough to engender with this beastly lust? *Origen* would
have it to be the Devil, saying, *Quod improbi hominis anima*

*diabolum maritum, ex quo ejusmodi edis sobolem, & conjuncto
animae nostrae fuit primo cum malo viro, & marito pessimo,
diabolo.* A wicked mans soul (saith he) is first joyned to a bad man,
and after married to a worse Devil, *out of which unclean matrimony
proceeds the filthy and polluted issue of sin* [Hom. 13 in Josuen]. . . .
Divers others there be of the opinion, that sin is produced of the
Devil, as Father thereof sowing his seed, and our Lust as a Mother
consenting, and receiving it. But the Devil can not be the party
meant in my text, that conceives together with our lust, for . . . he
hath not the power to do it; God hath limited and bounded his
power, not to go any futher than his Commission. This appears unto
us in the first and second of the sixth of *Job,* where tis shewed, that
the Devil could not tempt *Job* to any sin, until God had given him
leave. Nay, tis shewed in the Gospel, that the Devils had not power
to enter into a heard of *Swine,* until that our Saviour bad them go.
[Who or what then?] I answer, That it is the will of man which is in
this conception lust's Husband: for as the learned Divines which
were lately appointed, and imployed to set out Annotations upon all
the Books of the old and new Testament, in their exposition of my
Text do judiciously teach us: *Now lust may then be said to have
conceived, when the will entertains those evil motions with consent
and delight, which lust hath stirred up. . . .* To this purpose saies St.
Austin, *Noli consentire concupiscentiae tuae, non est unde con-
cipiat nisi de te. Consensisti? quare concubuisti in corde tuo. Let
not* (saith he) *thy Will consent to thy lust, thy lust cannot conceive
but by thy self, but if thou hast consented, thou hast already
engendred sin in thy heart.*[10]

It was not lust but man's will—will acting upon lust—which
originally was perverted and produced sin. In experiencing
motions of delight upon viewing the forbidden fruit, Adam and Eve
did not act "contrary to nature."[11] Nor was man's initial,
instinctive desire for knowledge in itself evil. Man was created
perfect but mutable. Otherwise, suggested the commentators,
man would have possessed the nature of God himself.[12] Lust
originally was not evil. "When *Adam* sinned," wrote Antony
Burgesse,

  it was not after the same manner, as we sinne; for when we sinne,
  this floweth from a corrupted nature within, *Jam.* 1.17, *Every one is
  tempted and drawn aside with the lust that is within him;* But in
  Adam there was no such vicious principle. It is therefore a false and
  dangerous position of the *Socinians* [Arminians], *That we sinne in
  the same manner that he did, That we have no more corrupted*

Nature in us, then he had, but as he had a free-will, by which he chose either good or evil, so it is with us. But this speaketh open defiance against the Scripture; For was *Adam* by nature the child of wrath? Were the imaginations of his thoughts only evil, and that continually? Could *Adam* say, He found a Law of sinne in his Members, warring against the Law of his mind? . . . In *Adam* there was no concupiscence in this sense [in his original nature]; The inferiour parts, though they did desire a sensible object, yet it was wholly in subordination, and under the command of the superior. It's true indeed *Eve* did look upon the forbidden fruit, and saw it was good and pleasant, whereupon she was tempted to eat of it, but this did not arise from any original [evil] lust in her, but from the mutability of her will, being not confirmed in what was good: Even as we see the Angels before their Apostasie, had sinfull desires in their will, through pride and affectation to be higher than they were, yet this did not arise from original lust in them. . . . It is therefore a false and an absurd Position, which *Molina* the Jesuite, one of the meer Naturalists affirmeth *(Quaest. 14. Disp. 45. de Concord. lib. Arb.)* where he saith, *Adam* had, *Innatum appetitium excellentiae ac laudis quo ad intellectum voluntatem*, &c. That he had this temptation within him, *viz.* an innate appetite to his own excellency and praise. For how could this consist with that holiness and righteousness God created him in? Indeed he saith in another place of the same book *(Quaest. 14. Disp. 45.) Ex contemplatione rei amabilis, &c.)* from the contemplation of any lovely object, and which is of concernment to be obtained, there doth naturally rise in the will a certain motion, whereby the will is affected to it; which motion is not a volition, but an affection of the will to that object, whose goodness it is allured with. And this he maketh to be in men, yea in the Angels before they fell. But what is this but to say that in men and Angels, even before their fall, there was a concupiscential inclination to delightsome objects: and so *Adam* and Angels must according to this Text be tempted away, and enticed by their own lusts? An horrible Position, highly derogating from God's honour, who created them holy and righteous.[13]

The position advanced by Burgesse might be supported by quotations from Bullinger, Turnbull, Salkeld, Downame, Du Moulin and other Protestant theologians of the seventeenth century.[14] Further quotation would seem unnecessary, however, for a basic position has been established: Many Protestant commentators objected to the Augustinian view of original sin. Instead, rejecting the Catholic distinction between venial and mortal sin, a considerable number of Milton's contemporaries chose the view which, according to the Council of Trent, had been the view of the Church from the beginning:[15] Adam was created perfect in every respect. Yet he sinned. The effective cause of his sin was his will. The proximate cause was lust. For lust to become sin, consent was first required. In Paradise, therefore, Adam and Eve remained unaffected by evil until, deliberately and voluntarily, they chose to eat of the tree of knowledge of good and evil.

It is this view which underlies the puzzling "pretemptation" scene which Milton presents in P.L. IV, 799–809, and V, 30–121. In Paradise Satan "tempts" Eve in a dream which is composed of the various elements of Eve's experience (P.L. V, 30–93). Eve's fancy is filled with numerous motions of lust. That these impulses were only potentially evil and that Eve had the inner strength to control lust, however, Milton makes unmistakably clear:

> ... know that in the Soule
> Are many lesser Faculties that serve
> Reason as chief; among these Fansie next
> Her office holds; of all external things,
> Which the five watchful Senses represent,
> She forms Imaginations, Aerie shapes,
> Which Reason joyning or disjoyning, frames
> All what we affirm or what deny, and call
> Our knowledge or opinion; then retires
> Into her private Cell when Nature rests.
> Oft in her absence mimic Fansie wakes
> To imitate her; but misjoyning shapes,
> Wilde work produces oft, and most in dreams,
> Ill matching words and deeds long past or late....
>
> ... yet be not sad.
> Evil into the mind of God or Man
> May come and go, so unapprov'd, and leave
> No spot or blame behind.
>   (P.L. V, 100–113, 116–119)

The elements of lust which filled Eve's fancy produced no harmful effects. So long as Eve retained control of her will, Eve's concupiscential faculty or fancy could not become evil.

A problem exists, however. Could "mimic Fansie," directed by Satan, have corrupted Eve? Could Satan have entered into Eve's sensitive faculty while she was asleep? This possibility Milton was almost forced to consider, for both theologically and physiologically it was possible that Satan might have corrupted Eve against her will. This was the view, in fact, expressed by Deacon and Walker, joint authors of *Dialogicall Discourses of Spirits and Divels* (1601):

> [Admittedly] there can be no *actual* accomplishment of the worke of sinne, before the *mind* it selfe (being first conuict) be made to consent; yet doth it not follow, but that (notwithstanding al this) a man may *outwardlie* be tempted to sinne, and tormented also of *Satan*, though *inwardlie*, the *mind* it selfe be neuer subdued. And, although it be vndoubtedlie true, that *euerie man (being tempted) is inticed and drawen by his owne concupiscence,* namely, by the *concupiscible faculty* of his proper *mind; [Iam. 1.14. August. super Genes. ad Litram cap. 11. Lyra in Genes. cap. 3.1]* yet, this is also as certeinly true, namely, that, euen the *concupiscible facultie* also it selfe, is first set a worke by meanes of the *phantasie,* or interiour *sensitiue power.* Which said *sensitiue power* (receyuing an impression of such *sensible things* as are offred vnto her from the exteriour *obiectes* of the exteriour *senses*) doth foorthwith set the *concupiscible* facultie a worke, and makes it to lust after those *sensible things* in *conceipte.* As for example, whensoeuer the *diuel* entendeth to worke mans *mind* to his mischeauous purpose, he first makes an assault vpon that which we cal the *sensitiue facultie;* and (by offring some deceaueable *obiect* vnto the *exteriour* senses) endeuoureth to circumuent the *sences* them selues, and, so he bewitcheth the *mind [Caluinus, in Gen. 3.6].* And, euen after this sorte he seduced the *ears,* and the *eies* of *Euah* her selfe: telling her confidentlie, they should *knowe good and euill,* making her also beleeue, that the forbidden fruite *was fayre to behold,* and thereby subdued her *sensitiue* facultie.

In the same manner, according to Deacon and Walker, degree by degree, Satan entered and conquered Eve's concupiscible, intellective, and irascible faculties, and finally the will itself.[16]

To this variation of Augustinianism Milton objected. Susceptibility to internal temptation did not cause Eve to sin. Nor did susceptibility to external temptation cause Eve (or Adam) to sin. Not even if Eve—or Christ, the second Adam—had been exposed to Satan's temptation while "mimic Fansie" had access to the sensitive faculty could external temptation be considered the cause of sin:

> [When *Adam,* and much more Christ, was tempted by Satan,] The temptation was only external, not internal; there was no inward lust within; yea the very external temptation of *Adam* and Christ was different from ours in a further respect. For the Devil had not power by his suggestions to move or disturb their phansie, as he doth in us. Though the Devil cannot force our wils, yet he can make bodily commotions of the phantasie, and so thereby man is the more easily carried away to evil. But neither Christ or *Adam* had their imaginations so disturbed. For although they might understand by phantasmes, yet all was at the command of deliberate judgement. A mans imagination was then in his own power: so that those inferiour faculties in their operation could not hinder the superiour. Whether *Adam* in the state of integrity would have had dreames, is uncertain; but if he had, learned men conclude, they would alwayes have been good, and not without the present use of reason, as *Rivet* thinketh *(in cap.* 3. Genes.).[17]

Burgesse's position (1658) was stated earlier by Rivetus (in 1651):

> We say therefore that Christ, who in himself had no corrupt desires [concupiscence], as well as our first parents in their innocent state, could not be tempted with internal temptation, neither through their own flesh, because it was completely subjected to guided reason, nor through the suggestion of the Devil, producing a fantasy within. For the faculty of imagining of such beings received no apparitions except those which were under the deliberate control of their reason. And in such a state, in which the reason was perfectly subjected to God, much less in Christ was it possible that the movement or operation of any inferior power might supersede the command of the ruling reason. Moreover, change of fancy cannot come through apparitions, without the operation of the fancy itself. For if anyone should say that evil dreams then could also occur to a man (even though this contention is uncertain, nevertheless if it should be conceded), we shall say that there would always be future agreement, at least habitual agreement, to those things under the control of the guided reason because such dreams would always be good.[18]

The view expressed by each of these commentators is basically the same as that expressed by Milton in P.L. V, 117–119:

> Evil into the mind of God or Man
> May come and go, so unapprov'd, and leave
> No spot or blame behind.

Lust may become evil—provided man allows it to become evil.
First, however, Adam and Eve must be warned that they are
mutable creatures. They must be warned that they possess
freedom of will. (As Basil Willey suggests, although perfect
beings, Adam and Eve actually could not have been "happy"—
could not have existed in a state of well-being in which there were
no contradictory desires or wishes—until after they had exercised
their freedom of choice.)[19] Book IV began with a plea that Adam
and Eve be warned of the approach of Satan. This warning has not
yet been given. Nor will it be given until, in P.L. VI, 900–912,
Raphael advises Adam *"of his enemy near at hand"* ("Argument" to Book V). In the interim, theoretically at least, man was
vulnerable to temptation. To remove even this possibility (that, by
controlling man's "mimic Fansie," Satan might have forced
Adam and Eve to sin), Milton maintained that, in the interval
between their creation and their warning by Raphael, Adam and
Eve were protected by God. As Zanchius wrote (in 1591):

> I doubt not therefore (I will tell you mine opinion, without the
> preiudice of others) I doubt not, I say, but that the Sonne of God
> [Raphael in *Paradise Lost*] taking vpon him the shape of man, was
> occupied that whole seuenth day in most holy colloquies with
> Adam; and that he did also fully make himselfe known vnto Adam
> and Eue, and did reueale the manner and order, which he had vsed
> in creating of all things: and did exhort them both to meditate vpon
> those works, and in them to acknowledge their Creator, and to
> praise him. And that by his own example he did admonish them to
> occupie themselues especially in this exercise of godliness, setting
> all other business aside: and also that they would so instruct and
> teach their children. To be short, I doubt not, but that in that
> seuenth day he did teach them all diuinitie; and did hold them
> occupied in hearing of him, and in praising and giuing thankes to
> God their Creator for so many and so great benefits.[20]

Until Raphael had completed his discussion with Adam, man
could not sin. Evil may have existed in Adam's and Eve's
environment and fancy. Lust may have been unruly (for by the will
of God Adam and Eve were developing characters). Yet evil could

not conceive—lust could not bring forth sin—until, deliberately ignoring God's warning, Adam and Eve chose to violate the law of God. First Adam and Eve must misuse their freedom of will. Then—and only then—could the "two monsters, Lust and Sin, mutually begetting each other,"[21] become Actual Evil.

Satan sought to be like God. Eve sought to be like Adam. Adam sought to express his love for Eve. None of these desires were evil in themselves. Why these initially good desires became perverted Milton made no attempt to explain. Nor does the Bible. To Milton, since man has a finite mind, ultimate causes were inexplicable. What was significant was that, unless God was to be censured for allowing his creatures freedom of choice, God could not possibly be blamed for sin. Unaltered by their environment, given sufficient strength to remain uncorrupted, warned by God of the penalty for choosing evil, Satan, Adam, and Eve sinned because they deliberately chose to create evil out of good.

CHAPTER SEVEN

Justice and Mercy

                              To Heav'n thir prayers
Flew up, nor missd the way, by envious windes
Blow'n vagabond or frustrate: in they passd
Dimentionless through Heav'nly dores; then clad
With incense, where the Golden Altar fum'd,
By thir great Intercessor, came in sight
Before the Fathers Throne: Them the glad Son
Presenting, thus to intercede began.
  See Father, what first fruits on Earth are sprung
From thy implanted Grace in Man, these Sighs
And Prayers, which in this Golden Censer, mixt
With Incense, I thy Priest before thee bring,
Fruits of more pleasing savour from thy seed
Sow'n with contrition in his heart, then those
Which his own hand manuring all the Trees
Of Paradise could have produc't, ere fall'n
From innocence. Now therefore bend thine eare
To supplication, heare his sighs though mute;
Unskilful with what words to pray, let mee
Interpret for him, mee his Advocate
And propitiation, all his works on mee
Good or not good ingraft, my Merit those
Shall perfet, and for these my Death shall pay.
Accept me, and in mee from these receave
The smell of peace toward Mankinde, let him live
Before thee reconcil'd, at least his days
Numberd, though sad, till Death, his doom (which I
To mitigate thus plead, not to reverse)
To better life shall yeeld him, where with mee

> All my redeemd may dwell in joy and bliss,
> Made one with me as I with thee am one.
>
> (P.L. XI, 14–44)

The last act of the heavenly cycle begins. Leaving Sin and Death at the Gates of Hell, Satan flies through Chaos, the upper Abyss, past Limbo,[1] to the site of the Garden of Eden (P.L. IV, 1–12; Ezek. 28:12–16; II Thess. 2:7–11; Rev. 9:15, 12:12, 13). Apprehended by the Angelic Guard led by Gabriel, at first Satan decides to resist:

> ... now dreadful deeds
> Might have ensu'd, nor onely Paradise
> In this commotion, but the Starrie Cope
> Of Heav'n perhaps, or all the Elements
> At least had gon to rack, disturbd and torne
> With violence of this conflict, had not soon
> Th' Eternal to prevent such horrid fray
> Hung forth in Heav'n his golden Scales, yet seen
> Betwixt *Astrea* and the *Scorpion* signe,
> Wherein all things created first he weighd,
> The pendulous round Earth with ballanc't Aire
> In counterpoise, now ponders all events,
> Battels and Realms: in these he put two weights
> The sequel each of parting and of fight;
> The latter quick up flew, and kickt the beam....
>
>   The Fiend lookt up and knew
> His mounted scale aloft: nor more, but fled
> Murmuring, and with him fled the shades of night.
>
> (P.L. IV, 990–1004, 1013–1015)

It has been suggested that this scene also represents useless machinery.[2] The criticism is far from being accurate. Structurally, that is, solely from the point of view of narrative art, the scene of Satan's "capture" and resulting flight from the Garden of Eden (the first "day" of the War on Earth) was decidedly necessary.

In P.L. VI, 44–55, at the beginning of the War in Heaven, God commissioned Michael and Gabriel to drive Satan and his followers from Heaven. This commission has not been executed.

It was Christ, not the angels, who drove Satan from Heaven (P.L.
VI, 680–718, 853–866). Yet the command to Michael and Gabriel
has not been revoked. It is still the responsibility of the angels to
bind Satan and to cast him into hell. Structurally, in the passage
quoted above, Milton "ties up" this unresolved aspect of his plot.
The time has not yet come for Gabriel (or Michael) to execute
God's commission. First Christ must appear (metaphorically) on
earth and, in his victory over Sin and Death on the cross,

> . . . bruise the head of *Satan,* crush his strength
> Defeating Sin and Death, his two maine armes. . . .
> Then to the Heav'n of Heav'ns he shall ascend
> With victory, triumphing through the aire
> Over his foes . . . ; there shall surprise
> The Serpent, Prince of aire, and drag in Chaines
> Through all his Realme, and there confounded leave.
> (P.L. XII, 430–431, 451–455)

Later, in the fullness of time, Christ will appear to destroy the
power of the devil completely and finally. Then, at the Day of
Judgment, Gabriel will execute the commission originally assigned him by God. "The summoning Arch-Angels" will proclaim
the "dread Tribunal":

> . . . Hell, her numbers full,
> Thenceforth shall be for ever shut. Mean while
> The World shall burn, and from her ashes spring
> New Heav'n and Earth, wherein the just shall dwell,
> And after all thir tribulations long
> See golden days, fruitful of golden deeds,
> With Joy and Love triumphing, and fair Truth.
> (P.L. III, 325–326, 332–338; cf. XII, 458–465)

This is the meaning of the scales which God causes to appear in
the heavens. God has not "changed his mind." Satan may tempt
and pry. He has been given permission to "break" his chains and
to appear again in the unsullied light of God's creation. His scale,
however, has "kickt the beam." Ultimately, therefore, he will be
trampled "as mire." At the Day of Judgment, Gabriel will execute
his commission. Satan and his followers will be driven "out from

God and bliss, Into thir place of punishment" (P.L. VI, 52–53), the pit of hell, where, bound and sealed, they must remain for eternity (Rev. 20:10). Then the heavenly cycle will be complete. Christ will return to reign, on earth as in heaven, as "universal King" (P.L. III, 317).

Structurally, from the point of view of plot construction, Milton was required to explain Michael's and Gabriel's failure to execute God's command. Milton might have avoided this difficulty, of course, by restating God's original commission. Theologically, however, this was impossible. According to I Thessalonians 4:16, Matthew 25:31–32, and Matthew 13:36–43, the angels are God's agents of justice:

> . . . the execution of that last Iudgement is commonly ascribed to the holy Angels; *The Lord shall descend from heauen with a shout; and with the Voyce of the Arch-angell, and with the Trumpet of God.* And again, *When the Sonne of man shall come in his glory, the holy Angels shall also come with him, then shall the sheepe bee separated from the Goates.* That this shall bee done by Angels, is euident in the Parable of the Haruest; *The Haruest is the end of the world, the Reapers are the Angels.* And to this same purpose Angels heere are brought in, as executors of the last Iudgement, to ouer-turne the world.[3]

Moreover, according to Revelation 9:1–4 and 7:1–4, the commission to act as instruments of God's justice was given to the angels in eternity. The proof texts, Revelation 9:1–4 and 7:1–4, should be quoted in full:

> 1 . . . and I [John] saw a star fall from heaven unto the earth: and to him was given the key of the bottomless pit. 2 And he opened the bottomless pit; and there arose a smoke out of the pit, as the smoke of a great furnace; and the sun and the air were darkened by reason of the smoke of the pit. 3 And there came out of the smoke locusts upon the earth: and unto them was given power, as the scorpions of the earth have power. 4 And it was commanded them that they should not hurt the grass of the earth, neither any green thing, neither any tree; but only those men which have not the seal of God in their foreheads (Rev. 9:1–4).

> 1 And after these things I saw four angels standing on the four corners of the earth, holding the four winds of the earth, that the wind should not blow on the earth, nor on the sea, nor on any tree. 2 And I saw another angel [Christ] ascending from the east, having

the seal of the living God: and he cried with a loud voice to the four
angels, to whom it was given to hurt the earth and the sea, 3 Saying,
Hurt not the earth, neither the sea, nor the trees, till we have sealed
the servants of our God in their foreheads. 4 And I heard the
number of them which were sealed: and there were sealed an
hundred and forty and four thousand of all the tribes of the children
of Israel (Rev. 7:1–4).

The four angels who stand "on the four corners of the earth"
(definite figures which are to be interpreted indefinitely) are the
angels to whom power was given in eternity to drive Satan and his
followers (the "winds") from heaven.[4] Milton could not have
rephrased God's original command without violating his concept
of the *literal* meaning of Revelation. According to Revelation 9:4
and 7:3, Michael and Gabriel, the commanders of the Hosts of
Heaven, were commissioned in eternity to execute God's
(Christ's) judgment upon Satan and his followers.

The scene of Satan's capture and flight is, then, scarcely useless
machinery. It is in this scene that Milton rises to the second
triumphant climax of the heavenly cycle: "Hurt not the earth,
neither the sea, nor the trees, till we have sealed the servants of our
God in their foreheads," Gabriel is commanded. The time has not
yet come for Satan's (and the world's) destruction. Of this fact,
however, Gabriel (and presumably Michael) has not yet been
informed.

> The Angels being thus in readinesse to fold vp the world like an old
> *Garment,* as S. *Dauid* cals it: and it being as easie to them to doe it,
> as it is for foure men hauing the foure ends of a sheet, to fold it
> together, are now discharged by a commandement from Iesus
> Christ, till the seruants of God bee sealed in their foreheads [Rev.
> 7:3, 9:4, 12:12; Ps. 102:26; Isa. 51:16; II Thess. 1:11–12; Heb.
> 1:11–14].[5]

Gabriel is not to proceed to judgment. The time of the Second
Coming is future, not present. God is a god of mercy and love as
well as a god of wrath and retribution.

The commandment applies to Satan as well as to Gabriel. Satan
may break his fetters. He may enter the Garden of Eden. He may
not, however, destroy God's creation by acts of violence (P.L. II,
362–370). Nor, until after Adam and Eve have been "sealed," may

he deceive ("seduce") mankind by secretly entering Eve's fancy in a dream (P.L. I, 645–649).[6] From these activities Satan has been bound: "God has limited and bounded his power, not to go any further than his Commission."[7] Satan may tempt Adam and Eve—but only when they are in full control of their faculities. First Adam and Eve must be told that Sin exists and that will can be perverted. The "servants of God"—all who will follow the law of God—must be sealed.[8] Then, and only then, may Satan tempt mankind.

As in heaven, so on earth. On the second "day" of the War on Earth, Adam and Eve are conquered by Satan (Gen. 3:6; II Thess. 2:7–11; Rev. 12:13). On the third "day," however, when the battle seems lost, when

> man with the wofull issues of the conquest, was either cast downe wallowing in bloud, or scattered with pursuing crueltie . . . Now one man commeth into the field in the right of Millions (that could not stand in their owne quarrell) challengeth the victors, with singular compassion calleth backe the scattered, raiseth a mightie expectation, exposeth himselfe to the danger, with incredible fury is encountred, one with Millions or Legions of Deuils, of incomprehensible rage, and long beaten experience. . . .[9]

Satan cannot destroy the new creation of God.

Adam and Eve will fall. Lust, originally good, will become evil. Satan, however, will not—can not—prevail. He can only flee miserably, ingloriously, murmuring, to heap further damnation upon himself (P.L. IV, 1013–1015; X, 504–521). For man God has ordained a different course.

In the sky God has placed a pair of "golden Scales." The scales are an instrument of creation (P.L. IV, 999–1001; Isa. 40:12). They are a sign of continued creation, of re-creation, of the coming of Christ—first as the Son of Man, and finally, at the Day of Judgment, as the Son of God (Gen. 3:15; Matt. 24:29–31).[10] To Satan the scales (balances) are a portent of impending doom. To mankind, the scales are a prophecy of mercy and grace.[11] Sealed by God, Adam and Eve may repent (P.L. XI, 14–44; II Tim. 2:19; Rev. 8:1–5).[12] All men may repent, insists Milton, if they will (P.L. III, 173–197). Waiting patiently in heaven with a "golden censer,"

Christ, the Messiah, stands ready to offer the "prayers of all saints" upon the altar which exists before the throne of God:

> 3 And another angel [Christ] came and stood at the altar, having a golden censer; and there was given unto him much incense, that he should offer it with the prayers of all saints upon the golden altar which was before the throne. 4 And the smoke of the incense, which came with the prayers of the saints, ascended up before God out of the angel's hand. 5 And the angel took the censer, and filled it with fire of the altar, and cast it into the earth: and there were voices, and thunderings, and lightnings, and an earthquake (Rev. 8:3–5; cf. 14:5).

> To Heav'n thir prayers
> Flew up, nor missd the way, by envious windes
> Blow'n vagabond or frustrate: in they passd
> Dimentionless through Heav'nly dores; then clad
> With incense, where the Golden Altar fum'd,
> By thir great Intercessor, came in sight
> Before the Fathers Throne: Them the glad Son
> Presenting, thus to intercede began. . . .
>   (P.L. XI, 14–21)

Satan has lost the War in Heaven. Whether Satan wins or loses his battle for earth depends upon the response of the individual to the grace of God.

To Milton, this was the plain and uncomplicated meaning of the Book of Revelation.

Conclusion

Emphasis in this study has been placed upon the view that the structure of the heavenly cycle of *Paradise Lost* is based upon the Book of Revelation. Of necessity this view is controversial. Modern criticism of Milton's epic is rather thoroughly imbued with the concept of "the less said about the theology of *Paradise Lost*, the better." If the proper approach is literary, then, of course, the theology of *Paradise Lost* should be minimized and if possible ignored. This view is unfortunate. Certainly the heavenly cycle of Milton's epic is poetic and literary. *Paradise Lost* is a poem, not a formal theological treatise. An understanding of the imagery, tonal effects, epic devices—all of the various poetic techniques which Milton employs in *Paradise Lost*—is essential if the greatness of Milton's epic is to be recognized. Poetry, however, contains more than imagery and style. Poetry contains thought, theological or otherwise. The basis of Milton's thought in the heavenly cycle of *Paradise Lost* is the Bible, particularly the Book of Revelation.

In the Book of Revelation Milton found answers to many of the problems which vexed the theologians of his day. Why did Lucifer rebel against God? (What was the cause of sin?) Revelation 12:5 (Rev. 5:5; Ps. 2:7, 110:1) answered this question. Lucifer rebelled against the elevation of Christ as the Lion or as the Son of God. But this was merely the external cause of evil. What was the internal origin of sin? To this question the Book of Revelation also gave Milton a plain, uncomplicated answer: The internal cause of evil was the will. In heaven Lucifer sought to be like God (Rev. 12:7; Isa. 14:13–15). This desire (lust), an aspiration which in itself was good, Lucifer deliberately perverted into Sin and Death (Rev. 6:8; James 1:15). As the result, Evil (actual and living) and rebellion (Rev. 12:7, 6:1–8, 12–17, 8:6–13, 9:17–21; Joel 2:1–11; Ezek. 1:4–28; Isa. 14:13–15) sprang into existence. War was fought in heaven. Lucifer (Satan) and his followers were defeated and driven from heaven.

What happened to Satan when he was cast into the cosmos? Was Satan permitted to roam unpunished and unrestricted through the "air" until the time of Christ's appearance upon earth? Or was he punished and cast into hell immediately after his rebellion and defeat in heaven? Where was hell? What limitations (if any) were placed upon Satan's power to tempt and to corrupt mankind? Could Adam and Eve have withstood the temptations of the devil? These questions, to which Renaissance theologians gave confusing and often contradictory answers, Milton answered by interpreting the Book of Revelation literally. According to Revelation 12:9 (Rev. 9:1, 20:1–3; II Peter 2:4; Isa. 14:9–19), Satan was cast into hell (the "pit") and "bound" (punished) *immediately* after his expulsion from heaven. Later, with the permission of God, Satan broke his chains (Rev. 12:12, 9:14–15, 20:1–3; II Thess. 2:3–12). Before he was permitted to tempt mankind, however, Satan was severely restricted ("bound" a second time, Rev. 12:12b, 7:1–11, 20:3; II Tim. 2:19), first in heaven, when Christ accepted his mediatorial office as Saviour of mankind (Rev. 7:4, 5:6, 13:8), then on earth, when Adam and Eve were warned of the existence of Sin and Death.

The pattern inaugurated in heaven was repeated on earth. On the second day of the War on Earth, Adam, Eve, and mankind face temptation and fall (Rev. 12:13, 6:4; Gen. 3:6). Like Satan, Adam and Eve create sin deliberately, voluntarily, by their own will. Death is the inevitable result. Milton ends his account of the heavenly cycle triumphantly, however. Both as King (the Lion) and as Mediator (the Lamb), Christ has the power to destroy the forces of Sin and Death, Satan's comrades-at-arms (Rev. 8:1–5; Gen. 3:15; I Cor. 15:54–57). Ultimately, metaphorically as well as literally, victory belongs to Christ, not to Satan.

This is the bare outline of the narrative which Milton presented in the heavenly cycle of *Paradise Lost*. Twenty-five quotations from twenty-one Renaissance theologians furnish evidence that the thread of Milton's narrative was based on sixteenth- and seventeenth-century interpretations of Scripture. The quotations, with page numbers indicated for convenience of reference, are from Suárez (pp. 15–16), Fulke (pp. 22–23), Bullinger (p. 32), Pareus (pp. 36, 94), Foxe (pp. 37–38), Brightman (p. 42), Goodwin (pp. 48–49), Dent (p. 51), Tyndale (p. 56), Gyffard (p. 74), Erasmus (pp. 75–76), Carleton (pp. 79–80), Marlorat (pp. 62, 82–83), Bale (pp. 87–88), à Lapide (pp. 89–90), Mayer (p. 93), Noble (pp. 102–103), Burgesse (pp. 103–104), Rivetus (p. 107), Zanchius (p. 108), and Cowper (p. 113). The structure which binds the thread of the narrative of *Paradise Lost* into a coherent whole Milton based upon the writings of Pareus, Cowper, Mayer, and other commentators who expressed similar views (text, pp. 35–37; see Appendix A).

To Milton, the point of view presented in *Paradise Lost* was scarcely "theological fiction." *Paradise Lost* is considerably more than a brilliant poetic effort, based upon literary sources, to explain the unexplainable. To Milton, the narrative of Christ's initial "begetting" as the Son of God, the War in Heaven, the begetting of Sin and Death, the construction of the Bridge Across Chaos, the description of Satan's flight from Gabriel were incidents which were as profoundly true as the Book of Revelation itself. Of this book, it should be recalled, John described the angel as saying, "If any man shall add unto these things, God shall add unto him the plagues that are written in this book: And if any man shall take away from the words of the book of this prophecy, God shall take away his part out of the book of life" (Rev. 22:18–19). Only by adopting the opinion that "Milton was never primarily a religious poet" may we conclude, I think, that in his account of the events of the heavenly cycle Milton lacked seriousness of purpose.

Milton's view of the structure of the Book of Revelation is not a modern view. The Miltonic interpretation was based upon four assumptions: First, that Christ was begotten (exalted visibly) in heaven as the Son of God, inferior to God only in his visibility, before he was begotten on earth as the Son of Man, the mediator between God and man. Second, that the Bible should be interpreted consistently, in context, literally when the context is literal, metaphorically when the context is metaphorical. Third, that the Book of Revelation is composed of a series of visions which are related in time, place, and action. Fourth, that the Book of Revelation contains an explanation of God's hidden or secret decrees, decrees which were foreordained and published before the foundation of the world.

Modern commentators would challenge each of these assumptions. Questions as to the nature of the Son of God, the proper method of interpreting the Bible, the meaning of the Book of Revelation are no less controversial today than they were in the seventeenth century. It is not the purpose of this study, therefore, to determine whether Milton's interpretation of the Book of Revelation was (and is) either valid or invalid. The purpose of this study will have been achieved if *Paradise Lost* is recognized as a literary work, an epic poem, in which theology is basic. Point by point, from introduction to conclusion, Milton built the structure of the heavenly cycle of *Paradise Lost* upon the related visions of the Book of Revelation. Into this structure Milton introduced various texts of the Bible which, according to Renaissance Protestant commentators, were pertinent or relevant. (Many of the parallel passages appear in the marginal references of the King James Version of the Bible.) Primarily the heavenly cycle of *Paradise Lost* is a commentary upon the Book of Revelation. Indeed, *Paradise Lost* is the only Renaissance Protestant commentary on the Book of Revelation which is still read with profit and delight.

Appendix A

THE STRUCTURE OF THE HEAVENLY CYCLE

```
(Begetting: Literal)
5: 1- 5  5--12: 1- 5          War in Heaven

                                6: 1- 2 (Third Day)----        ----------------8: 6- 7----------
                                6: 3- 4 (First Day)-----          6:8 (Sin)     ----8: 8- 9--13:3 (Satan Wounded)--
                                6: 5- 6 (Second Day) --         -6:12 (Earthquake)----8:10-11--- 9:17-18 (Artillery)------
                                6: 7- 8 (Third Day)----          20:1-7 (Binding—Loosing)      8:12-13---------
                 12: 7-10       6:12-17 (Third Day---                                  9: 1-12 9:13-21--13: 1, 11-(12:3)
                                        Expulsion) -----          -7:1-3 (Abdiel)------------(Hell) (Loosing) (Sin and Death)
                                6: 9-11 (Limbo)-------                              -(8:1- 6)-----------

                                                                       (Golden Altar)

   (Eternity)
   Rev. 4: 1-11                 War on Earth

                                6: 1- 2 (Third Day)----         6:8 (Potential Sin & Death)---8: 6- 7--5:8--------
                                6: 3- 4 (First Day)-----                                  -8: 8- 9-----------
(Office: Literal)               6: 5- 6 (Second Day) --         -6:12 (Earthquake)---------8:10-11----------
5: 6-14--12:11-17               6: 7- 8 (Third Day)----          20:1-7 (Binding—Loosing       8:12-13---------
                                6:12-17 (Third Day---                       Potential)    9: 1-12--9:13-21--13: 1, 11-(12:3)
                                        Expulsion) ------         -7:1-3 (Sealing) ---------(Earth)------18:5 (Bridge)-----
                                6: 9-11 (Mercy of ------                                    -8: 1- 5 (5:8)-----------
                                        Christ)

                                                                       (Golden Altar)

Begetting: Metaphorical------------
Office: Metaphorical
POTENTIAL
```

Appendix B

THE BINDING OF SATAN

The background and significance of seventeenth-century interpretations of Revelation and Daniel are discussed by Louise Fargo Brown, *The Political Activities of the Baptists and Fifth Monarchy Men in England During the Interregnum* (Washington, 1912); H. H. Rowley, *Darius The Mede And The Four World Empires In The Book of Daniel* (Cardiff, 1959; 1st ed., 1935); Le Roy Edwin Froom, *The Prophetic Faith Of Our Fathers* (Washington, 1948); Dietrich Korn, *Das Thema Des Jüngsten Tages in Der Deutschen Literature Des 17. Jahrhunderts* (Tübingen, 1957); Michael Fixler, *Milton And The Kingdoms Of God* (1964); Peter Toon, ed., *Puritans, The Millenium And The Future Of Israel: Puritan Eschatology 1600 to 1660* (Cambridge, 1970); and B. S. Capp, *The Fifth Monarchy Men* (1972). Excellent though these studies are, they fail to indicate that for more than a century prior to 1650 Renaissance theologians pointed directly to the second half of the seventeenth century as a time when the world would undergo a "shaking and an overturning." Basing their calculations upon Revelation and Daniel, from 1544 to 1650 more than twenty Protestant commentators (listed below) maintained that the Day of Judgment, the Second Coming, the Reign of Christ or of the Saints, the Conversion of the Jews, and/or the Fall of Antichrist would occur between 1650–1700.[1]

Andreas Oisander	*Coniectures of the ende* (1548; 1st Latin ed., 1544)	Day of Judgment	1657–1677
		Fall of Antichrist (Pope)	1772
David Chytraeus	*Auslegung der Offenbarung Johannis* (1572)	Fall of Antichrist (Pope)	1672 (or 1866)

[1]The list excludes numerous references to the Parousia or the destruction of Antichrist as "imminent," "at hand," or "soon to come." Asterisks indicate commentators who dated the thousand-year binding of Satan (Rev. 20) specifically from 1650 to 1700.

Lambert Daneau	*Tractatus de Antichristo* (1582)	Fall of Antichrist (Pope)	1666
Bartholomäus Ringwalt	*Lauter Warheit* (1588)	Reign of Christ	1684
John Napier	*Reuelation of John* (1593)	Day of Judgment	1688–1700
Philipp Nicolai	*Chronologia Sacra* (1630; 1st Latin ed., 1596)	(Conversion of the Jews) Fall of Antichrist (Pope), Fall of Antichrist (Turks), and Reign of Christ	(1600) 1670
T. L[upton]	*Babylon is Fallen* (1597)	Fall of Antichrist (Pope)	1666
Robert Pont	*A New Treatise* (1599)	Day of Judgment	1688–1700
Peter Du Moulin	*Accomplishment Of Prophecies* (1613)	Fall of Antichrist (Pope)	1689
Thomas Brightman	*Exposition Of Daniel* (1614)	Fall of Antichrist (Turks)	1650–1695
Richard Fowns	*Trisagion* (1619; 1st ed., 1618)	Second Coming	1666
Henry Finch	*Worlds Great Restavration* (1621)	Reign of the Jews Fall of Antichrist (Turks)	1650 1650–1695
*Joseph Mede	*Key of the Revelation* (1643; 1st Latin ed., 1627)	Fall of Antichrist (Pope) and Reign of the Saints	1655–1665
*John Henry Alsted	*The Beloved City* (1643; 1st Latin ed., 1627)	Reign of Christ	1694
*Thomas Goodwin	*Exposition Of Revelation* (written in 1639)	Fall of Antichrist (Pope) Fall of Antichrist (Turks) Conversion of the Jews Reign of Christ	1650–1700 1655–1656 1700
*William Kiffin?	*Glimpse Of Sions Glory* (1641?)	Fall of Antichrist (Pope)	1650–1695
*John Archer	*Personall Reigne Of Christ* (1641)	Conversion of the Jews Fall of Antichrist (Pope)	1650–1656 1666
*Jeremiah Burroughs	*Exposition Of Hosea* (1643)	Fall of Antichrist (Pope)	1650–1660?
Ephriam Huet	*Prophecie Of Daniel* (1643)	Fall of the Turks and Conversion of the Jews	1650–1695
John Shawe	*A Broken Heart* (1643)	Conversion of the Jews	1650
*William Reynor	*Babylons Ruining– Earthquake* (1644)	Fall of Antichrist (Pope) and Reign of the Saints	1660

*T[homas]	*Glory of Christ*	Conversion of the Nations	1650–1700
C[ollier]	(1647)	Reign of Christ	1700
*George Foster	*Sounding Of The*	Fall of Antichrist	
	Last Trumpet (1650)	(Parliament) and Reign of	1650–1651
		the Saints	

Napier, Brightman, Mede, Alsted, Goodwin, Archer, Burroughs—in the seventeenth century these were men of repute. It was largely upon the writings of this group of scholars that Milton's contemporaries based their interpretations of Revelation and Daniel. In 1641 Milton agreed with those who "proclaimed the coming Kingdom of Christ and stripped the prelatical robe so that Antichrist's cloven hoof might stand revealed" (Fixler, p. 103). *Paradise Lost* expresses a different conviction. To Milton, in *Paradise Lost,* the "Antichrist" of Revelation and of Daniel is the devil (Lucifer), not a human being. The concept that Constantine was the agent of Antichrist's (Satan's) binding Milton rejects completely. He makes no use of the mystical numbers of Revelation and of Daniel, the figures upon which his contemporaries based their calculations of the binding of Satan and/or of the Second Coming (*). The texts which Milton employs in *Paradise Lost* are millennial texts. The interpretation of these texts is pre-Reformation (Toon, pp. 15, 31, 49–50; Tuveson, pp. 15–27). With its identification of the seals with the trumpets of Revelation (text, pp. 35–37 above), the structure of *Paradise Lost* is contemporary. Doctrinally, however, the concepts that inform Milton's interpretation of Revelation in *Paradise Lost* are those of traditional Christianity. In *Paradise Lost,* avoiding the millennial "new" theology of the seventeenth century, Milton deliberately returned to the long established interpretation of Augustine *(City of God,* XX, VII–VIII). The thousand years of Satan's binding (an indefinite figure) is equivalent to "the whole period of this world's history." To Milton, as to Augustine, the binding of Satan was both eternal (literal) and temporal (metaphorical).

Notes

Chapter 1 Before the Beginning

1 Page and line references to *The Christian Doctrine (De Doctrina Christiana), Paradise Lost,* and other works by Milton follow the numbering of *The Works of John Milton,* ed. James Holly Hanford and Waldo Hilary Dunn (1931–1938). Unless otherwise indicated, place of publication of all texts cited is New York or London.

2 Maurice Kelley, *This Great Argument* (Princeton, 1941), pp. 95–105; Allan H. Gilbert, "The Theological Basis of Satan's Rebellion and the Function of Abdiel in *Paradise Lost*," *MP,* XL (1942), 26; B. Rajan, *Paradise Lost & The Seventeenth Century Reader* (1947), pp. 31, 142–143; Kenneth Muir, *John Milton* (1955), p. 164; Robert Martin Adams, *Ikon: John Milton and the Modern Critics* (Ithaca, 1955), p. 143; Merritt Y. Hughes, ed., *John Milton Complete Poems and Major Prose* (1957), p. 316; William Empson, *Milton's God* (1961), pp. 99–102. See also Herbert J. C. Grierson, *Milton & Wordsworth, Poets and Prophets* (Cambridge, 1937), p. 99; Arthur Sewall, *A Study in Milton's Christian Doctrine* (Oxford, 1939), pp. 89–90, 98; C. S. Lewis, *A Preface to Paradise Lost* (Oxford, 1942), pp. 86–87; John S. Diekhoff, *Milton's Paradise Lost* (1946), pp. 79–80; Walter Clyde Curry, *Milton's Ontology, Cosmogony, and Physics* (Lexington, Ky., 1957), pp. 43–47, 207; John Peter, *A Critique of Paradise Lost* (1960), p. 66; William G. Madsen, *From Shadowy Types To Truth* (New Haven, 1968), pp. 5, 68–69, 84; and William B. Hunter, Jr., "Milton On The Exaltation Of The Son: The War In Heaven In *Paradise Lost*," *ELH,* XXXVI (1969), 215–231.

3 F. E. Hutchinson, *Milton and the English Mind* (1948), p. 168; Kelley (1941), p. 103; J. B. Broadbent, *Some Graver Subject* (1960), pp. 223–224. See also Denis Saurat, *Milton Man and Thinker* (1925), p. 209; Grant McColley, *Paradise Lost* (Chicago, 1940), p. 316; Arnold Williams, "The Motivation of Satan's Rebellion in *Paradise Lost*," *SP,* XLII (1945), 267; Mark Van Doren, "Paradise Lost," *The Noble Voice* (1946), p. 139; J. H. Adamson, "The War In Heaven: Milton's Version Of The Merkabah," *JEGP,* LVII (1958), 703; and Empson (1961), p. 99. The criticism was expressed as early as 1729 by Constantine de Magny, *Dissertation Critique Le Paradis Perdu* (Paris, 1729), p. 187.

4 Kelley (1941), p. 103; Saurat (1925), p. 206; McColley (1940), p. 28.

5 "Preface," *The History Of Sin and Heresie* (1698), sig. A2*v.*

6 *The Political History Of The Devil* (1726), pp. 74, 71. Compare John Dennis, *The Grounds Of Criticism In Poetry* (1704), p. 36; Anon., *Le Journal Littéraire*, IX (1717), in Herman Scherpbier, *Milton in Holland* (Paris, 1933), p. 127; de Magny (1729), p. 104; "Theophilus," *Gentleman's Magazine*, March, 1738, p. 124; Jacob Bodmer, *Critische Abhandlung von dem Wunderbaren in der Poesie und dessen Verbindung mit dem Wahrscheinlichen In einer Vertheidigung des Gedichtes John Miltons von der vehrlohrnen Paradeise* (Zurich, 1740), pp. 109–110; Filippo Scolari, *Saggio di Critica sul Paradiso Perduto* (Venezia, 1818), pp. 67–68, in Edward F. Kenrick, " 'Paradise Lost' and The 'Index' Of Prohibited Books," *SP*, LIII (1956), 495; François Chateaubriand, "Essai Sur La Littérature Anglaise" (1836), *Oeuvres Completes* (Paris, 1860), ed. Grenier Frères, XI, 696; and H. McLachlan, *The Religious Opinions of Milton, Locke, and Newton* (Manchester, 1941), pp. 17–18.

7 "Enarrationes In Psalmos," *Patrologiae Cursus Completus, Series Latina,* cited hereafter as *PL,* ed. J. P. Migne (Paris, 1865), 36, 70–71. A similar view was stated by Philo, Origen, Athanasius, Basil, Primasius, Aquinas, and other early commentators. See Göttlieb Lünemann, "The Epistle To The Hebrews," *Meyer's Commentary On The New Testament* (1885), tr. Maurice J. Evans, p. 402; and Brooke Foss Wescott, *The Epistle To The Hebrews* (1914; 1st ed., 1889), p. 21.

8 *The Commentaries of M. Iohn Calvin upon the Actes of the Apostles* (1585), tr. Christopher Fetherstone, pp. 313–314. See Chapter 3, p. 54, above.

9 Francis Vatablus, *Liber Psalmorvm Davidis* (1556), p. 6; [John Ball,] *A Short Treatise* (1646; 1st ed., 1629), p. 50; Iohn Boys, *Workes* (1629; 1st ed., 1622), p. 675; cf. p. 811; Solomon Gesner, *Commentationes In Psalmos Davidis* (Witebergae, 1629), p. 22; Paul Tarnov, *S. Johannis Evangelium Commentarius* (Rostochi, 1629), pp. 285, 301; William Ames, *Lectiones in CL psalmos Davidis* (1635), quoted by Gilbert (1942), p. 24; Richard Clerke, *Sermons* (1637), ed. Charles White, pp. 25–34. The label "1st ed." indicates the earliest edition listed in Darling, Wing, *British Museum Catalogue,* and other standard listings.

10 Henry Bullinger, *A Hvndred Sermons vp̄o the Apocalips* (1561), p. 352; Théodore Bèza, *The Psalmes Of Dauid* (1581; 1st ed., 1580), tr. Antonie Gilbie, p. 2; Immanuel Tremellius and Francis Junius, *Testamenti Veteris Biblia Sacra* (1585; 1st ed., 1580), III, 39–40; D. Victorinus Strigelius, *Part Of The Harmony Of King Davids Harp* (1582), tr. Richard Robinson, p. 16; [Thomas Wilcox,] *A very godly and learned Exposition, vpon the whole Booke of Psalmes* (1591; 1st ed., 1586), p. 5; Richard Webb, *Christs Kingdome* (1611; 1st ed., 1610), pp. 92–110; Henry Ainsworth, *Annotations Upon the Book of Psalmes* (2nd ed., 1617), sig. [A4]; William Cowper, "Pathmos: Or, A Commentary On The Revelation" (1619), *Workes* (1623), p. 1021; Thomas Goodwin, *The Great Interest Of States & Kingdomes* (1646), p. 35; *Johannis Piscatoris*

Commentarii In Omnes Libros Veteris Testamenti (Herbornae Nassoviorum, 1646), III, 113.

11 Agreement regarding the meaning of the word "literal" is not found in the commentaries. Commentators disagreed as to whether the context of various passages (particularly in the Book of Revelation) was earth (literal) or heaven (literal). For the sake of consistency, Milton's use of the word "literal" in *The Christian Doctrine* (V, 181, 13–16) has been followed throughout this study. The problems involved in the literal and metaphorical approaches to Scripture are considered at some length in Chapters 3 and 4.

12 In *The Christian Doctrine* Milton states that Christ's incarnation is a mystery which is beyond human understanding. "How much better is it," writes Milton, "to know merely that the Son of God, our Mediator, was made flesh, that he is called both God and Man, and is such in reality; which is expressed in Greek by the single and appropriate term Θεάνθρωπος" (C.D. XIV, 273, 9–12). In *Paradise Lost* Milton does not discuss the subject of Christ's dual nature. On earth Christ is the metaphorically begotten Son of God, God-man, the Mediator who by one "God-like act" (P.L. XII, 427) restores the relationship between God and man.

13 Allan H. Gilbert, *On the Composition of Paradise Lost* (Chapel Hill, 1947), p. 114; David Daiches, *Milton* (1957), p. 184.

14 Gilbert, "The Theological Basis of Satan's Rebellion" (1942), pp. 23, 24–26; Ruth Montgomery Kivette, *Milton On The Trinity* (unpublished Ph.D. dissertation, Columbia University, 1960), pp. 95–96, 100. Note the Vulgate reading of Psalm 110 (109):3b: "ex utero ante luciferum genui te" ("from the womb before the day star [Lucifer] I begot thee"). Compare Adolphe Napoleon Didron, *Christian Iconography* (1886; reprinted, 1968), completed by Margaret Stokes, II, 17–18, 230; and J. M. Neale and R. F. Littledale, *A Commentary On The Psalms* (3rd ed., 1887), III, 439, 447–450. In *Paradise Lost* Milton interpreted Psalm 2, 110, Revelation 5, 12, metaphorically as well as literally. See C.D. IX, XV, XXXIII, and pp. 37–38, 61–65, above.

15 Rajan (1947), p. 31; Kelley (1941), p. 98. See Saurat (1925), pp. 208–209; Davis P. Harding, *Milton And The Renaissance Ovid* (Urbana, 1946), p. 67; Hutchinson (1948), p. 123; Rex Warner, *John Milton* (1949), p. 14; Kester Svendson, *Milton and Science* (Cambridge, Mass., 1956), p. 239; Hughes (1957), p. 178; Sims (1962), p. 217; and Douglas Bush, *John Milton* (1964), pp. 142, 157.

16 Time, of course, indicates finitude. Other expressions, such as "infinite" time or "elder state" of time, however, are no more satisfactory. For discussion of the problem, see Laurence Stapleton, "Milton's Conception of Time in *The Christian Doctrine*," *Harvard Theological Review*, LVII (1964), 9–21; and (particularly) Augustine, *City of God*, XII, XV–XIX, tr. Philip Levine (Cambridge, Mass., 1966), IV, 65–93.

17 Thomas Goodwin, "An Exposition Of The Epistle To The Ephesians," *Works*(1681), ed. John C. Miller (Edinburgh, 1861), I, 473.

18 Bullinger (1561), p. 162; William Fulke, *Praelections vpon the Sacred and holy Reuelation of S. Iohn* (1573), tr. George Gyffard, fol. 33*v;* Iohn Mayer, *Ecclesiastica Interpretatio* (1627), p. 307; Gyffard, *Sermons Vpon The Whole Booke Of The Revelation* (1596), p. 122.

19 Iohn Bale, *The Image Of both churches* (1548?), ed. Henry Christmas, Parker Society (Cambridge, 1849), I, 298; Gyffard (1596), pp. 119–120; Arthur Dent, *The Rvine Of Rome Or An Exposition vpon the whole Reuelation* (1607; 1st ed., 1603), pp. 37, 47, 55; Cowper (1623; 1st ed., 1619), pp. 833, 840; Johann Piscator, "Apocalypseos Johannis," *Commentarii In Omnes Libros Novi Testamenti* (Herbornae Nassoviorum, 1638; 1st ed., 1621?), pp. 797–798; Boys (1629; 1st ed., 1622), p. 350; Mayer (1627), pp. 299, 306; Iohn Diodati, *Pious Annotations Upon The Holy Bible* (1643), note on Revelation 4:2; William Leo, *A Sermon Preached At Lambeth* (1645), p. 2.

20 According to Joseph Turmel, *Histoire Des Dogmas* (Paris, 1935), IV, 85, "Jusqu'à la fin du IVe siècle les anges étaient donc censés n'avoir connu le mystère de l'Incarnation qu'à l'epoque de l'ascension. Ou si, un ou deux docteurs tiennent un language un peu différent, c'est simplement pour dire que les esprits angliques furent informes du plan divin au moment de sa realisation. Augustin changea tout cela. Selon lui *(Genes. litter.* 5, 38) les anges eurent longtemps d'avance communication du mystère de l'Incarnation." See C.D. VII, 33–34, 8–10. According to Chrysostom, "Homily XV On John 1:18," before the Incarnation Christ was *angelis invisibilis.*

21 John Calvin, *The Institvtion Of Christian Religion* (1634; 1st ed., 1561), tr. Thomas Norton, I, XIV, 19, fols. 70, 122; John Downame, *The Summe of Sacred Diuinite* (1630?), p. 228; Arthur Jackson, *A Help For The Understanding Of the Holy Scripture* (1643), p. 7; John Wollebius, *The Abridgment Of Christian Divinity* (1656; 1st ed., 1650), tr. Alexander Ross, p. 64. For a modern translation of Wollebius' *Abridgment (Compendium Theologiae Christianae,* 1626), see John W. Beardslee, *Reformed Dogmatics* (1965), pp. 27–262.

22 Reginald Scot, *The Discovery of Witchcraft* (1665; 1st ed., 1584), [II,] 8–10, discusses nine scholastic views (and disagrees with each). See also Iohn Salkeld, *A Treatise of Angels* (1613), pp. 336–341; *R. P. Francisci Suárez E. Societate Jesu Opera Omnia* (Paris, 1856), tom. II, lib. VII, cap. XIII, #5–13, pp. 882–885; Mayer (1627), pp. 147–148; and Turmel (1935), IV, 91.

23 Zanchius, *De Operibvs Dei Intra Spacivm Sex Diervm Creatis* (Genevae, 1613; 1st ed., 1591), tom. III, col. 170, cited by Williams (1945), p. 264. The translation is by Edward Leigh, *A Treatise of Divinity* (1646), III, 106–107.

24 Wollebius (1656; 1st ed., 1650), p. 33. For discussion of Milton's indebtedness to Wollebius, Polanus, Zanchius, Calvin, Tremellius and

Junius, Bèza, Ames, and other authors, see Maurice Kelley, *Complete Prose Works Of John Milton* (New Haven, 1973), VI, 17–22, 107, *passim*.

25 Amandus Polanus, *The Svbstanec* [sic] *Of Christian Religion* (1600), pp. 11–12. Compare Bullinger (1561), p. 15; Fulke (1573), fol. 34; Robert Rollock, *A Treatise Of Gods Effectval Calling* (1603), tr. Henry Holland, pp. 231, 233; [Ball] (1646; 1st ed., 1629), p. 52; Tarnov (1629), p. 301; Conrad Vorstius, "Commentarivs In . . . Ephesios," *Commentarivs in Omnes Epistolas Apostolicas* (Amsterdami, 1631), pp. 279, 282; Edward Reynolds, *An Explication Of The Hvndredth And Tenth Psalme* (1632), pp. 77–80, 398–399; Edward Leigh, *A Treatise of the Divine Promises* (1633), p. 64; Nemsius, *The Nature Of Man* (1636), tr. George Wither, pp. 532–533. See, however, Kelley, *This Great Argument* (1941), p. 121, and *Complete Prose* (1973), VI, 208.

26 Calvin, *Institutes*, tr. Henry Beveridge (Grand Rapids, 1957), III, XXIII, 7; XXI, 5; cf. II, XII, 4–5. The subject is discussed at some length by Gary D. Hamilton, "Milton's Defensive God: A Reappraisal," *SP*, LXIX (1972), 87–100. Calvin objected to the "speculation" that Satan revolted "when he foresaw the Son of God was to be clothed in human flesh. . . . Since the Son of God was made man in order to restore us—then already lost—from our miserable overthrow, how could that be foreseen which would never have happened unless man had sinned." Quoted by McColley (1940), pp. 26–27. Unlike Suárez (see text below), however, Calvin insisted that God's original decree was a decree of complete election and reprobation. The hypothesis by William Hunter (1969), p. 223, that by the term "begot" Milton meant to suggest a combined metaphorical-literal exaltation of the Son, would seem invalidated by the statements of Calvin and Suárez.

27 Suárez (1856), tom. II, lib. VII, cap. XIII, #5, p. 882. Compare Karl Werner, *Franz Suarez und die Scholastik der letzten Jahrhunderts* (Regensburg, 1861), I, 224–225. The Suárez text reads as follows:

> juxta opinionem, quam multi D. Thomae attribuunt, Deus secundum ordinem rationis praedestinavit Incarnationem post peccantum Luciferi . . . ; ergo non potuit Lucerferi peccantum habere pro objecto Incarnationem, supposita Dei praescientia et praedestinatione. Antecedans probatur, quia Deus non praeordinavit Incarnationem, nisi post praevium peccatum Adae, quia principaliter, et quasi adaequate in remedium illis praeordinata est: ita ut si Adam non peccasset, ex vi praesentis decreti praedestinato non fieret, ut auctores hujus opinionis contendunt: sed peccatum Adae supponit peccatum Angelorum ordine causalitatis, quia malus Angelus fuit causa inducens hominem ad peccandum: ergo a fortiori peccantum Angeli praecessit in praevisione divina voluntatem Incarnationis; ergo non potuit Incarnatio esse objectum ejus.

28 In *The Christian Doctrine* (V, 185, 24–26), Milton wrote: ". . . however the generation of the Son may have taken place, it arose from no natural necessity, as is generally contended" (quoted by Kelley,

This Great Argument, 1941, p. 121). This view Milton repeated poetically in P.L. VIII, 419–421. Adam, conversing with the Almighty (Christ), explains man's need for a mate: "No need that thou Shouldst propagat, already infinite; And through all numbers absolute, though One." Professor Kelley (*This Great Argument,* p. 121; *Harvard Theological Review,* LIV, 202–203; cf. *Complete Prose,* VI, 110–111) regards Adam's request as clear proof of the existence in *Paradise Lost* of "at least one Arian statement . . . [thus] . . . champions of Milton's orthodoxy are consequently faced with the choice either of abandoning their Trinitarian theory of *Paradise Lost* or of admitting that the epic contains two contradictory views on the Son and the Father. . . ." Neither conclusion would seen necessary. First, before the fall of the angels, there was "No need" for Christ to be begotten literally (in heaven). God is "the necessitie of things" (P.L. VII, 172–173; III, 98–111). Second, before the fall of mankind, there was "No need" for Christ to be begotten metaphorically (on earth). Note the statement of Thomas Jackson, *A Treatise Of The Divine Essence* (1628), II, 191: "The incarnation of our blessed Saviour, was in the opinion of some of the Ancients, absolutely necessary before the creation of mankind, & should in time *infallibly* have been accomplished for confirming or augmenting that happy estate wherein *Adam* was created; if so he had continued stedfast in it untill the time appointed by God for his change or translation. But however the Schooles may determine or *wave* this question (I must confesse, neither very usefull nor in this place much necessary) there was no necessity questionlesse, that the *second Adam* should become a *bloudy sacrifice* for our sinnes, unlesse the first *Adam* had sinned: but after he, by his actuall transgression, had utterly cut off that *possibility* of perserverance, which the eternall decree had bestowed upon him, the *humiliation* and bitter *passion* of the *Sonne* of God, became as *necessary* in respect of Gods mercy and bounty towards man, and of his infinite justice which (notwithstanding his infinite mercy) was to be fully satisfied, as his incarnation." Third, before he was begotten visibly Christ existed invisibly as God (P.L. V, 835–841; III, 390–391). See also Richard Baker, *An Apologie For Lay-Mens Writing in Divinity* (1641), sigs. [K6r–K8], and footnote 25 above. The passage from *The Christian Doctrine* should not be misapplied.

29 Based on John 1:1–3, the view that Christ was "begotten" in eternity (the "twofold stage theory" of Christ's generation) was held by Theophilus, Tertullian, and Clement of Alexandria. According to Harry Austryn Wolfson, *The Philosophy Of The Church Fathers* (Cambridge, Mass., 1970; 1st ed., 1956), I, 217, this view—to which Milton may or may not have been indebted—disappeared from Christian theology after the fourth century. The subject is considered by Kelley, *Complete Prose* (1973), VI, 262; and C. A. Patrides, "An Open Letter . . . ," *Milton Quarterly,* VII (1973), 72–73.

30 Each of the texts refers to the same time, "eternity." In each of the texts, moreover, Christ is exalted ("begotten") in the presence of the "angels." Psalm 2 and Psalm 110, to be sure, refer to "kings" and to "heathen" rather than to "angels." To Milton, however, the allusion to Psalm 2:9 in Revelation 12:5 and to Psalm 2:5, 12, in Psalm 110:5 (as well as in Hebrews 1:2, 5, 13) furnished proof that the personages involved in each of these passages were the same. John himself, on the basis of divine authority, associated Psalm 2 (Ps. 110) with Revelation 12. Human authority—the authority of Renaissance Bible scholarship—justified the association of Revelation 12:5 with Revelation 5:5. Compare the similar poetic treatment of Revelation 5 (Ps. 2, 110) by Edward Henry Bickersteth, *Yesterday, Today, and For Ever* (1870; 1st ed., 1866), IV, 279–559, pp. 125–134, and note, p. 408. See Chapter 1, notes 7, 14, and 31; Chapter 2, notes 2, 17–20, and 33; and Chapter 3, notes 6, 8, and 12.

31 Many interpretations of the meaning of "the book" were suggested by Renaissance commentators: "The book" represented the Old and New Testaments (Augustin Marlorat, *A Catholike exposition vpon the Reuelation of Sainct Iohn,* 1574, fol. 79), the Book of Revelation itself (Mayer, 1627, p. 306), the history of the Church (Cowper, 1623, 1st ed., 1619, p. 851), or the hidden or secret decrees of God (Bullinger, 1561, p. 157; Iohn Foxe, *Eicasmi Sev Meditationes, In Sacram Apocalypsin,* 1587, p. 41; Francis Junius, *The Apocalyps, Or Revelation Of S. Iohn,* Cambridge, 1596, tr. T. B[arbar], p. 61; Piscator, "Apocalypseos," 1638, 1st ed., 1621?, p. 798). For the purpose of this study the most significant interpretation was that "the book" represented the secret decrees of God. The interpretation of Revelation 5:2–3 by Bale (1548?), I, sigs. [Hvii-Hviiᵛ], is particularly revelant: The "boke is Goddess heauenlye ordinaunce, contayninge not onelye all that hath bene created of God vysible & inuisible, but also the vniuersall contentes of the holy scripture. . . . no man was founde able [to open the book], neyther in heauen, nor in earth, nor vnder the earth, yet was there a dyligent serch made, and many did attempt it. The Angels that by apostasye fell from God, when they were in heauen wrought maistryes about it."

32 Gyffard (1596), p. 122. Compare Bullinger (1561), p. 157; Fulke (1573), fols. 33–34; Marlorat (1574), fol. 82; Foxe (1587), p. 11; Thomas Brightman, *The Revelation of S. Iohn* (Leyden, 1616; 1st ed., 1611), p. 255; David Pareus, *A Commentary Upon The Divine Revelation Of The Apostle And Evangelist Iohn* (Amsterdam, 1644; 1st Latin ed., Heidelberg, 1618), tr. Elias Arnold, pp. 99–100; Mayer (1627), p. 308.

33 ". . . when the scripture saith, that the Lord Jesus sitteth at the right hand of his Father, it understandeth it chiefly of his human nature which he took upon him. . . . [The text, however, has another signification.] Thus the right hand of God is infinite, neither may it be shut in; for God's might and power is incomprehensible. The kingdom of Christ also, which is

everlasting, is a kingdom of all worlds; and so is he of one substance, of one power and honour, with the Father, not bound to one place, but is every where." Otto Werdmueller, *The Hope of the Faythfull* (1544?), tr. Myles Coverdale, *Remains of Myles Coverdale,* ed. George Pearson, Parker Society (Cambridge, 1846), pp. 156, 163. Calvin's comment (*Institutes,* II, XV, 6) should also be noted: ". . . his [Christ's] sitting at the right hand of the Father has the same meaning as if he was called the vicegerent of the Father, intrusted with the whole power of government."

34 See notes 19 above and 35 below.

35 Marlorat (1574), fol. 71*v*; Brightman (1616; 1st ed., 1611), p. 218; Cowper (1623; 1st ed., 1619), pp. 840–842; Thomas Wilson, *A Christian Dictionary* (1622, 2nd ed.; 1616), [II] note on "Jasper Stone"; Nathanael Homes, *The New World Or The New Reformed Chvrch* (1641), p. 62; John Trapp, *A Commentary or Exposition upon all the books of the New Testament* (1656), ed. W. Webster (1865), p. 747. See P.L. VI, 757–759.

36 Bullinger (1561), pp. 145–153; Fulke (1573), fols. 34, 34v; Brightman (1616; 1st ed., 1611), pp. 257–258; Pareus (1644; 1st ed., 1618), p. 4; cf. pp. 87–88; Boys (1629; 1st ed., 1622), p. 811; Cornelius à Lapide, *Commentaria in Apocalypsin S. Iohannis Apostoli* (Antwerp, 1662; 1st ed., 1627), p. 80.

37 Ribera, *In sacram beati Ioannis Apostoli & Euangelistae Apocalypsin Commentarij* (Antverpiae, 1602), p. 203.

In hoc [Rev. 5:5–7] autem quod Christus venire dicitur ad Patrem, minor illo ostenditur, quatenus homo est, aequalem cum eo honorem non habens. Pater enim sedet, ipse stat, & ad Patrem venit non Pater ad eum, librum accipit, quasi sibi soli debitum vt aperiat, vt qui iudex & Dominus est omnium hominum, ipse poenas praenuntiet, & infligi iubeat.

See P. Luis de Alcazar, *Argvmentvm Apocalypseos qvo distinctione Capitvm observate indicatur totivs Libri Acolvthia* (1603), in à Lapide (1662; 1st ed., 1627), p. 80; and C. D. V, 291–293, 25–20. Alcazar's views were discussed repeatedly and at length both by à Lapide (1662; 1st ed., 1627) and Pareus (1664; 1st ed., 1618), *passim.*

38 Compare the Socinian interpretation of Revelation 4–5 by Iohn Crellius, *De Vno Deo Patre* (Racoviae, 1631), II, 82: "Nam primùm, si Christus secundùm naturam potiorem [Rev. 5:5–7], secundùm quam solam persona esse creditur, idem cum sedente in throno esset [Rev. 4:2–5], non posset ab eo simpliciter distingvi. Id enim perinde esset; ac si simpliciter negaretur esse sedens in throno." "For first, if Christ had a second more evident human nature, a nature which alone is human, he was the same when sitting on the throne; he could not be distinguished from that simply. When sitting on the throne he can not be distinguished from one who is not sitting on the throne." By distinguishing between "office" and "begetting," Milton avoided the anti-Trinitarian interpretation noted by Kelley, *Complete Prose* (1973), VI, 110.

39 Louis Racine, *Life of Milton Together With Observations On Paradise Lost* (1930; 1st ed., Paris, 1754), tr. Katherine John, p. 150.

40 Throughout the preceding pages emphasis has been placed on the view that the underlying concepts of both *Paradise Lost* and *The Christian Doctrine* are essentially the same. A caveat should be issued against identifying the two works completely. *The Christian Doctrine* is an Arian (or, more accurately, an anti-Trinitarian) document. (The better term is "subordinationist." See Kivette, 1960, p. 107; and Patrides, 1973, pp. 72–73.) *Paradise Lost* is not. In *The Christian Doctrine* Milton dwells at length upon the "proof" of his belief that Psalm 2 with its related passages cannot possibly be used to show that Christ was "begotten" from eternity. In *Paradise Lost* the issue is not raised. The "begetting" of Christ in P.L. V, 603–608, does not refer to Christ's ultimate or initial origin. According to Abdiel, Christ created the angels. Thus Christ existed before he was "begotten." Note Calvin's statement *(Institutes,* I, XIII, 17): "The words, Father, Son, and Holy Spirit, certainly indicate a real distinction, not allowing us to suppose that they are merely epithets by which God is variously designated from his works. Still they indicate distinction only, not division. . . . it is clear that the only begotten Son previously existed in the bosom of the Father (John i.18). For who will dare to affirm that the Son entered his Father's bosom for the first time, when he came down from heaven to assume human nature?" So far as the reader is concerned, in *Paradise Lost,* both before and after his initial appearance, Christ is God, God is Christ. In P.L. V, 603–608, Milton states that the Son is "begotten" by the Father. In that Christ is "begotten" he is inferior to the Father. By immediately declaring that Christ is the Son of God, however, Milton removes the Arian (subordinationist) implications. As the quotation from Crellius indicates, Milton had every opportunity to write an Arian or a Socinian poem. He did not avail himself of the opportunity.

CHAPTER 2   THE WAR IN HEAVEN

1 Samuel Morland, *The Urim of Conscience* (1695), p. 14, quoted by Robert H. West, *Milton And The Angels* (Athens, Ga., 1955), p. 118; Anon., *Le Journal Littéraire,* IX (1717), quoted by John Martin Telleen, *Milton Dans La Littérature Française* (Paris, 1904), p. 10; John Dennis, "Letters on Milton and Wycherley" (1721–1722), *Critical Works* (Baltimore, 1943), ed. Edward Niles Hooker, II, 224; [Defoe] (1726), pp. 74–76; Voltaire, "Essai Sur La Poésie Epique" (1726), *Oeuvres* (Paris, 1834), ed. M. Beuchot, X, 485; de Magny (1729), pp. 116–117, 125–126; John Clarke, *An Essay Upon Study* (2nd ed., 1737), p. 194; Abbé Goujet, *Bibliotheque Françoise* (Paris, 1744), pp. 202–204; Racine (1930; 1st ed., 1754), tr. John, pp. 142, 158; José Cadalso, "Eruditos a la Violeta" (1772), *Obras* (Madrid, 1818), I, 31, in E. Allison Peers, "Milton In Spain," *SP,* XXIII

(1926), 172; J. A. Aiken, ed., *The Poetical Works of John Milton* (1808), I, 27; Robert Pollok, "Introductory Notice," *The Course of Time* (Philadelphia, 1864; 1st ed., 1827), p. xxiv; Egerton Brydges, ed., *The Poetical Works of John Milton* (1835), II, 287; Walter Bagehot, "John Milton" (1859), *Works and Life* (1915), ed. Russell Barrington, III, 210–211; Matthew Arnold, "A French Critic On Milton," *Mixed Essays* (1904; 1st ed., 1879), pp. 195–199; Mark Pattison, *Milton* (1879), p. 185; William H. Stifler, "Some Phases Of Theology In The 'Paradise Lost,' " *The Baptist Quarterly Review*, V (1883), 136–137, 139; Saurat (1925), pp. 208–209; Grierson (1937), p. 118; A. J. A. Waldock, *Paradise Lost And Its Critics* (Cambridge, 1947), p. 112; R. J. Zwi Werblowsky, *Lucifer and Prometheus* (1952), pp. 7–8; Peter (1960), p. 78.

2 "Out of the manner of their rebellion and conspiracie, in that they did band themselues, and sit in counsell against the Lord and his Annointed, we collect this doctrine, that there are Counsels and Parliaments held as well against the Lord, as for the Lord, and cleane contrary vnto his truth, as for his truth." Webb (1611; 1st ed., 1610), p. 60. According to Gesner (1629), p. 14, the reference to "the kings of the earth" in Psalm 2:2 should be translated as Molech: "Hinc est nomen idoli מֶלֶךְ Molech seu Molock, quod Saturni fuisse putatur." "Rulers," according to John of Damascus, *Exposition of the Orthodox Faith* (c. 725), are the first of the last triad in the nine-fold division of the celestial hierarchy. (See Gustav Davidson, *A Dictionary of Angels,* 1967, p. 247.) "Christ" is the reading for "anointed" in the Geneva version of the Bible.

3 Most Protestant commentators on Revelation identified Michael symbolically as Christ (Rajan, 1947, p. 146; West, 1955, p. 125). The "literal" interpretation was presented, however, by such reputable Protestant commentators as Bale (1548?), II, [Evi]; Foxe (1587), p. 200; Mayer (1627), p. 394; Joseph Mede, *The Key of the Revelation* (1643; 1st Latin ed., 1627), tr. Richard More, II, 40; Symon Patrick, "Two Sermons On Michaelmas Day, 1672," *Works,* ed. Alexander Taylor (Oxford, 1858), p. 281; and Leslie (1698), p. 2. See also Andrew Willet, *Hexapla In Danielem* (1610), p. 384; and McColley (1940), p. 22.

4 Bullinger (1561), p. 355; Patrik Forbes, *An Exqvisite Commentarie Vpon The Revelation* (1613), pp. 102–104; Pareus (1644; 1st ed., 1618), p. 263; Cowper (1623; 1st ed., 1619), p. 1023; Mayer (1627), p. 392; Thomas Taylor, *Christs Victorie Over The Dragon* (1633), pp. 290–291.

5 N. Byfield, *An Exposition Vpon the Epistle To the Collosians* (1628; 1st ed., 1615), p. 69. The description is metaphorical. See also Iohn Iewell, *An Exposition Vpon the two Epistles of the Apostle Saint Paul to the Thessalonians* (1594; 1st ed., 1583), pp. 336–338; Edward Elton, *An Exposition Of The Epistle Of St. Pavl To The Colossians* (1620; 1st ed., 1615), pp. 321–330; and Bickersteth (1870; 1st ed., 1866), VIII, 78–594, X, 104–320, pp. 253–271, 315–323.

6 The view that "Earth [may] Be but the shaddow of Heav'n" (P.L. V, 574–575) is derived from many sources. Primary are Romans 1:20, "For the invisible things of him [God] from the creation of the world are clearly seen, being understood by the things that are made, even his eternal power and Godhead . . . ," and II Peter 3:8, "one day is with the Lord as a thousand years, and a thousand years as one day" (Ps. 90:4). Applied to the six days of creation, II Peter 3:8 was used to prove that the earth would exist precisely 6,000 years before the "second creation," or the great Day of Judgment, would occur. The concept that history is cyclic necessarily followed. For discussions of the tangled Christian-Platonic background of the cyclic view (the *Annus Magnus*), compare Lactantius, *Divine Institutes*, VII, 14; Pierre Duhem, *Le Système du Monde* (Paris, 1914), vols. II, III, VII, VIII, see Index; Lynn Thorndyke, *A History Of Magic And Experimental Science* (1929), vols. I–II, Index; Karl Löwith, *Meaning In History* (Chicago, 1949), pp. 165, 248; Albert R. Cirillo, "Noon-Midnight and the Temporal Structure of *Paradise Lost*," *ELH*, XXIX (1962), 372–375, 387–390; and Alastair Fowler, *Spenser And The Numbers Of Time* (1964), pp. 40, 193. Theologians objected to Plato's view (*Statesman*, 269–274) that time is composed of endless cycles. The concept, if accepted, would mean that Adam and Eve, recreated endlessly, must fall and fall again. Thus Christ must die repeatedly on the cross. Milton's view was scarcely Platonic.

7 Pseudo-Augustine, "Expositio In Apocalypsim B. Joannis," *PL*, 35, 2425. Cornelius à Lapide (1662; 1st ed., 1627), p. 120, cites Tyconius, Primasius, Bede, Haymo, Lyra, Aquinas, Ioachim, Aureolus, Pannonius, Ribera, Viegas, and Peterius as advocates of this view. See also *Caesarii Arelatensis Opera Varia* (Maretioli, 1942), II, 225; *Dionysii Cartusiani Opera Omnia* (Monstrolii, 1901), XIV, 272; Foxe (1587), p. 41; Cowper (1623; 1st ed., 1619), p. 872; and Nicholas Zegerus, "Annotationes in Novum Testamentum," cited by John Pearson, ed., *Annotata ad Actus Apostolicos, Epistolas & Apocalypsin* (1660), VII, 4754.

8 Bullinger (1561), p. 355.

9 Gyffard (1596), p. 228.

10 Fulke (1573), fols. 39, 84*v;* [T. Hayne,] *The General View Of The Holy Scriptures* (1640; 1st ed., 1607), pp. 349–350; Mede (1643; 1st ed., 1627), p. 52.

11 Fulke (1573), fol. 87; Marlorat (1574), fol. 185*v;* Pareus (1644; 1st ed., 1618), p. 272; Cowper (1623; 1st ed., 1619), p. 1035; Taylor (1633), pp. 128–129; Georges Duriez, *La Théologie Dans Le Drame Religieux En Allemagne Au Moyen Age* (Lille, 1914), p. 598; and Dennis H. Burden, *The Logical Epic* (Cambridge, Mass., 1967), p. 53.

12 According to Pareus (1644; 1st ed., 1618), "The greater part of interpreters both Papists & Protestants . . . understand this *mountaine* to be Satan the prince of the world, who burning with the fire of envie at the

preaching of the Gospel, is cast into the sea of this world" (p. 159). Pareus, however, explained the mountain of Revelation 8:8 as a symbol of the Antichrist. The view that the mountain was a symbol for Satan was held by Primasius, Caesariensis, Cartusianus, Hugo Cardinalus, and Viegas (Cowper, 1623, 1st ed., 1619, p. 938).

13 Iohn Deacon and Iohn Walker, *A Svmmarie Answere* (1601), p. 144; Miles Mosse, *Ivstifying And Saving Faith Distingvished from the faith of the Deuils* (1613), p. 9; William Greenhill, *An Exposition Of the five first Chapters Of The Prophet Ezekiel* (1645), p. 104. The view is that of Tertullian, "Apologeticus Adversus Gentes Pro Christianis," *PL*, 1, XXII, 466.

14 McColley (1940), pp. 21–29.

15 See *The Reason Of Church-governement Urg'd against Prelaty* (1641–42), III, 238, 1–7; "Preface" to *Samson Agonistes* (1671), I, 331, 16–20. The text of *The Works of John Milton,* ed. Hanford and Dunn, is used throughout this study.

16 According to Theodore Banks, *Milton's Imagery* (1950), pp. 176–177, Milton derived the largest proportion of his images from the Book of Revelation. Milton's use of imagery from the Book of Revelation is not simply decorative or occasional, however. Rather it is structural. The imagery of *Paradise Lost* is the imagery of the Book of Revelation.

17 Pareus (1644; 1st ed., 1618), p. 24.

18 Cowper (1623; 1st ed., 1619), p. 826.

19 Mayer (1627), p. 338; cf. pp. 253–255. To Pareus, Cowper, and Mayer, the vials (Rev. 16), which were "particular" visions, were not parallel in meaning with the seals (Rev. 6–7) and the trumpets (Rev. 8–9), which were "universal" visions. See pp. 61–62, above. In *Paradise Lost* Milton paralleled the seals with the trumpets but not with the vials. Milton probably would have agreed with the statement of Stephen Marshall, *The Song Of Moses The Servant Of God, And The Song Of The Lambe* (1643), p. 44: "All Protestant Writers do agree, that we are under the pouring out of some *one* or more of these seven vialls." In *Paradise Lost,* however, except as a source for details Milton does not refer to Revelation 14–19. The subject matter of the vials (the history of the Church in the last age or in the period prior to the Day of Judgment) is not the subject matter of *Paradise Lost.*

20 Fulke (1573), fol. 52; Marlorat (1574), fols. 120, 123; Taylor (1633), pp. 141, 238–244; *A Briefe Explanation Of The XX. Chapter Of The Revelation of Saint John* (1641), p. 9; Hezekiah Holland, *An Exposition . . . Upon the Revelation of Saint John* (1650), sig. [al]. Pareus (p. 21) acknowledged indebtedness to Nicholaus Collado, *Exposition On The Revelation* (1584). The Recapitulation Theory dates from the fourth century. See Victorinus, "Commentary on the Apocalypse of the Blessed John," in Edwin Froom, *The Prophetic Faith Of Our Fathers* (1950), I, 340–341; Tyconius, "Book of Rules," cited by Augustine, "Christian

Instruction," *Writings of Saint Augustine,* tr. John J. Gavigan (1947), IV, XXXVI, 102; Richard a Saint Victore, "In Apocalypsim Joannis Libri Septem," *PL,* 196, 780–781; Martin Legionensis, "Expositio Libri Apocalypsis," *PL,* 209, 347–348; Rvpert Tvitiensis, *Commentariorvm In Apocalypsin, Libri XII* (Noremberge, 1526), pp. 215–216; Henri de Lubac, *Exégère Médiévale Les Quatre Sens de L'Ecriture* (Aubier, 1959), II, 505; Friedrich Düsterdieck, *Critical And Exegetical Handbook To The Revelation of John* (1887), tr. Henry E. Jacobs, pp. 13–18; and A. T. Robertson, *Syllabus For New Testament Study* (Nashville, 1923; 1st ed., 1915), pp. 265–271. In the twentieth century the view has been advocated by John Wick Bowman, *The Drama Of The Book of Revelation* (Philadelphia, 1955), p. 63; and J. Sidlow Baxter, *Explore The Book* (Grand Rapids, Mich., 1967; 1st ed., 1960), pp. 344–345.

21 Pareus (1644; 1st ed., 1618), p. 266. According to McColley (1940), p. 21, by emphasizing "the revolt of the angels, he [Milton] sacrificed the support of contemporary Protestant theology." The statement should be qualified. Most Protestant theologians explained the "war in heaven" metaphorically as the earthly war of the Church against evil. Other Protestant commentators (as John Foxe and the authors of the semi-official *Sermons* of 1559), however, interpreted the "war in heaven" traditionally or literally. See text above and below and notes 22–24 following.

22 "An Homilee agaynst disobedience and wylfull rebellion," *Certayne Sermons appoynted by the Queenes Maiestie* (1559), [II,] 545.

23 Foxe's text (p. 203) reads:

Age, & quo tēpore incidit hic Draconis casus? Post partumnè mulieris, an ante partem [Rev. 12:1–7]? Si à partu, quid igitur ijs respōdebimus, qui ex loco Iudae fratris Iacobi, ex Esaia, receptáque veterum opinione, de lapsu Luciferi, Angelorúmque ruina disputant, quos multo ante Christum natum, non seruantes originem suam, è coelesti domicilio concidisse autumant? [Marginal Gloss: Solutio. Duplex Luciferi lapsus è coelo.] Cui vt respondeam obiectioni: vt id non negamus, deturbatum de coelo Luciferum, cum suis Angelis, ante aeditum in mundo seruatorem: at nihil id obstat tamen, quin verum sit, quod de vtroque tempore Luciferinae ruinae commemoratur, sed alia atq.

24 Tymme, *A Silver Watch-Bell* (13th impression, 1619; 1st ed., 1605), p. 71; Manton, *A Practical Commentary . . . On the Epistle of Jude* (1658), pp. 284–285; à Lapide (1662; 1st ed., 1627), pp. 205–217. Compare Martin Luther, *Luther Still Speaking . . . A Commentary on the first five chapters of the Book of Genesis* (1544), tr. Henry Cole (Edinburgh, 1868), pp. 44–46; [Dudley Fenner,] *The Sacred Doctrine Of Divinitie* (1613; 1st ed., 1599), p. 9; Mayer (1627), pp. 391–393; Thomas Case, *Gods Rising, His Enemies Scattering* (1644; 1st ed., 1642), p. 7; *The Rebells Catechisme* (1643), p. 2, quoted by George Wesley Whiting, *Milton's Literary Milieu*

(Chapel Hill, 1939), p. 232; Thomas Grantham, *Christianismvs Primitivus* (1678), I, 108–109; Leslie (1698), pp. 1–2; and Ernest Lee Tuveson, *Millennium and Utopia* (Berkeley, 1949), pp. 15–16, 26–27.

25 Taylor (1633), p. 238.

26 Cowper (1623; 1st ed., 1619), p. 872. The Geneva version of the Bible (1560), gloss to Revelation 6:2, reads: "He that rideth on the white horse, is Christ." See note 7 above.

27 Saurat (1925), p. 208.

28 Clarke (1737), p. 198.

29 Pareus (1644; 1st ed., 1618), p. 114; Fulke (1573), fol. 39*v*; Diodati (1643), note on Revelation 6:5. For a summary of the structural differences between Pareus' and Milton's interpretations of the Book of Revelation, see Appendix A and pp. 61–62, above.

30 Pareus objected to identifying the "great star" of Revelation 8:10 as Satan. See, however, Zegerus, in Pearson (1660), VII, 4775; Alcuin, "Commentariorum In Apocalypsin," *PL,* 100, 1137; and Haymo, "Expositionis In Apocalypsin B. Joannis," *PL,* 117, 1048.

31 Brightman (1616; 1st ed., 1611), pp. 420–421.

32 Richard Bernard, *A Key Of Knowledge For the Opening Of . . . Revelation* (1617), p. 197; Pareus (1644; 1st ed., 1618), p. 190; Cowper (1623; 1st ed., 1619), p. 984; Mede (1643; 1st ed., 1627), pp. 116–117; Henry Hammond, *A Paraphrase And Annotations Upon all the Books of the New Testament* (1681; 1st ed., 1653), p. 902; Trapp (1656), p. 756. The interpretation was expressed frequently in eighteenth- and nineteenth-century commentaries. See, for example, Thomas Newton, *Dissertation On The Prophecies* (1752), ed. W. S. Dobson (Philadelphia, 1832), p. 492; Adam Clarke, *Commentary* (1809), ed. Robert Earle (Grand Rapids, Mich., 1970), p. 1345; Andrew Fuller, "Expository Discourse On The Apocalypse" (1815), *Works,* ed. Andrew Gunton (Boston, 1833), II, 39; and Matthew Henry, "An Exposition Of The Revelation" (1714?), completed by William Tong (1838), *Comprehensive Commentary Acts—Revelation,* eds. William Jenks and Joseph A. Warne (Philadelphia, 1869), p. 696.

33 Merritt Y. Hughes, "Satan and the 'Myth' of the Tyrant," *Ten Perspectives On Milton* (New Haven, 1965), pp. 170–172.

34 See Pareus (1644; 1st ed., 1618), p. 170; and Taylor (1633), p. 697. A number of commentators regarded Revelation 6:9–11 (the fifth seal) as an interruption in the order of the narrative or "history" of Revelation 6:1–12. Revelation 6:12 represented the continuation of Revelation 6:8. See Chapter 7, note 1; Bullinger (1561), pp. 181–193, 205; Foxe (1587), p. 56; Gyffard (1596), p. 139; and Forbes (1613), pp. 41–43, 69. See also John A. Himes, "The Plan of Paradise Lost," *New Englander,* LXII (1883), 196–211; and Michael Fixler, "The Apocalypse within *Paradise Lost,*" *New Essays on Paradise Lost,* ed. Thomas Kranidas (Berkeley,

1969), pp. 164–165. With the argument of these articles the present study is largely in disagreement.

35 Thomas Hall, *An Exposition...On...Amos* (1661), p. 489. According to John M. Steadman, *Milton's Epic Characters* (Chapel Hill, 1968), pp. 183–185, patristic exegesis identified "the giants [הַגִּבֹּרִים, Nephilim or giants] in the earth" of Genesis 6:4 with the fallen angels. The appearance of the Titans in heaven also may be justified by Proverbs 9:18 (Vulgate): "and giants [וּרְפָאִים, Rephaim or giants] were there..." (in hell). Compare Isaiah 14:9. These were "Monstrous men, that would dart thunder at God himselfe; and raise vp mountaines of impietie against Heauen." Thomas Adams, *The Diuells Banket* (1614), p. 175.

36 Taylor (1633), p. 141; cf. pp. 697–698.

37 An example of Milton's humor. The devils are herded from heaven like goats because, עַתּוּדֵי אָרֶץ .., they are goats. Dr. Johnson ("Milton," 1779, *Works*, ed. Arthur Murphey, 1796, IX, 177) seems to have missed the point in his criticism of this passage.

38 Cowper (1623; 1st ed., 1619), p. 889. See Marlorat (1574), fol. 102; and Mayer (1627), pp. 321, 323.

39 "An Exposition Of The Revelation" (written in 1639), *Works* (1692), ed. John C. Miller (Edinburgh, 1861), III, 47–48. Goodwin's exposition involved two frequently combined theological views: 1) that "the gods of the nations are devils" (אֱלִילִים), Ps. 96:5, and 2) that the names assumed by the devils originally were those of "men departed." See Augustine, *City of God*, VIII, XXIV, XXVI; Lactantius, I, 6; Joseph Mede, *The Apostasy Of The Latter Times* (1642; 1st ed., 1641), p. 12; *Works* (1648), pp. 461–465, 76–79. P.L. I, 361–375, states the interpretation indicated above. P.L. VI, 838–877, presents the opposite interpretation. The first passage is metaphorical; the second, literal.

40 Dent (1607; 1st ed., 1603), p. 42. Compare Fulke (1573), fols. 28v–29; Tremellius and Junius (1585; 1st ed., 1580), III, 128; Foxe (1587), pp. 32–33; Iohn Foord, *Apocalypsis Iesv Christi, Revelata Per Angelvm* (1597), p. 26; Cowper (1623; 1st ed., 1619), pp. 845–847; Mayer (1627), pp. 303–306; Thomas Adams, *The Spiritvall Navigator* (1615), pp. 56–58; Greenhill (1645), pp. 130–133, 181; John Carter, *The Wheel turned by a voice from the throne of Glory* (1647), pp. 59–104. See Thomas Keightley, *Account of the Life and Writings of Milton* (1855), pp. 474–479; Turmel (1935), IV, 75–76; West (1955), p. 157; Hughes, *Milton* (1957), p. 80; Adamson (1958), pp. 690–703; and George Wesley Whiting, *Milton and This Pendant World* (Austin, 1958), pp. 96–104. Considerable scholarship has been expended on Milton's use of Ezekiel as the basis for his description of the Chariot of the Son. The fact is that Protestant commentators on Revelation frequently identified the visible throne of God with the "likeness of the [a] throne" in Ezekiel 1:4–28 and 10:1–22 (Rev. 4:2–9). Milton seems to have followed the Latin rather than the

THE VISION OF EZEKIEL,

A. The whirlewind that came out of the North, or Aquilon.

B. The great cloudes.

C. The fire wrapped about it.

D. The brightnes abous it.

E. The likenesse of Amber, or the pale colour.

F. The forme of the foure beastes.

G. Their feete like Calues feete.

H. Hands comming out from vnder their winges.

I.K.L.M. The fashion of the foure faces of euerie beast.

N. Their winges ioyned one to another.

O. Their two wings, which couered their bodies.

P. Fire running among the beastes.

Q. Wheeles hauing euerie one foure faces.

R. The rings of the wheeles which were full of eyes.

S. The firmament like vnto cristall.

T. The throne, which was set vpon the firmament.

V. Where sate like the appearance of a man.

X. The appearance of amber aboue, and beneath the man

Y. The fire aboue him.

Z. The brightnesse of fire like the rainebowe.

Midi, Or the South.

Hebrew interpretation of Ezekiel 1:4–28 and 10:1–22. Although the "fourfold-visag'd Foure" living creatures move with "One Spirit" with the "living Wheels" of the Chariot of Paternal Deity, the cherubim are separate from the wheels themselves (Latin interpretation). Apparently the wheels, which are described as being "undrawn," are not interconnected or combined into an "Orb" with a common center (Hebrew interpretation). See James Strachan, *Early Bible Illustrations* (Cambridge, 1957), pp. 18–21, and figs. 21, 39, 40, 43, 112; and *The Bible* (Geneva version, 1602; 1st ed., 1560), fol. 344v (above). Milton's description of Satan as "a stripling Cherube" and of Zephon as "youthful" follows an alternate explanation of the meaning of the word "cherub," כְּרוּב, "a youth" (P.L. III, 636, IV, 845). According to II Chronicles 3:10 (Geneva version), the cherubim of Solomon's temple were "wrought like children."

41 Wilson (1622, 2nd ed.; 1616), [II,] note on "Foure Beastes." Compare Fulke (1573), fol. 29; Gyffard (1596), pp. 115–117; Junius (1596), p. 81; Gasper Sanchez, *Sacarum literarum Interpretis In Ezechielem & Danielem* (Lvgdvni, 1619), pp. 26–34; Mayer (1627), pp. 301–305; William Pemble, "A Short and Sweete Exposition Vpon The First Nine Chapters of Zecharie" (1629), *Workes* (3rd ed., 1635), pp. 424, 426; and Iohn Preston, *Life Eternall Or, A Treatise Of the knowledge of the Divine Essence* (1631), pp. 34–35. See, however, Adamson (1958), pp. 694, 703.

42 The view of Kivette (1960), p. 112 note, that Christ's role in *Paradise Lost* "is that of a puppet-monarch manipulated by a higher power," is somewhat less than satisfactory.

CHAPTER 3   ORTHODOXY AND CONFUSION

1 [Defoe] (1726), p. 70; cf. pp. 77–80. See John Cowper Powys, *Enjoyment Of Literature* (1938), p. 261; Rajan (1947), p. 144; Waldock (1947), pp. 92–95; and West (1955), p. 124.

2 Bernard Routh, *Lettres Critiques a M^r Le Comte *** Sur Le Paradis Perdu* (Paris, 1731), pp. 144–147; de Magny (1729), pp. 193–207; Jacques de Lille, tr., *Paradis Perdu* (Paris, 1805), I, 6. See Walter Raleigh, *Milton* (1900), pp. 85–86; and Saurat (1925), pp. 207–208.

3 *Gentleman's Magazine*, March, 1738, p. 124. See also *Journal de Trévoux* (1710), quoted by Telleen (1904), p. 8; H. G. Rosedale, "Milton: His Religion And Polemics, Ecclesiastical As Well As Theological," *Milton Memorial Lectures, 1908* (1909; reprinted, 1964), ed. Percy W. Ames, pp. 184, 187; John Erskine, *The Delight of Great Books* (Indianapolis, 1928; 1st ed., 1916), pp. 159–160; John Middleton Murry, *Keats* (1955; 1st ed., 1930), pp. 257, 266; Lord David Cecil, ed., *The Oxford Book Of Christian Verse* (Oxford, 1940), pp. xxi, xxii; Frank Allen Patterson, ed., *The Student's Milton* (1947), pp. 47–48.

4 *Milton Criticism* (1950), p. 6. Compare John Walter Good, *Studies In The Milton Tradition* (Urbana, 1915; reprinted, 1967), pp. 220, 221, 259–260; and George F. Sensabaugh, *Milton in Early America* (Princeton, 1964), pp. 229, 238, 278, 300–304.

5 Lewis (1942), p. 92; John Bailey, *Milton* (1915), pp. 144–148; E. M. W. Tillyard, *The Miltonic Setting* (1947; 1st ed., 1938), p. 73; Wylie Sypher, *Partisan Reader* (1946), pp. 567–581, cited by Malcolm Mackenzie Ross, *Poetry & Dogma* (New Brunswick, N.J., 1954), pp. 185–187; Rajan (1947), pp. 19, 35–36; Muir (1955), p. 164; Howard Schultz, *Milton and Forbidden Knowledge* (1955), p. 119; Douglas Bush, ed., *The Complete Poetical Works Of John Milton* (1965), p. 204.

6 See Chapter 1, notes 7 through 10.

7 Banks (1950), pp. 142–148.

8 Phillip Melanchthon, *Loci Commvnes Theologici* (Lipsiae, 1556; 1st ed., 1521), p. 30; Ainsworth (1617, sig. Hh; Boys (1629; 1st ed., 1622), pp.

811, 816; Gesner (1629), p. 742; Reynolds (1632), pp. 6, 16–17, 22–23; George Abbot, *Brief Notes Upon the whole Book of Psalmes* (1651), pp. 538–539.

9 Tremellius and Junius (1585; 1st ed., 1580), III, 100; [Wilcox] (1591; 1st ed., 1586), p. 433; Polanus (1600), p. 157; Boys (1629; 1st ed., 1622), pp. 811–813, 823; [Ball] (1646; 1st ed., 1629), pp. 83, 92. See F. F. Bruce, "The Epistle To The Hebrews," *The New International Commentary* (Grand Rapids, Mich., 1964), pp. 7–8, 4–5, 17–18, and 23–26.

10 Zanchius (1613; 1st ed., 1591), tom. III, col. 69; King James I, *Daemonologie* (1603; 1st ed., 1597), III, 75; Salkeld (1613), p. 336; Mayer (1627), p. 147; Clerke (1637), p. 118; Piscator, *Commentarii* (1646), III, 50; Jeremiah Whitaker, *The Danger of Greatnesse* (1646), p. 27; Jeremy Taylor, *A Course of Sermons* (1668; 1st ed., 1653), p. 242. See P. E. Dustoor, "Legends of Lucifer in Early English and in Milton," *Anglia,* LIV (1930), 229.

11 Wolfgang Musculus, *Common places of Christian Religion* (1563), tr. John Man, fols. 11–11v; Edward Dering, *XXVII. Lectvres, or readings, vpon . . . Hebrues* (1590; 1st ed., 1576), fol. 85; Gyffard (1596), p. 229; Brightman (1616; 1st ed., 1611), p. 356; Iohn Donne, *Sermons* (1624), ed. Evelyn M. Simpson and George R. Potter (Berkeley, 1953), VI, 69; Downame (1630?), p. 227; Thomas Adams, *A Commentary Or, Exposition Upon . . . St. Peter* (1633), p. 358; Diodati (1643), note on Isaiah 14:9–13; Manton (1658), p. 277.

12 Foxe (1587), p. 30; Forbes (1613), pp. 10–31; Cowper (1623; 1st ed., 1619), p. 835; Piscator, "Apocalypseos" (1638; 1st ed., 1621?), p. 797; Mayer (1627), pp. 299–310.

13 John Napier, *A Plaine Discouery of the whole Reuelation of Saint Iohn* (Edinburgh, 1593), pp. 26–27, 63; Mede, *The Key of the Revelation* (1643; 1st ed., 1627), pp. 31–34; Goodwin, "An Exposition Of The Revelation" (1639), III, 2; Hvgo Grotius, "Annotationes In Apocalypsin," *Opervm Theologicorvm* (Basileae, 1732; 1st ed., 1644), III, 1174–1176; Hammond (1681; 1st ed., 1653), p. 883.

14 Augustine, *Of The Citie Of God* (1610), tr. J. H., XX, IX, pp. 803–804; Foxe (1587), pp. 203–204; Brightman (1616; 1st ed., 1611), pp. 517–520; Pareus (1644; 1st ed., 1618), p. 272; Cowper (1623; 1st ed., 1619), pp. 1015–1028; Mayer (1627), pp. 390–395. See Schultz (1955), pp. 228–234; and Michael Fixler, *Milton And The Kingdoms of God* (1964), pp. 13–45.

15 See Chapter 2, notes 21–23.

16 Bullinger (1561), pp. 242–250; Fulke (1573), fols. 51v–60v; Gyffard (1596), pp. 158–164; Dent (1607; 1st ed., 1603), pp. 89–92; Cowper (1623; 1st ed., 1619), p. 934.

17 Gyffard (1596), pp. 161–180; Forbes (1613), sigs. A1v–A2; Pareus (1644; 1st ed., 1618), p. 166; Thomas Taylor (1633), pp. 238–240; Holland (1650), p. 54. Most Protestant commentators on the Book of Revelation interpreted Revelation in terms of historical events (as the invasion of

NOTES TO PAGES 56-58

Italy by the Huns, the machinations of the various emperors and popes, the coming of Wycliffe, Hus, or Luther, etc.) from the time of Christ to the end of the world. Apparently Grotius (1732; 1st ed., 1644) was the first prominent Protestant scholar who maintained the Revelation should be explicated in terms of first-century Christianity.

18 *The Obedience of a Christen man* (1535; 1st ed., 1528), sigs. R1v–R111.

19 Iohn Marbeck, *A Booke Of Notes and Common places* (1581), p. 400; Iohn Deacon and Iohn Walker, *Dialogicall Discourses of Spirits and Divels* (1601), p. 112; Thomas Adams, *The Diuells Banket* (1614), sigs. A3v–A4; [Iohn Day,] *Day's Descant On Davids Psalmes* (Oxford, 1620), pp. 37–38; Thomas Jackson, *The Knowledg Of Christ Jesus* (1634), p. 77; Wollebius (1656; 1st ed., 1650), p. 12; Jeremy Taylor (1668; 1st ed., 1653), pp. 192–194; Robert Fludd, *Mosaicall Philosophy* (1659), sig. Aiv; others. See Joshua McClennen, "On the Meaning and Function of Allegory in the English Renaissance," *The University of Michigan Contributions in Modern Philology*, VI (1947), 22–36; Theodore Long Hugelet, *Milton's Hermeneutics: A Study Of Scriptural Interpretation In The Divorce Tracts And In "De Doctrina Christiana"* (unpublished Ph.D. dissertation, University of North Carolina, 1959), pp. 120–124ff.; D. C. Allen, "Milton and the Descent to Light," *JEGP*, LX (1961), 614, reprinted, *Milton, Modern Essays*, ed. Arthur E. Barker (1965), p. 177; U. Milo Kaufmann, "Puritan Hermeneutics," *The Pilgrim's Progress And Traditions In Puritan Meditation* (New Haven, 1966), pp. 25–60; and Kelley, *Complete Prose* (1973), VI, 581–582. Although faulty, the most useful recent discussion of Milton's use of metaphorical language is that of Madsen (1968), pp. 5, 54–84.

20 Taylor (1668; 1st ed., 1653), p. 194.

21 *A Disputation on Holy Scripture* (1610; 1st ed., 1588), Parker Society, p. 404, quoted in part by Charles K. Cannon, "William Whitaker's *Disputatio de Sacra Scriptura:* A Sixteenth-Century Theory of Allegory," *HLQ*, XXV (1961–1962), 132–133; and Kaufmann (1966), p. 30.

22 See note 13.

23 Desiderius Erasmus, *The Paraphrase of Erasmus vpon the newe testament* (1549), II, vi; Napier (1593), p. 27; Hvgh Brovghton, *A Revelation Of The Holy Apocalyps* ([Middleburgh,] 1610), p. 206; Boys (1629; 1st ed., 1622), pp. 355, 792; Zegerus, in Pearson (1660), VII, 4741. The view was held by Irenaeus, Athanasius, Anselm, Gregory, Bede, Haymo, Rupert, Richard, Aureolus, Cartusianus, and other writers upon the Book of Revelation.

24 Bullinger (1561), p. 208; Fulke (1573), fols. 53v, 55, 76v; Marlorat (1574), fols. 121, 170; Forbes (1613), pp. 65–66, 69; Cowper (1623; 1st ed., 1619), pp. 951, 1020; Wilson (1622, 2nd ed.; 1616), [II,] note on "Locusts."

25 Bullinger (1561), p. 259; Foxe (1587), pp. 84–87; Napier (1593), p. 3;

Forbes (1613), p. 71; Pareus (1644; 1st ed., 1618), pp. 175–178; Cowper (1623; 1st ed., 1619), pp. 950–962.

26 Bullinger (1561), p. 265; Dent (1607; 1st ed., 1603), pp. 95–100; Cowper (1623; 1st ed., 1619), p. 955; Mayer (1627), pp. 345–346; William Guild, *The Sealed Book Opened* (1656), pp. 74–75. Protestant commentators generally maintained that the "star" of Revelation 9:1 was the Antichrist, specifically the Pope of Rome. Catholic commentators replied by identifying the "star" with Luther and Calvin.

27 See note 12.

28 Junius (1596), pp. 98–100; Thomas Adams, *A Commentary* (1633), p. 528; Zegerus, in Pearson (1660), VII, 4754, 4775. According to Foxe (1587), p. 83, the "locusts" were regarded as devils by Aretas, Bede, Aquinas, Rupert, Haymo, and Primasius.

29 Théodore Bèza, *The Newe Testament* (1579), tr. L. Tomson, fol. 391v; Junius (1596), p. 98; Tymme (1619; 1st ed., 1605), p. 71; Pareus (1644; 1st ed., 1618), p. 171; Wilson (1622, 2nd ed.; 1616), [II,] note on "Bottomlesse Pit"; Diodati (1643), notes on Isaiah 14:9 and Revelation 9:1; cf. Henry Barclay Swete, *The Apocalypse of St. John* (Grand Rapids, 1908; reprint), pp. 114–115, 22.

30 Bullinger (1561), pp. 140–175, 355; Fulke (1573), fols. 28v, 75–78; Gyffard (1596), pp. 113–122, 219–220; Junius (1596), pp. 54–65, 144–148; Dent (1607; 1st ed., 1603), pp. 38–40, 156.

31 Fulke (1573), pp. 53–60, 131; Foxe (1587), pp. 83–88, 206; Brightman (1616; 1st ed., 1611), pp. 369–378, 647–649; [Thomas Cartwright,] *A Plaine Explanation Of The Whole Revelation Of Saint John* (1622), pp. 46–47, 121.

32 *Clavis Apocalyptica* (1651), p. 154.

33 *Of Reformation . . . In England* (1641), III, 4–5, 24–13; *The Reason Of Church-governement Urg'd against Prelaty* (1641–42), III, 246, 5–6; and *Eikonoklastes* (1649), V, 306–307, 11–4.

34 Deacon and Walker, *Dialogicall Discourses* (1601), p. 114; Forbes (1613), pp. 102–103; Thomas Taylor (1633), pp. 403–404; and Joseph H. Summers, *The Muses Method* (1962), p. 198. See *Animadversions Upon The Remonstrants Defence* (1641), III, 140, 19–25, and Hugelet (1959), pp. 23–24. Revelation 12:9 and 20:2 are the only passages in the Bible which clearly identify Satan as the serpent (Gen. 3:1–6).

35 Marlorat (1574), fol. 174v; Bale (1548?), II, 32, 33v. Compare notes 17 and 34 and pp. 37–38, above. Most Protestant commentators began the history of Revelation with the coming of Christ. The older, patristic (Augustinian) view that Revelation contained a metaphorical account of the fall of Adam and Eve was not uncommon, however.

CHAPTER 4   FLIGHT AND FRUSTRATION

1 Augustine, *Confessions,* XI, 12, cited by Calvin, *Institutes* (1561), XIV, 1. Similarly, in C. D. VII, 3, 2–5 (cf. *Tetrachordon,* IV, 168, 14–17),

Milton commented, "As to the actions of God before the foundation of the world, it would be the height of folly to inquire into them, and almost equally so to attempt a solution to the question." See pp. 96–98, above.

2 Zanchius (1613; 1st ed., 1591), tom. III, col. 174; Tymme (1619; 1st ed., 1605), p. 81; Thomas Adams, *The Diuells Banket* (1614), p. 186; Henry Greenwood, *Tormenting Tophet: Or A terrible Description of Hel* (1615; 2nd ed., 1614), p. 42; *A Learned Summary Upon the famous Poeme of William of Saluste Lord of Bartas* (1621), tr. T. L[odge], I, 30, II, 54; Wollebius (1656; 1st ed., 1650), p. 88; Christopher Love, *Hell's Terror* (1653), III, 36.

3 *A Conference of the Catholike and Protestante Doctrine* (Douai, 1631), quoted by C. A. Patrides, "Renaissance and Modern Views on Hell," *Harvard Theological Review,* LVII (1964), 222.

4 [Simon Episcopius,] *The Confession Or Declaration Of The...Remonstrants* ([1676;] 1st ed., 1622), p. 100; Mayer (1627), p. 149; William Ames, *An Analyticall Exposition Of...Peter* (1641), p. 199; Richard Bernard, *The Article Of Christs Descension Into Hell* (1641), p. 16; Manton (1658), p. 285; Nathanael Homes, *The Resurrection-Revealed* (1661), pp. 209–211.

5 Napier (1593), p. 237; Henry Lawrence, *Of Our Commvnion And Warre With Angels* (1646), p. 56; Manton (1658), p. 286. See Love (1653), III, 35.

6 Napier (1593), p. 237; Wilson (1622, 2nd ed.; 1616), [II,] note on "Bottomlesse Pit"; Iohn Mayer, *A Commentarie Vpon The New Testament* (1631), I, 365; Thomas Phillips, *The Booke of Lamentations* (1639), p. 21; T. Hayne, *Christs Kingdome On Earth, Opened according to the Scriptures* (1645), p. 75; Lawrence (1646), p. 56; Alexander Ross, *The New Planet No Planet* (1646), p. 58. The most frequently advocated view of both patristic and scholastic writers, states Joseph Bautz, *Die Hölle* (Mainz, 1905; 1st ed., 1882), pp. 30, 36, was that hell is located in the interior of the earth.

7 Pareus (1644; 1st ed., 1618), p. 171. See C. D. XXXIII, 375, 2–11, pp. 70–71 above. According to Grant McColley, "The Book of Enoch and Paradise Lost," *Harvard Theological Review,* XXXI (1938), 33, "The idea that hell is located outside the earth rather than within it was of course a commonplace. . . . however, it was not a commonplace to regard hell as located within a chaos beyond heaven and earth." See, for example, Aquinas, *Summa Theologica,* Part III (Supplement), Q. 97, Art. 7, 1922 ed., vol. 21, pp. 180, 181–182; and Love (1653), III, 35. Some commentators maintained that Satan had not yet been confined to hell. Hell was the future, rather than the past or present, place of confinement for the devil. The principal advocate of this view was the "learned" Joseph Mede, *Works* (1648), pp. 68–72. See also [Richard Overton,] *Man wholly Mortel* (1655; 1st ed., 1643), p. 66. Other theologians postulated the existence of two hells, the one temporary, the other final. First, following his expulsion from heaven, Satan was confined in the hell (variously

located) of II Peter and Jude. This was (and is) a temporary place of confinement. In the future, after the Day of Judgment, Satan will be confined permanently in his second, final place of punishment, the "pit" of Revelation 20. See Napier (1593), p. 237; Cowper (1623; 1st ed., 1619), pp. 1025–1026; Mayer, *Ecclesiastica Interpretatio* (1627), pp. 148–149; Diodati (1643), note on II Peter 2:4; and Lawrence (1646), pp. 57–58.

8 See John Calvin, *Institutes* (1561), III, XXV, 12, cited by Roland Mushat Frye, *God, Man, And Satan* (Princeton, 1960), p. 39; Zanchius (1613; 1st ed., 1591), tom. III, cols. 174–176; Nicholas Gibbens, *Qvestions And Dispvtations Concerning The Holy Scriptvre* (1601), p. 133; William Perkins, "An Exposition Vpon The Epistle Of Jude" (1606), *Workes* (1631), III, 529; Cowper (1623; 1st ed., 1619), p. 1025; Mayer, *Ecclesiastica Interpretatio* (1627), pp. 148–149; Diodati (1643), note on II Peter 2:4; Lawrence (1646), pp. 56–58; Trapp (1656), p. 738.

9 Phillips (1639), pp. 37, 27; Isaac Ambrose, *Prima, Media, & Vltima* (1650), III, 135–149; Love (1653), II, 18–19; VII, 107. See also Tobias Swinden, *An Enquiry Into The Nature and Place Of Hell* (1714), pp. 83, 199–204, 210–212, 13–16, 35–36, 41–58; cf. pp. 73–74, 133, 135.

10 Junius (1596), p. 98; Love (1653), II, 19, 20; Thomas Lye, *The King of Terrors* (1660), p. 14. See Louis Coulange, *The Life Of The Devil* (1930), tr. Stephen Hadon Guest, pp. 60–64.

11 Gyffard (1596), pp. 235, 386; Dent (1607; 1st ed., 1603), pp. 155–157, 264–266; Brightman (1616; 1st ed., 1611), p. 517; Thomas Taylor (1633), pp. 425, 437–438, 693; T. B., *The Saints Inheritance After the Day of Ivdgement* (1643), p. 12. A variant reading of σειραῖς ζόφου, "chains of darkness" (II Peter 2:4), it should be noted, is σειροῖς ζόφου, "pits" or "dens of darkness."

12 Iohn Alsted, *The Beloved City Or, The Saints Reign On Earth A Thovsand Yeares* (1643; 1st Latin ed., 1627), p. 35; John Archer, *The Personall Reigne Of Christ Upon Earth* (1661; 1st ed., 1641), p. 40; Jeremiah Burroughs, *Moses His Choice* (1650; 1st ed., 1641), p. 453; Mede, *Works* (1648), pp. 68–74. See Appendix B.

13 Fulke (1573), fol. 131; Gyffard (1596), p. 395; Dent (1607; 1st ed., 1603), p. 270; Pareus (1644; 1st ed., 1618), p. 501; Diodati (1643), note on Revelation 20:3. The view basically is that of Augustine, *City of God*, tr. William Chase Greene (1960), XX, VII–IX, vol. VI, pp. 283–317.

14 John Foxe, *Actes and Monuments* (1583; 1st ed., 1563), p. 101; Napier (1593), p. 62; Junius (1596), p. 257; Robert Abbot, *Antichristi Demonstrato* (1603), p. 88; Hammond (1681; 1st ed., 1653), p. 998. See William Haller, *The Elect Nation* (1963), pp. 136–137; and C. A. Patrides, "Renaissance and Modern Thought On the Last Things: A Study In Changing Conceptions," *Harvard Theological Review*, LI (1958), 169–185.

15 Patrides, "Renaissance Estimates of the Year of Creation," *HLQ*,

XXVI (1963), 316–318; Lycosthenes, *Prodigiorum Ac Ostentorum Chronicon* (Basil, 1557), sig. [b2v]. Patrides lists 43 dates of creation suggested by 108 writers. Ninety of the writers dated creation from 4004 to 3928 B.C. Lycosthenes lists 29 dates advocated by 43 authorities (6 noted by Patrides). Twenty of these authorities dated creation from 4004 to 3928 B.C. Fourteen advocated dates from 6984 to 4103. A combination of the two lists yields a median date of 3969 B.C.

16 Wrote Hartlib (1651), pp. 26–27, 132, for example: "The Chronologer's supposition in general is this; that this present one thousand six hundred fiftieth year, since the birth of Christ, is the five thousand five hundred ninetie ninth year since the creation of the world. But if wee do well consider the Chronological numbers expressed in the Scripture, it will evidently appear, that in this present one thousand six hundred fiftieth year of our lord, the five thousand nine hundred ninetie fifth year since the Creation of the world, doth expire; and the six thousand year of the world will end with the one thousand six hundred fiftie fifth year of our Lord.... the seventh Trumpet shall sound in the one thousand six hundred fiftie fifth year." According to the Bible, maintained Hartlib, 1) Abram was born when Terah was 205 instead of 145 years old, 2) the patriarchs dwelt in Canaan 215 years before they began the 430 years of their sojourn in Egypt, and 3) the period from the Exodus to the building of the Temple by Solomon was 580 instead of 480 years. The significance of Hartlib's chronology becomes apparent if one subtracts Hartlib's corrected date of the world's duration (4345 + 1650), from 6000, the accepted period of the age of the world. In 1650, according to Hartlib, of the 6000 years which God had allotted to his creation, less than five years remained.

17 See Appendix B.

18 George Foster, *Sounding Of The Last Trumpet* (1650), p. 49; Hartlib (1651), p. 132; Henry More, *Synopsis Prophetica* (1664), pp. 202–204; John Rogers, *Sagir, Or Doomes-day* (1653), quoted by A. J. D. Farrar, "The Fifth Monarchy Movement," *Transactions of the Baptist Historical Society,* II (1911), 171; Napier (1593), p. 16. Specific dates (1650–1700) for the Fall of Antichrist, the Conversion of the Jews, and/or the Second Coming were stated also by Mary Cary, *Little Horns Doom* (1651), pp. 140–144; William Lilly, *Monarchy Or No Monarchy* (1651), pp. 7, 13; Christopher Love, *Heavens-Glory* (1653), pp. 59, 76; William Aspinwall, *The Fifth Monarchy* (1653), p. 14; J. Tillinghast, *Generation-Worke,* 3rd part (1654), pp. 62–63, 171ff.; John Cotten, *Exposition . . . Upon Revelation* (1655), p. 93; Christopher Feake, *A Beam of Light* (1659), pp. 315–317; R. Codrington, tr., *The Prophecies of Christopher Kolterus* (1664), p. 19; Increase Mather, *The Mystery Of Israel's Salvation* (1669), p. 144; Hanserd Knollys, *The World that Now is* (1681), p. 170; others. For discussion of earlier dates, see John Swan, *Speculum Mundi*

(Cambridge, 1635), pp. 16–23; Ronald H. Bainton, *Early and Medieval Christianity* (Boston, 1962), pp. 83–94; and Paul H. Kocher, *Science and Religion in Elizabethan England* (1969), pp. 76–81.

19 See William Haller, *Liberty and Reformation in the Puritan Revolution* (1955), pp. 47–51.

20 Arthur E. Barker, *Milton And The Puritan Dilemma 1641–1660* (Toronto, 1942), pp. 195–205; Fixler (1964), pp. 94–109; A. S. P. Woodhouse and Douglas Bush, *A Variorum Commentary on The Poems of John Milton* (1972), II (I), 94.

21 Pareus (1644; 1st ed., 1618), p. 171. The etymology was noted by William Massey, *Remarks Upon Milton's Paradise Lost* (1761), pp. 227–228.

22 Hayne, *Christs Kingdome* (1645), p. 75.

23 Patterson (1947), p. 80. See Merritt Y. Hughes, "Myself Am Hell," *MP*, LIV (1956), 85, 87; and C. D. XXXIII, 371–373, 7–11.

24 Calvin, *Institvtion* (1634; 1st ed., 1561), III, XXV, 12, fol. 4; *Commentarii in Isaiam* (1551), p. 305, cited by D. P. Walker, *The Decline of Hell* (Chicago, 1964), p. 62. According to Walker (p. 62), "Among the Fathers only a small minority, headed by Origen, are in favor of interpreting hell-fire figuratively as remorse, regret, etc." This "minority," however, includes such authorities as Tertullian, Augustine, Jerome, Eusebius, and Gregory the Great (Bautz, 1905, 1st ed., 1882, p. 43).

25 Thomas Adams, *The Diuells Banket* (1614), p. 190.

26 Isaac Ambrose (1650), [III,] 148. Compare P.L. I, 61–68; Bautz (1905; 1st ed., 1882), pp. 152–175; Merritt Y. Hughes, "Milton And The Sense Of Glory," *PQ*, XXVII (1949), 117–119 and 119 note; John M. Steadman, "Milton and Patristic Tradition: The Quality of Hell-Fire," *Anglia*, LXXVI (1958), 116–128. Ambrose (p. 149) comments further: "It is (I confesse) a question whether devils suffer by *fire?* and how may that be? some are of opinion, that they are not onely spirits, but have bodies, not organicall as ours, but aereall or somewhat more subtil then [than] the air it self: this opinion howsoever most denie, yet Austin [*De Civit. Dei.* lib. 21. cap. 10] argues for it; for if men and devils (saith he) are punished in the same *fire,* and that *fire* be corporeall, how are Devils capable of the suffering unlesse they have bodies, (like men) fit for the impression? And yet if we deny them to have bodies, I see no impossibilitie, but that spirits may suffer in hell fire: is it not as easie with God to joyn spirits and fire, as souls and bodies? as therefore the soul may suffer through the body, so likewise may these spirits be tormented by fire."

27 Pareus (1644; 1st ed., 1618), p. 502.

28 Erasmus (1549), II, xxxii; Bullinger (1561), pp. 588–591; Marlorat (1574), fol. 274; Immanuel Tremellius, *Iesv Christi Domini Nostri Novvm Testamentvm* (1585), fol. 197; Foxe, *Eicasmi* (1587), p. 206; Napier

(1593), p. 237; Junius (1596), p. 255; Gyffard (1596), pp. 386–387. See note 11.

29 Erasmus (1549), fols. xi–xiv.

30 Tremellius and Junius, *Testamenti Veteris Biblia Sacra* (1585; 1st ed., 1580), III, 39; Richard Sibbes, *Beames of Divine Light* (1639), pp. 315–318; John Vicars, *Decapla in Psalmos* (1639), p. 4; Himes (1883), pp. 199–200; Augustine, *City of God,* tr. Levine (1966), XIII, XXIV, vol. 4, pp. 253, 255.

31 "These locusts," writes Stanley Eugene Fish, *Surprised by Sin* (1967), p. 314, "if they were placed under a microscope, would be seen to have 'shapes . . . like unto horses', and 'hair as the hair of women' and 'breastplates of iron' and 'tails like unto scorpions' (Revelation ix. 7–10)."

32 Marjorie Nicolson, *John Milton A Reader's guide to his poetry* (1963), pp. 196–198, 204–205. See Milton, *Of Reformation . . . In England* (1641), III, 4–5, 24–13; *Considerations Touching The likeliest means to remove Hirelings out of the church* (1659), VI, 81, 14–19; *A Treatise Of Civil power In Ecclesiastical causes* (1659), VI, 6–8, 24–6.

33 Richard Gilpin, *Daemonologia Sacra. Or, A Treatise Of Satans Temptations* (1677), I, 19; and Maximillian Redwin, *Der Teufel in den deutschen Spielen des Mittelalters* (Göttingen, 1915), p. 82.

34 Thomas Carleton, *Theologiae Scholasticae* (Leodii, 1659), I, 367. Compare the similar view of Aquinas, *Summa Theologica,* 1922 ed., Part I, Q. 109, Art. 2. Carleton's text reads:

> in Luciferi electionem conspirasse, eumáue sibi praefecisse, tum quia omnium erat naturâ praestantissimus, tum ex odio Dei, utpote qui eum plus caeteris offenderat, aliosáue ad illum offendendum induxerat, tum etiam ex malevolentiâ & invidiâ erga homines, cujus nimirum industria & artibus, & per se, & ministros à se constitutos, homines in gravissimas Dei offensiones, acerbissimosáue tandem inferni cruciatus pertractum iri sperabant.

> Imò coelum, res inanimata, multisáue gradibus homine, leone, ac caeteris animantibus, imò plantis etiam & arboribus, ut multi putant, inferius, in his tamen omnibus suum habet influxum. Deinde quivis Angelus inferior esset Angeli perfectioris subditus, sicáue infimus Angelus tot dominos haberet, quot Angelos se perfectiores.

35 *De Natura Legis Naturae* (1461–1463), *Works* (1869), ed. Lord Clermont, I, 322, quoted by E. M. W. Tillyard, "The Chain of Being," *The Elizabethan World Picture* (1960), pp. 25–26.

36 Love, *Hell's Terror* (1653), III, 40–41. See, however, Marianna Woodhull, *The Epic of Paradise Lost* (1907), pp. 260–262; and Walker (1964), pp. 29–32. Augustine's identification of Satan with "Behemoth," whom God "made to be a laughing-stock for his angels" (Job 40:19), and with the Leviathan, the "serpent which thou [God] didst form to be a laughing-stock" (Ps. 104:26), further justifies the harshness which God

expresses in this passage *(City of God,* tr. David S. Wiesen, 1968, XI, XV, vol. III, p. 487; compare Neale and Littledale, 3rd ed., 1887, vol. III, pp. 335–336). Milton rejected the view of the "merciful doctors" (principally Origen, "De Principiis," *The Ante-Nicene Fathers,* ed. Alexander Roberts, 1926, I, V–VI, vol. IV, pp. 256–262) that eventually even the devil might be saved. The doctrine of universal salvation was advocated by at least six British theologians between 1648 and 1662 (Walker, pp. 93, 104–105, 124, and 126).

37 Augustin Marlorat, *A Catholike and Ecclesiasticall exposition of the holy Gospell after S. Iohn* (1575), pp. 14, 290, quoted by Marbeck (1581), pp. 632–633. See also Steadman, *Milton's Epic Characters* (1968), pp. 282–285 ff. According to Mede, "Discourse 40," quoted by John Brand, *Observations On The Popular Antiquities of Great Britain,* rev. by Henry Ellis (1849), II, 518, "The devil could not appear in humane shape, while man was in his integrity; because he was a spirit fallen from his first glorious perfection, and therefore must appear in such shape which might argue his imperfection and abasement, which was the shape of a beast; otherwise, no reason can be given why he should not rather have appeared to Eve in the shape of a woman than of a serpent."

38 Marbeck (1581), p. 631. Compare Didron (1886; reprinted 1968), II, 110–111 (fig. 166), 266.

39 Pareus (1644; 1st ed., 1618), pp. 304–305.

CHAPTER 5 SIN AND DEATH

1 Bowman (1955), p. 85.

2 Marlorat, *Reuelation* (1574), fol. 154*v,* quoted by Marbeck (1581), p. 102. See Chapter 2, note 11, above.

3 Bale (1548?), II, [fviiii*v,* giiii–giiii*v*].

4 Geruase Babington, *Certaine Plaine, briefe, and comfortable Notes, vpon euery Chapter of Genesis* (1596; 1st ed., 1592), p. 4; Humphrey Sydenham, *Sermons vpon Solemne Occasions* (1637), p. 169; [S. Franck,] *The Forbidden Fruit. Or A Treatise Of the Tree of . . . Good & Evill* (1640), p. 34.

5 Richard Sibbes, "The Gloriovs Feast of the Gospel" (1650), *Works,* ed. Alexander Grosart, Nicol's Series Of Standard Divines (Edinburgh, 1862), II, 471.

6 Cowper (1623; 1st ed., 1619), p. 882; cf. pp. 955–956.

7 À Lapide (1622; 1st ed., 1627), p. 34. Compare Mathias Rissi, *Time And History* (Richmond, Va., 1966; 1st ed., Zurich, 1965), tr. Gordon C. Winsor, pp. 104–105. À Lapide's text reads:

Mortem & infernū in Apocalypsi per prosopopoeiam, qua si duas personas in comoediam iuduci, quae Ecclesiae & Christianis necem & excidium minabantur. Mors enim inducitur quasi praeuisa, & occidens; infernus verò subsequens, & deuorans eos quos mors occidit: vnde mors inducitur quasi sagittas vibrans, infernus quasi fauces hiantes pandens, & occisos. Nam eorum corpora sepulchris, animas verò in imis terrae visceribus constrictas detinet. Hinc ait Sapiens Prouerb 1.12. *Deglutiamus* eum, *sicut infernus*. Et Isaias cap. 5.14. *Dilatauit infernus animam suam,* quasi cerberus triceps tres fauces, & tria guttura pandens. hic est enim Gentilium Pluto, mortuorum deuorator.

8 In Revelation 20:14, "death and hell" are said to be cast into the "lake of fire" or hell. But hell (which existed before the angels fell from heaven, Isa. 14:9–15, 5:14; Job 41) cannot be cast into hell. In Revelation 20:14, stated the commentators, "hell" must be interpreted as "second" or "spiritual" death. Milton chose to identify "hell" as Sin. The interpretation was not distinctly different from that of his contemporaries. See, for example, Gyffard (1596), p. 411; Wilson (1622, 2nd ed.; 1616), [II,] note on "Hell"; and (for inconographic representation of hell as a place) Robert Hughes, *Heaven and Hell in Western Art* (1968), pp. 175–201.

9 Critics frequently cite Virgil, *Aeneid,* III, 424; Ovid, *Metamorphoses,* XIV, 59; Hesiod, *Theogony,* 298; Edmund Spenser, *Faerie Queen* (1590), I, i, 14–15; and Phineas Fletcher, *The Locusts, Or Appollyonists* (1627), I, 10; *The Purple Island* (1633), XII, 27, as sources for the details with which Milton has elaborated his description of Sin. Actually descriptions of Sin (Envy, Lust) are relatively common in Renaissance poetry. See, for example, Thomas Peyton, *The Glasse Of Time* (1623; 1st ed., 1620), pp. 28–30; [Samuel Avstin,] *Avstins Vrania, Or, The Heavenly Mvse* (1629), pp. 26–27; J. A. Rivers, *Devovt Rhapsodies* (1647), p. 41; [Thomas Jenner,] *The Ages of Sin, or Sinnes Birth & groweth* (165–), pp. 1–9; and H. J. Todd, ed., *The Poetical Works of John Milton* (3rd ed., 1826), II, 155–156, 158. For prose descriptions of Sin (Scylla), see Chrysostom, "Homily IX On First Corinthians," cited by J. F. Gillam, "Scylla and Sin," *PQ,* XXIX (1950), 346; and Natale Conti, *Mythologiae* (Paris? 1600), pp. 915–916.

The view that Sin was a monster ($\dot{\alpha}\mu\alpha\rho\tau\acute{\iota}\alpha$) was a Renaissance commonplace. See A. B. Chambers, " 'Sin' and 'Sign' in *Paradise Lost,*" *HLQ,* XXVI (1963), 381–382. Drawings of monstrous yet human devils with second faces located in their stomachs or chests, hell-hounds occasionally peering from the mouths of the second faces, appear frequently in Medieval-Renaissance texts. See, *inter alios,* Hughes (1968), pp. 37, 176, 208, 228, 230, 231; Theodore Spencer, "Chaucer's Hell," *Speculum,* II (1927), 188; Ian Fleming, ed., *The Seven Deadly Sins* (1962), [p. 3]; and (particularly) Paul Carus, *The History of the Devil* (Chicago, 1900), p. 441.

Milton's description of the body of Sin reflects the Medieval-Renaissance tradition that Satan appeared to Eve in a half-serpentine, half-feminine form. Compare Michelangelo, "Temptation and Expulsion," Sistine Chapel (1509–1510); and the illustration from Carleton (1659), sig. [i], below. As on earth, so in heaven and at the Gates of Hell. The "sting" of Sin is derived from I Corinthians 15:55. According to the Geneva version of the Bible (1560; reprinted, 1969), I Corinthians 15:55, may be translated either as "O death, where *is* thy stīg! ô graue [hell] where *is* thy victorie!" or as *O death, where is thy victorie! o graue* [hell] *where is thy sting!"* In early manuscripts "sting" and "victory" were transposed. Milton justifiably identified Sin as Athena, the offspring of Zeus, for, according to *Les Images Ov Tableavx De Platte Peinture Des Devx Philostrates...Et Ses Statvres De Callistrate,* tr. Blaise de Vigenère (Paris, 1615), p. 511, Athena was the pagan representation of the Logos. Compare Justin Martyr, *Apology,* I, 67.

"Hell," represented as a monstrous head (misshapen, with wide gaping mouth) which follows the fourth horseman, appears frequently in Renaissance Bible illustrations of Revelation 6:8. See Gerhard Schmidt, *Die Illustration der Lutherbibel 1522–1700* (Basel, 1962), figs. 39, 42, 47, 64,

72, 145, 170, and 246; and Strachan (1957), fig. 16 (below, from the Cologne Bible, 1478–80). Hell appears as a three-headed monster in Florens Deuchler, *Forty paintings from an early 14th century manuscript of the Apocalypse* (Zurich, 1969), [plate 7]. Less imaginative than it is generally considered, Milton's description of the activities of Satan, Sin, and Death is considerably more than a "myth, an imaginative embodiment of a moral truth" which Milton "created to parallel the historical [biblical] account of the fall of man" (Robert C. Fox, "The Allegory of Sin and Death in *Paradise Lost*," *MLQ*, XXIV, 1963, 362). To Milton the account of Satan, Sin, and Death was founded upon biblical fact.

10 Vicars (1639), Commentary on Psalm 68:23, p. 196.

11 Mayer, *Ecclesiastica Interpretatio* (1627), pp. 9–10.

12 Babington (1596; 1st ed., 1592), p. 4; Richard Bernard, *Contemplative Pictures* (1610), p. 67; Sydenham (1637), pp. 169–170; Richard Coppin, *The Exaltation Of All things in Christ* (1649), p. 43. See John M. Steadman, "Milton and St. Basil: The Genesis of Sin and Death," *MLN*, LXXIII (1958), 83–84.

13 Antony Burgesse, *The Doctrine Of Original Sin* (1658), IV, 457.

14 *Ibid.*, II, 157.

15 Pareus (1644; 1st ed., 1618), p. 460. Compare the similar statements of Brightman (1616; 1st ed., 1611), p. 962; Peter Du Moulin, *The*

Accomplishment Of The Prophecies (Oxford, 1613), p. 250; and Piscator, "Apocalypseos" (1638; 1st ed., 1621?), p. 818. See, however, E. M. W. Tillyard, "The Causeway from Hell to the World in the Tenth Book of Paradise Lost," *SP*, XXXVIII (1941), 266–270. Dr. Johnson's objection ("Milton," 1779, *Works*, ed. Murphey, 1796, IX, 176) to the Bridge Across Chaos (the *"mole* of *aggravated soil*, cemented with *asphaltus"*) as "a work too bulky for ideal architects" would seem largely negated also by the statements cited above.

16 Cited by Burgesse (1658), IV, 459.

CHAPTER 6   LUST AND WILL

1 *Summa Theologica*, Part I, Q. 63, Art. 3, 1922 ed., vol. 3, p. 149. Commenting upon Isaiah 14:13–14, Aquinas remarked (p. 148) that Lucifer's desire to "be like the most High" might be explained either as a desire for equality or as a desire for likeness. Lucifer could not have sinned initially by seeking to be equal to God, for "by natural knowledge he knew that this was impossible; and there was no habit preceding his first sinful act, nor any passion fettering his mind, so as to lead him to choose what was impossible by failing in some particular." Initially, then, Lucifer's attempt to imitate God was based upon a desire to be like God, a desire which in itself was good. In Book II, similarly, Moloc, Belial, and Mammon proposed courses of action in which the underlying motives were, respectively, honor or glory, humility, and purposeful activity, motives which were evil only when they were perverted.

2 Augustine, *City of God*, tr. Levine, XII, VI, vol. 4, p. 33.

3 Saurat (1925), pp. 152, 155ff.; Tillyard, *Milton* (1934), p. 262, *Studies in Milton* (1951), pp. 11–13; Waldock (1947), p. 61; Millicent Bell, "The Fallacy of the Fall in Paradise Lost," *PMLA*, LXX (1955), 1187–1197; Broadbent (1960), pp. 197–198; John M. Patrick, *Milton's Concept of Sin as Developed in Paradise Lost*, Utah State Monograph Series (1960), VII, 29, *passim;* and Fredson Bowers, "Adam, Eve, and the Fall in 'Paradise Lost,' " *PMLA*, LXXXIV (1969), 269–273.

4 *City of God*, tr. Levine, XIV, XIII, vol. 4, pp. 335–339; cf. XIV, X, vol. 4, pp. 319–323.

5 William Ames, *The Marrow Of Sacred Divinity* (1642), p. 49, reprinted as *The Marrow Of Theology* (Boston, 1968), tr. John Dykstra Eusden, p. 114; Iohn Mayer, *Ecclesiastica Interpretatio* (1627), p. 11; William Pemble, "Vindiciae Fidei" (1625), *Workes* (3rd ed., 1635), pp. 207–208; Edward Reynolds, *A Treatise Of The Passions And Faculties Of the Soule of Man* (1640), pp. 61–64, quoted by Lily B. Campbell, *Shakespeare's Tragic Heroes* (1930; 1965 reprint), pp. 71–72; John Wollebius (1656; 1st ed., 1650), p. 74, quoted by Kelley, *Complete Prose* (1973), VI, 116. See also Calvin, "The Adultero-German Interim..." (1547), in *Defense Of The Reformed Faith*, tr. Henry Beveridge (Grand

Rapids, 1958), p. 193; ... *Commentaries of D. Peter Martir Vermilius ...
vpon the Epistle of S. Paul* (1568), tr. H. B., fols. 118*v*–190; Cowper,
"Combate Of Christ With Satan" (1623), *Workes* (1626), p. 608; David
Dickson, *Expositio Analytica Omnium Apostolicarvm Epistolarvm*
(Glasguae, 1645), pp. 683–684; and Barbara Kiefer Lewalski, "Innocence
and Experience In Milton's Eden," *New Essays* (1969), ed. Kranidas, pp.
97–98.

6 Wollebius (1656; 1st ed., 1650), p. 78.

7 Cowper, "Heaven Opened" (1611?), *Workes* (1629), p. 26, quoting
from the First Decree of the Fifth Session of the Council of Trent. For
defense of the Catholic position, see Robert Bellarmine, "Secunda
Controversia Generalis," *De Controversiis Christianae Fidei* (Neapoli,
1858; 1st ed., 1587–1589), lib. IV, cap. XI–XII, cols. 161–169; and
Carleton (1659), tom. I, disp. LXXIX, pp. 356–359. As Aquinas notes,
Summa Theologica, Part II (I), Q. 24, Art. 2, 1922 ed., vol. 6, pp. 295–296,
debate concerning the nature of the emotions goes back to the Peripatetic
and Stoic controversies of the early and pre-Christian era.

8 James Arminius, "Articulo perpendendi, cap. de peccato origines"
(1608), *The Writings of James Arminius,* tr. James Nicols (Grand Rapids,
1956), II, 492, quoted by Burgesse (1658), IV, 479. The context of the
quotation raises doubt as to whether Arminius actually advocated the
view he was charged with advocating. See, however, Deacon and Walker,
Dialogicall Discourses (1601), pp. 18, 43–45; Peter Du Moulin, *The
Anatomy of Arminianisme* (1630; 1st ed., 1620), pp. 36, 41; Cowper,
"Combate Of Christ With Satan" (1623), *Workes* (1626), pp. 608–609; and
Iohn Owen, *A Display Of Arminianisme* (1643), pp. 88–89. An excellent
analysis of the difficulties involved in the Augustinian-Arminian view of
man's original sin appears in Jonathan Edwards, "Freedom of the Will"
(1754), *The Works of Jonathan Edwards,* ed. Paul Ramsay (New Haven,
1957), I, I, 1–5, 171–194.

9 Owen (1643), p. 89.

10 *The Conception And Birth of Sin* (1655), pp. 7–8, 10. Aquinas'
reconciliation of Augustine's apparently contradictory view should be
quoted: "The cause of original sin must be considered with respect to the
cause of original justice, which is opposed to it. Now the whole order of
original justice consists in man's will being subject to God: which
subjection, first and chiefly, was in the will, whose function it is to move all
the other parts to the end, as stated above (Q. IX, A. I), so that the will
being turned away from God, all the other powers of the soul become
inordinate. Accordingly the privation of original justice, whereby the will
was made subject to God, is the formal element in original sin; while every
other disorder of the soul's powers, is a kind of material element in respect
of original sin. Now the inordinateness of the other powers of the soul
consists chiefly in their turning inordinately to mutable good; which
inordinateness may be called by the general name of concupiscence.

Hence original sin is concupiscence materially, but privation of original justice formally." *Summa Theologica,* Part II, Q. 82, Art. 3, 1922 ed., vol. 7, p. 418. Aquinas, however, was not wholly consistent in his view that the misuse of the will initiated sin. See, for example, Part I, Q. 94, Art. 4, vol. 4, p. 315.

11 Chaos, with its "visage incompos'd" (P.L. II, 989), is the prime example of "disorderly motions" (lust) in *Paradise Lost.* If "disorderly motions" originally were evil, then Chaos originally must have been evil also. Since man was made of the resolved elements of Chaos, then man must have been created of evil elements. Objection to this variation of the Augustinian view (which Augustine rejected) furnishes the theological basis for the confrontation of Chaos with Satan in P.L. II, 890–1009. Other than for this note this subject is not considered in this study. The subject has been discussed competently and thoroughly by Walter Clyde Curry, "Milton's Chaos and Old Night," *JEGP,* XLVI (1947), 38–52. To Milton, no creation of God (angel, man, or Chaos personified) originally was evil.

12 William Perkins, *A Golden Chaine, Or The Description of Theologie* (1592; 1st ed., 1591), sig. B8; Greenwood (1615), p. 2; Cowper, "Combate Of Christe With Satan" (1623), *Works* (1626), p. 608; Thomas Jackson, *A Treatise Of The Divine Essence* (1628), I, 188.

13 Burgesse (1658), I, 23; II, 160; IV, 462–463. See, however, Murray W. Bundy, "Eve's Dream And The Temptation In *Paradise Lost,*" *Research Studies Of The State College Of Washington,* X (1942), 290–291; Steadman, *Milton's Epic Characters* (1968), pp. 139–150; and Aquinas, *Summa Theologica,* Part II, Q. 82, Art. 3, 1922 ed., vol. 7, p. 418, above.

14 Henry Bullinger, *Decades* (1584; 1st English ed., 1577), II, 324; Richard Turnbull, *An Exposition Vpon the Canonicall Epistle Of Saint Iames* (1591), fols. 43v, 47v–48; [John Salkeld,] *A Treatise Of Paradise* (1617), pp. 178–181, 294–295; John Downame (1630?), p. 118; Du Moulin, *The Anatomy of Arminianisme* (1630; 1st ed., 1620), pp. 41–47. See also Peter de la Primaudaye, *The French Academie* (1586), tr. T. B., p. 28; Thomas Wright, *The Passions of the Minde* (1601; 1973 reprint), pp. 27–40; Bernard, *Contemplative Pictures* (1610), p. 67; and Sydenham (1637), pp. 27–28. Compare *The Doctrine And Discipline Of Divorce* (1643), III, 396, 13–24, and C.D. VII, 25, 5–13; XI, 181, 19–22; 193, 10–18; 195, 1–8; 197, 17–18, 24–28. B. A. Wright, *Milton's 'Paradise Lost'* (1962), p. 142, notes that the meaning of P.L. X, 585–588, is that "sin was potentially in Paradise from the beginning, was actually there with the first act of disobedience, and finally was there in the consequent lust of Adam and Eve, the carnal desires with which all their posterity would be afflicted." Compare the similar statement of Thomas Newton, ed., *Paradise Lost* (4th ed., 1757), note on P.L. X, 586.

15 For adverse Protestant comment upon the Council of Trent, see Calvin, "Acts of the Council of Trent with the Antidote" (1547), in *Defense Of The Reformed Faith,* tr. Beveridge (1958), p. 88; Rollock (1603), p. 145; Cowper, "Heaven Opened" (1611?), *Workes* (1629), p. 26. The position adopted by Burgesse and others was basically (but not identically) that held by Aquinas. For distinctions between the views held by Aquinas and Augustine, see John Reesing, *Milton's Poetic Art* (Cambridge, Mass., 1968), pp. 151–153; and Joseph E. Duncan, *Milton's Earthly Paradise* (Minneapolis, 1972), pp. 55, 72–73.

16 Deacon and Walker, *Dialogicall Discourses* (1601), pp. 43–44, 44–45. In P.L. IV, 799–809, Satan, disguised as a toad, pours (whispers) venom into Eve's ear. The episode apparently is a parody of Catholic representations of the Annunciation. According to Augustine, "Deus per angelum loquebatur et Virgo per aurem impregnabatur" *(Sermo de Tempore,* XXII). In scenes of the Annunciation the beak of the dove (Paraclete) frequently is directed toward the ear of the Virgin. "This attitude of the dove, which is quite common and indeed almost universal, in medieval and early modern pictures of the Annunciation," states E. P. Evans, *Animal Symbolism In Ecclesiastical Architecture* (1896; reprinted, 1969), p. 98, reflects the view held "by patristic and later theologians, that the conception of Christ was effected supernaturally through the Virgin's ear, so that she remained perfectly pure and immaculate, and her maidenhood intact." See Svendsen (1956), p. 265. As unfallen Adam is a type of Christ, so unfallen Eve is a type of the Virgin.

17 Burgesse (1658), IV, 462–463.

18 Andraeus Rivetus, *Opervm Theologicorum* (Roterdami, 1651), I, 116. Compare Aquinas, *Summa Theologica,* Part I, Q. 94, Art. 4, 1922 ed., vol. 4, pp. 313–315. Rivetus' text reads:

> Dicimus ergo Christum qui in se nullam habuit concupiscentiam vitiosam, & primos parentes in innocentiae statu, non potuisse tentari interna tentatione, neque per carnem, quia perfectè rationi rectae subjiciebatur, neque per suggestionem Dioboli, phantasiam intus moventis. Nam talium imaginandi facultas, nulla recipiebat phantasmata, nisi ex deliberato rationis judicio. Et in tali statu, in quo ratio perfectè subjiciebatur Deo, multo minus in Christo fieri poterat, ut motus vel operatio inferioris cujusdam facultatis, nutum dominantis rationis praeveniret. Non sit autem phantasiae per phantasmata mutatio, sine ipsius phantasiae operatione. Quod si quis dicat tum homini etiam insomnia potuisse accidere, etsi id incertum sit, tamen si concedatur, dicemus ad ea semper fuisse futurum rectae rationis consensum, saltem habitualem, quia somnia semper fuissent bona. . . .

19 *The Seventeenth Century Background* (1934), pp. 247, 256. When Willey suggests that "Milton does not really believe" that Adam's unfallen state was preferable to his fallen state, however, a demurral must be entered. In a sense the fall was fortunate; yet Adam could have been

(would have been) "Happier, had it suffic'd him to have known Good by it self, and Evil not at all" (P.L. XI, 88–89). The view that man originally might have been "happy" without experiencing evil is not negated by P.L. XI, 25–30, and XII, 585–587.

20 Zanchius, "De Hominis Creatione," *De Operibvs Dei Intra Spacivm Sex Diervm Creatis* (1613; 1st ed., 1591), tom. III, col. 539, tr. Nicholas Bownd, *Sabbathvm Veteris Et Novi Testamenti* (1606; 1st ed., 1595), p. 19. Zanchius text reads:

> Ego itaque non dubito (dico meam sententiam, sine aliorum praeiudicio) non dubito, inquam, quin Filius Dei, humanam faciem indutus; toto hoc septimo die occupatus fuerit in sanctissimus cum Adamo colloquiis: quin illi & Euae sese plane patefecerit, modum & ordinem quo vsus fuerat in creandis rebus omnibus, reuelarit: ad haec opera contemplanda inque eis suum creatorem, & Deum verum cognoscendum, ac laudandum hortatus fuerit: & vt suo examplo, septimo quoque die in hoc potissimum pietatis exercitio, operibus aliis omnibus posthabitis, sese occuparent, docuerit: atque vt ita suos etiam liberos instituerent, monuerit: quae vita, item quae foelicitas eos maneret in Coelo: vti perpetua & vera quies est, patefecerit. Denique non dubito, quin eos illo die totam Theologiam condocefecerit, & in audiendo se, laudibúsque suum Deum ac creatorem celebrando, atque gratias pro tot tantisq; beneficius agendo occupatos tenuerit.

Compare Cornelius à Lapide, *Commentaria in Pentatevchvm Mosis* (Antverpiae, 1630; 1st ed., 1616), p. 14; [John Salkeld,] *A Treatise Of Paradise* (1617), p. 196; Thomas Broad, *Tractatvs De Sabbato* (1627), p. 2; Gilbert Ironside, *Seven Qvestions Of The Sabbath Briefly Dispvted* (Oxford, 1637), pp. 5–6, 8; and Hamon L'Estrange, *Gods Sabbath Before the Law and Under the Gospel* (Cambridge, 1641), p. 31. According to Ironside (p. 8), "Divines generally affirme that he [Adam] knew not, that he should fall, or need a Redeemer, though perhaps the fall of Angells was revealed unto him." Disagreement with the view that Adam had been warned of Satan's fall was expressed frequently. Compare Andrew Willet, *Hexapla in Genesin* (1608; 1st ed., 1605), p. 37, quoted by Arnold Williams, *The Common Expositor* (Chapel Hill, 1948), p. 84; Swan (1635), p. 498; George Walker, *The Doctrine Of the Sabbath* (Amsterdam, 1639; 1st ed., 1638), pp. 5–12; [T. Hayne,] *The General View Of The Holy Scriptures* (1640), p. 25. According to Willet (p. 37), since Adam "fell the same day of his creation," he could not have known of the fall of the angels. The controversy involved the interpretation of two passages, Ecclus. 17:6–7 and Ps. 49:12 (אָדָם, Adam, man).

21 Noble (1655), p. 5.

Chapter 7 Justice and Mercy

1 Milton's satire upon Limbo or the Paradise of Fools was in part based upon Ariosto, *Orlando Furioso,* C, XXIV, 70. The primary source,

however, was Revelation 6:9. In Revelation 6:9, after the four horses and their riders have been described in Revelation 6:8, before the heavens open and Satan falls from heaven in Revelation 6:13–17, John inserts a passage which seems out of context: "And when he [Christ] had opened the fifth seal, I saw under the altar the souls of them that were slain for the word of God, and for the testimony which they held." This passage Catholic theologians interpreted as a reference to Limbo. See, for example, Ribera (1602), p. 237; and à Lapide, *Commentaria in Apocalypsin S. Iohannis* (1662; 1st ed., 1627), pp. 125–127. According to Ribera, "sinus Abrahae intedum à sanctis patribus dicitur locus, in quo nunc Sancti quiescunt in coelo, quoniam ante mortem Christi ita dicebatur Limbus, in quo purgatae animas manebunt." Following his source, the Book of Revelation, Milton was almost obliged to discuss Limbo at this point in his poem. The passage is discussed briefly by Milton in C. D. XIII, 243, 16–21.

2 Empson (1961), pp. 118, 110: "As a believer in the providence of God, Milton could not possibly have believed in the huge success-story of Satan fighting his way to Paradise. The chains of Hell, Sin, Death, Chaos, and an army of good angels hold Satan back, but all this stage machinery is arranged by God to collapse as soon as he [Satan] advances. . . . [The angels] knew, and they knew that God knew that they knew, that this tiresome chore was completely useless." The view that in this scene the angels are little more than "stage machinery" is expressed frequently. See also West (1955), pp. 107–109; Broadbent (1960), pp. 190–193; Peter (1960), pp. 80–82; Fish (1967), pp. 174–175. The criticism seems to have been stated originally by Voltaire (1726), X, 486.

3 Cowper, "Pathmos" (1623; 1st ed., 1619), pp. 893–894.

4 The meaning of the symbols was disputed. According to Napier (1593), p. 118; Junius (1596), p. 80; and Mayer, *Ecclesiastica Interpretatio* (1627), pp. 325–326, for example, the "four angels" of Revelation 7:1–4 were good or loyal angels. The "winds" were a symbol of the devil. Zanchius (1613; 1st ed., 1591), tom. III, col. 186; Pareus (1644; 1st ed., 1618), pp. 137–139; and Grotius (1732; 1st ed., 1644), III, 1183, advocated the opposite point of view. In hell, according to Milton, the "winds" were loosed (P.L. II, 514–520) immediately after the Infernal Council approved Satan's decision to invade earth.

5 Cowper, "Pathmos" (1623; 1st ed., 1619), p. 894. Compare Junius (1596), p. 82; William Symonds, *Pisgah Evangelica* (1606; 1st ed., 1605), p. 20; Mayer, *Ecclesiastica Interpretatio* (1627), p. 326. See, however, Todd (3rd ed., 1826), II, 362–364.

6 See Chapter 4, notes 11 and 26, and p. 75, above.

7 Noble (1655), p. 7. See C. A. Patrides, "Milton and His Contemporaries on the Chains of Satan," *MLN,* LXXIII (1958), 257–260; and R. H. Charles, *Commentary On The Revelation,* The International Critical Commentary (1920), I, 205–206. In P.L. V, 270–277, the appearance of

Raphael as a phoenix (ὥς φοίνιε, phoenix, palm tree, sand; Ps. 92:12, Job 29:18) restates God's promise that "Man...shall find grace, The other none," P.L. III, 131–132. The phoenix is a symbol of resurrection. See Tertullian, *On the Resurrection of the Flesh*, XIII; James Paterson, *A Complete Commentary...On Milton's Paradise Lost* (1744), pp. 336–337; Evans (1896; reprinted, 1969), pp. 66, 69–70, 83, 137; and note 8 below.

8 Were Adam and Eve upheld by "supernatural grace" before they fell? Milton's answer to this question apparently was "yes." Restricted or bound by the Golden Scales (prevenient grace) as well as by the Bridge Across Chaos (ultimate law), Satan could not have tempted Adam and Eve until after they had been "sealed." Did Adam (Eve) sin, then, because "God was pleased, for the magnifying of his name, to withdraw himselfe from him, and so left him under the power of temptation, by which he was overcome"? J[ohn] G[reene], *The First Man, Or A Short Discourse Of Adams State* (1643), p. 9; cf. Saurat (1925), p. 124. To this question, Milton's answer was a definite "no!" After warning Adam and Eve of the potential existence of Sin and Death, God did not withdraw his protection. Adam and Eve were upheld by "supernatural grace" both before and after their sealing. See the discussion of this point by Steadman, *Milton's Epic Characters* (1968), pp. 150–154ff. Adam and Eve fell not because God withdrew his power but because, voluntarily and deliberately, they *chose* to fall.

9 Byfield (1628; 1st ed., 1615), p. 69. See pp. 30–31, above.

10 Bullinger, *A Hundred Sermons vpō the Apocalips* (1561), p. 218; Fulke (1573), fols. 43v–44; Foxe, *Eicasmi* (1587), p. 65; Gyffard (1596), pp. 143–149; Pareus (1644; 1st ed., 1618), pp. 140–142, 154; Mayer, *Ecclesiastica Interpretatio* (1627), p. 326; Boys (1629; 1st ed., 1622), p. 813. See E. M. W. Tillyard, *The English Epic And Its Background* (1954; reprinted, 1966), pp. 435–437.

11 Augustin Marlorat, *A Catholike And Ecclesiasticall exposition of the holy Gospell after S. Mathewe* (1570), tr. Thomas Tymme, fols. 577–579; Pareus (1644; 1st ed., 1618), p. 141; Boys (1629; 1st ed., 1622), pp. 86, 88, 813; Thomas Temple, *Christs Government In and over his People* (1642), p. 35; Jeremy Taylor (1688; 1st ed., 1653), pp. 8–9. The literary antecedents of the "golden Scales" *(Iliad,* VIII, XXII; *Aeneid,* XII) are discussed by Davis P. Harding, *The Club of Hercules* (Urbana, 1962), pp. 46–50; for negative criticism see Nicolson (1963), p. 244. The "golden Scales" are considerably more than a "pagan device" (Nicolson), however. Their primary source is Revelation 7:1–4 (9:1–4). A conflation of Revelation 7:1–4 (9:1–4) with Ezekiel 28:12–16 also may be involved. Apparently Milton translated Ezekiel 28:16 (14), אַבְנֵי־אֵשׁ, "stones of fire," as "balances of the sun." (Compare Joel 1:19, 20, 2:3–5.) Thus Satan, the "anointed cherub" who deceives Uriel, the "angel...in the Sun," is depicted as walking "up and down" in Eden before he

approaches Eve (Ezek. 28:14, 13: Rev. 19:17; P.L. III, 588–742, IV, 131–408), as being detected by Ithuriel and Zephon, the "guardian cherub[im]" of Eden (Ezek. 28:16, Septuagint; Rev. 7:1; P.L. IV, 799–856), and as being judged by the "golden Scales" which are hung in the sky (Ezek. 28:16, 14; Rev. 7:1–4; P.L. IV, 990–1015)—not by Michael (Dan. 5:27) but by God. For discussion of the scales as symbols of judgment and of salvation, see Evans (1896; reprinted, 1969), pp. 327–329, 330; and A. Caiger-Smith, *English Medieval Mural Paintings* (Oxford, 1963), pp. 29, 32, 59, 61, 63, 130–182.

12 C. A. Patrides, "Milton and the Protestant Theory of Atonement," *PMLA*, LXXIV (1959), 7–13. See Revelation 8:1–5: "After that provision was made for the safegarde of the Church, least it should faint vnder so great a burthen of euills, the seuen Aungels do straitway prepare themselues to sound these trumpets, whereby we may easelye gather, that they were stayed before, so long as Christ made intercession for the safetie of the Church, & with his giftes might arme the faithfull to beare all aduersities whatsoeuer. . . ." Fulke (1573), fol. 51*v*. Compare Marlorat, *Reuelation* (1574), fol. 116; Gyffard (1596), pp. 158–161; Dent (1607; 1st ed., 1603), pp. 87–88; Symonds (1606; 1st ed., 1605), pp. 20–25; Brovghton (1610), p. 59; Pareus (1644; 1st ed., 1618), p. 154; Cowper, "Pathmos" (1623; 1st ed., 1619), pp. 930–931; Mayer, *Ecclesiastica Interpretatio* (1627), pp. 325–326; [Edward Fisher,] *The Marrow Of Modern Divinity* (1645), pp. 35–36, 42; Hammond (1681; 1st ed., 1653), p. 897; and G. A. Wilkes, *The Thesis Of Paradise Lost* (Melbourne, 1961), pp. 4–5.

Revelation 7:1–4   Revelation 8:3–5

in [Hans Sebald Beham,] *Imaginvm In Apocalypsi Iohannis descriptio, cum enarratione vera, pia, & apta, quae potest esse vice iusti Commentarij, & lectu digni: Elegiaco Carmine Condita* (Vitebergae, 1575; 1st ed., 1539?), pp. 490, 492.

Indexes

Bibliographical Index

Spelling of names has been normalized to agree with Renaissance practice. Titles of works written after 1720 have not been listed.

Abbot, George, *Brief Notes Upon the whole Book of Psalmes*, 142.

Abbot, Robert, *Antichristi Demonstrato*, 146.

Adams, Robert Martin, 1, 125.

Adams, Thomas, 73; *A Commentary Or, Exposition Upon ... St. Peter*, 142, 144; *The Diuells Banket*, 72, 139, 143, 145, 148; *The Spiritvall Navigator*, 139.

Adamson, J. H., 125, 139, 141.

Aiken, J. A., 134.

Ainsworth, Henry, *Annotations Upon the Book of Psalmes*, 126, 141.

À Lapide, Cornelius, 22, 119; *Commentaria in Apocalypsin S. Iohannis Apostoli*, 89–90, 132, 135, 137, 150, 159; *Commentaria in Pentatevchm Mosis*, 158.

Alcazar, P. Luis de, 23; *Argvmemtvm Apocalypseos qvo distinctione Capitvm observate indicatur totivs Libri Acolvthia*, 132.

Alcuin, "Commentariorum In Apocalypsin," 138.

Allen, D. C., 143.

Alsted, John, 124; *The Beloved City Or, The Saints Reign On Earth A Thovsand Yeares*, 123, 146.

Ambrose, 54.

Ambrose, Isaac, 73; *Prima, Media, & Vltima*, 72, 146, 148.

Ames, Percy W., 141.

Ames, William, v, 54, 101, 129; *Lectiones in CL psalmos Davidis*, 126; *An Analyticall Exposition Of ... Peter*, 145; *The Marrow Of Sacred Divinity*, 101, 154; *The Marrow Of Theology*, 154.

Andreas, 94.

Anselm, 143.

Apostles Creed, The, 20.

Aquinas, Thomas, 15, 126, 135, 144, 157; *Summa Theologica*, 97, 145, 149, 154, 155–156, 157.

Archer, John, 124; *The Personall Reigne Of Christ Upon Earth*, 123, 146.

Arelatensis, Caesarius, *Opera Varia*, 135.

Aretas, 144.

Ariosto, Ludovico, 26, 27, 43, 50; *Orlando Furioso*, 39, 158.

Arminius, James, "Articulo perpendendi," 102, 155.

Arnold, Elias, 131.

Arnold, Matthew, 134.

Aspinwall, William, *The Fifth Monarchy*, 147.

Athanasius, 126, 143.

Augustine, 4, 15, 36, 54, 68, 81, 101, 102, 103, 104, 106, 144, 148, 155, 156, 157; "Christian Instruction," 136; *Confessions*, 144; *De Genesi ad litteram*, 15, 106, 128; "Enarrationes In Psalmos," 126; *Of The Citie of God*, 67, 100–101, 124, 127, 139, 142, 146, 148, 149, 150, 154; *Sermo de Tempore*, 157.

Aureolus, 135, 143.

[Austin, Samuel,] *Avstins Vrania, Or, The Heavenly Mvse*, 151.

Babington, Gervase, *Certaine Plaine, briefe, and comfortable Notes, vpon euery Chapter of Genesis*, 150, 153.

Bagehot, Walter, 134.

Bailey, John, 141.

Bainton, Ronald H., 148.

Baker, Richard, *An Apologie For Lay-Mens Writing in Divinity*, 130.

Bale, John, 119; *The Image Of both churches*, 62, 87–88, 128, 131, 134, 144, 150.

[Ball, John,] *A Short Treatise*, 126, 129, 142.

Banks, Theodore, 136, 141.

B[arbar,] T., 131.

Barker, Arthur E., 143, 148.

Barrington, Russell, 134.

Basil, 126.

Bautz, Joseph, 145, 148.

Baxter, J. Sidlow, 137.

Beardslee, John W., 128.
Bede, 135, 143, 144.
[Beham, Hans Sebald,] *Imaginvm In Apocalypsi Iohannis descripto,* 161.
Bell, Mellicent, 154.
Bellarmine, Robert, "Secunda Controversia Generalis," 155.
Bernard, Richard, 42; *The Article Of Christs Descension Into Hell,* 145; *Contemplative Pictures,* 153, 156; *A Key Of Knowledge For The Opening Of... Revelation,* 138.
Beuchot, M., 133.
Beveridge, Henry, 129, 154, 157.
Bèza, Théodore, 54, 60, 89, 129; *The Newe Testament,* 144; *The Psalmes Of Dauid,* 126.
Bickersteth, Edward Henry, 131, 134.
Bodmer, Jacob, 126.
Bowers, Fredson, 154.
Bowman, John Wick, 87, 137, 150.
Bownd, Nicholas, *Sabbathvm Veteris Et Novi Testamenti,* 158.
Boys, John, 22, 54; *Workes,* 126, 128, 132, 141, 142, 143, 160.
Brand, John, 150.
Briefe Explanation Of The XX. Chapter Of The Revelation of Saint John, A, 136.
Brightman, Thomas, 22, 42–44, 119, 124; *Exposition Of Daniel,* 123; *The Revelation of S. Iohn,* 42, 43, 131, 132, 138, 142, 144, 146, 153.
Broad, Thomas, *Tractatvs De Sabbato,* 158.
Broadbent, J. B., 2, 125, 154, 159.
Broughton, Hugh, *A Revelation Of The Holy Apocalyps,* 143, 161.
Brown, Louise Fargo, 122.
Bruce, F. F., 142.
Brydges, Egerton, 134.
B., T., *The Saints Inheritance After the Day of Ivdgement,* 146.
Bullinger, Henry, 22, 73, 104, 119; *Decades,* 156; *A Hvndred Sermons vpō the Apocalips,* 12, 32, 126, 128, 129, 131, 132, 134, 135, 138, 142, 143, 144, 148, 160.
Bundy, Murray W., 156.
Burden, Dennis H., 135.
Burgesse, Antony, 104, 119, 157; *The Doctrine Of Original Sin,* 93, 96, 103–104, 107, 153, 154, 156, 157.
Burroughs, Jeremiah, 124; *Exposition Of Hosea,* 123; *Moses His Choice,* 146.
Bush, Douglas, 127, 141, 148.
Byfield, N., *An Exposition Vpon the Epistle To The Collosians,* 30–31, 115, 134, 160.
Cadalso, José, 133.
Caesariensis, 136.
Caiger-Smith, A., 161.
Calvin, John, 4, 15, 54, 68, 94, 106, 128, 144; "Acts of the Council of Trent with the Antidote," 157; "The Adultero-German Interim," 154; *The Commentaries of M. Iohn Calvin upon the Actes of the Apostles,*

126; *Commentarii in Isaiam,* 148; *The Institutes of the Christian Religion,* 15, 67, 72, 128, 129, 132, 133, 144, 146, 148.
Campbell, Lily B., 154.
Cannon, Charles K., 143.
Capp, B. S., 122.
Cardinalus, Hugo, 136.
Carleton, Thomas, 119; *Theologiae Scholasticae,* 79–80, 83, 149, 152, 155.
Carter, John, *The Wheel turned by a voice from the throne of Glory,* 139.
Cartusianus, Dionysius, 136, 143; *Opera Omnia,* 135.
[Cartwright, Thomas,] *A Plaine Explanation Of The Whole Revelation Of Saint John,* 144.
Carus, Paul, 151.
Cary, Mary, *Little Horns Doom,* 147.
Case, Thomas, *Gods Rising, His Enemies Scattering,* 137.
Cecil, Lord David, 141.
Chalcocondalar, Laonicus, 42.
Chambers, A. B., 151.
Charles, R. H., 159.
Chateaubriand, François, 126.
Christmas, Henry, 128.
Chrysostom, "Homily XV On John 1:18," 128; "Homily IX On First Corinthians," 151.
Chytraeus, David, *Auslegung der Offenbarung Johannis,* 122.
Cirillo, Albert R., 135.
Clarke, Adam, 138.
Clarke, John, 40, 133, 138.
Clement of Alexandria, 130.
Clerke, Richard, 54; *Sermons,* 126, 142.
Clermont, Lord, 149.
Codrington, R., *The Prophecies of Christopher Kolterus,* 147.
Cole, Henry, 137.
Collado, Nicholaus, *Exposition On The Revelation,* 136.
C[ollier,] T[homas,] *The Glory of Christ,* 124.
Constantine, 69, 124.
Conti, Natale, *Mythologiae,* 151.
Coppin, Richard, *The Exaltation Of All things in Christ,* 153.
Cotten, John, *Exposition... Upon Revelation,* 147.
Coulange, Louis, 146.
Council of Trent, The, 102, 105, 155, 157.
Coverdale, Myles, *Remains of Myles Coverdale,* 132.
Cowper, William, 35, 36, 37, 42, 119; "Combate Of Christ With Satan," 154, 155, 156; "Heaven Opened," 102, 155, 157; "Pathmos: Or, A Commentary On The Revelation," 36, 38, 89, 113, 114, 126, 128, 131, 132, 134, 135, 136, 138, 139, 142, 143, 144, 146, 150, 155, 159, 161.
Crellius, John, 133; *De Vno Deo Patre,* 132.
Curry, Walter Clyde, 125, 156.

Daiches, David, 11, 127.
Daneau, Lambert, *Tractatus de Antichristo,* 123.
Darling, James, 126.
Davidson, Gustav, 134.
[Day, John,] *Day's Descant On Davids Psalmes,* 143.
Deacon, John, and Walker, John, *Dialogicall Discourses of Spirits and Divels,* 106, 143, 144, 155, 157; *A Svmmarie Answere,* 136.
[Defoe, Daniel,] 3, 4, 5, 53, 126, 133, 141.
De Lille, Jacques, 53, 141.
De Lubac, Henri, 137.
De Magny, Constantine, 53, 125, 126, 133, 141.
Dennis, John, *The Grounds Of Criticism In Poetry,* 126, 133.
Dent, Arthur, 119; *The Rvine Of Rome Or An Exposition vpon the whole Reuelation,* 51, 128, 139, 142, 144, 146, 161.
Dering, Edward, *XXVII. Lectvres, or readings, vpon . . . Hebrues,* 142.
Deuchler, Florens, 153.
Dickson, David, *Expositio Analytica Omnium Apostolicarvm Epistolarvm,* 154.
Didron, Adolphe Napoleon, 127, 150.
Diekhoff, John S., 125.
Diodati, John, *Pious Annotations Upon The Holy Bible,* 41, 128, 138, 142, 144, 146.
Dobson, W. S., 138.
Donne, John, *Sermons,* 142.
Downame, John, 104, *The Summe of Sacred Diuinitie,* 128, 142, 156.
Du Bartas, William, 26, 145.
Duhem, Pierre, 135.
Du Moulin, Peter, 104; *The Accomplishment Of The Prophecies,* 123, 153; *The Anatomy of Arminianisme,* 155, 156.
Duncan, Joseph E., 157.
Duriez, Georges, 135.
Düsterdieck, Friedrich, 137.
Dustoor, P. E., 142.
Earle, Robert, 138.
Edwards, Jonathan, 155.
Ellis, Henry, 150.
Elton, Edward, *An Exposition Of The Epistle Of St. Pavl To The Colossians,* 134.
Empson, William, 1, 125, 159.
[Episcopius, Simon,] *The Confession Or Declaration Of The . . . Remonstrants,* 68, 145.
Erasmus, Desiderius, 73, 76, 119; *The Paraphrase of Erasmus vpon the newe testament,* 75–76, 143, 148, 149.
Erskine, John, 141.
Eusden, John Dykstra, 154.
Eusebius, 54, 148.
Evans, E. P., 157, 160, 161.
Evans, Maurice J., 126.
Farrar, A. J. D., 147.
Feake, Christopher, *A Beam of Light,* 147.
[Fenner, Dudley,] *The Sacred Doctrine Of Divinitie,* 137.

Fetherstone, Christopher, 126.
Finch, Henry, *Worlds Great Restavration,* 123.
Fish, Stanley Eugene, 149, 159.
[Fisher, Edward,] *The Marrow Of Modern Divinity,* 161.
Fixler, Michael, 122, 124, 138, 142, 148.
Fleming, Ian, 151.
Fletcher, Phineas, *The Locusts, Or Appollyonists,* 151; *The Purple Island,* 151.
Fludd, Robert, *Mosaicall Philosophy,* 143.
Foord, John, *Apocalypsis Iesv Christi, Revelata Per Angelvm,* 139.
Forbes, Patrik, *An Exqvisite Commentarie Vpon The Revelation,* 134, 138, 142, 143, 144.
Fortesque, Sir John, *De Natura Legis Naturae,* 80, 149.
Foster, George, 69, 70; *The Sounding Of The Last Trumpet,* 124, 147.
Fowler, Alastair, 135.
Fowns, Richard, *Trisagion,* 123.
Fox, Robert C., 153.
Foxe, John, v, 60, 73, 119, 137; *Actes and Monuments,* 146; *Eicasmi Sev Meditationes, In Sacram Apocalypsin,* 37–38, 131, 134, 135, 137, 138, 139, 142, 143, 144, 148, 160.
[Franck, S.,] *The Forbidden Fruit. Or A Treatise Of the Tree of . . . Good & Evill,* 150.
Frères, Grenier, 126.
Froom, Edwin, 122, 136.
Frye, Roland Mushat, 146.
Fulke, William, 22, 119; *Praelections vpon the Sacred and holy Reuelation of S. Iohn,* 12, 22–23, 41, 128, 129, 131, 132, 135, 136, 138, 139, 141, 142, 143, 144, 146, 160, 161.
Fuller, Andrew, 138.
Gavigan, John J., 137.
Gesner, Solomon, *Commentationes In Psalmos Davidis,* 126, 134, 142.
Gibbens, Nicholas, *Qvestions And Dispvtations Concerning The Holy Scriptvre,* 146.
Gilbert, Allan H., 1, 11, 125, 126, 127.
Gilbie, Antony, 126.
Gillam, J. F., 151.
Gilpin, Richard, *Daemonologia Sacra,* 149.
Good, John Walter, 141.
Goodwin, Thomas, 49, 119, 124; "An Exposition Of The Revelation," 48-49, 123, 139, 142; "An Exposition Of The Epistle To The Ephesians," 12, 128; *The Great Interest Of States & Kingdomes,* 126.
Goujet, Abbé, 133.
Grantham, Thomas, *Christianismvs Primitivus,* 138.
G[reene,] J[ohn,] *The First Man, Or A Short Discourse Of Adams State,* 160.
Greene, William Chase, 146.
Greenhill, William, *An Exposition Of the five first Chapters Of The Prophet Ezekiel,* 136, 139.

Greenwood, Henry, *Tormenting Tophet: Or A terrible Description of Hel*, 145, 156.
Gregory, 143, 148.
Grierson, Herbert J. C., 125, 134.
Grosart, Alexander, 150.
Grotius, Hugo, 60; "Annotationes In Apocalypsin," 142, 143, 159.
Guest, Stephen Hadon, 146.
Guild, William, *The Sealed Book Opened*, 144.
Gunton, Andrew, 138.
Gyffard, George, 12, 73, 119, 128; *Sermons Vpon The Whole Booke Of The Revelation*, 12, 19–20, 32, 74, 75, 128, 131, 135, 138, 141, 142, 144, 146, 149, 151, 160, 161.
Hakewill, George, *An Apologie or Declaration Of The Power And Providence Of God in the Gouernment of the World*, 43.
Hall, Thomas, *An Exposition . . . On . . . Amos*, 45, 139.
Haller, William, 146, 148.
Hamilton, Gary D., 129.
Hammond, Henry, 42; *A Paraphrase And Annotations Upon all the Books of the New Testament*, 138, 142, 146, 161.
Hanford, James Holly, and Dunn, Waldo Hilary, 125, 136.
Harding, Davis P., 127, 160.
Hartlib, Samuel, 69, 70; *Clavis Apocalyptica*, 59, 144, 147.
Haymo, 135, 143, 144; "Expositionis In Apocalypsin B. Joannis," 138.
Hayne, T., 71; *Christs Kingdome On Earth, Opened according to the Scriptures*, 71, 145, 148; *The General View Of The Holy Scriptures*, 135, 158.
Henry, Matthew, 138.
Hesiod, 26, 45, 50; *Theogony*, 40, 151.
Hilary, 54.
Himes, John A., 138, 140.
Holland, Henry, 129.
Holland, Hezekiah, *An Exposition . . . Upon the Revelation of Saint John*, 136, 142.
Homer, 26, 27, 33, 45, 50; *Iliad*, 33, 40, 160.
Homes, Nathanael, *The New World Or The New Reformed Chvrch*, 132; *The Resurrection-Revealed*, 145.
"Homilee agaynst disobedience and wylfull rebellion, An," 37, 137.
Hooker, Edward Niles, 133.
Huet, Ephriam, *Prophecie Of Daniel*, 123.
Hugelet, Theodore Long, 143, 144.
Hughes, Merritt Y., 1, 125, 127, 138, 139, 148.
Hughes, Robert, 151.
Hunter, William B., Jr., 125, 129.
Hus, John, 143.
Hutchinson, F. E., 2, 125, 127.
Irenaeus, 143.
Ironside, Gilbert, *Seven Qvestions Of The Sabbath Briefly Dispvted*, 158.
Jackson, Arthur, *A Help For The Understanding Of the Holy Scripture*, 128.

Jackson, Thomas, *The Knowledg Of Christ Jesus*, 143; *A Treatise Of The Divine Essence*, 130, 156.
Jacobs, Henry E., 137.
James I, *Daemonologie*, 142.
Jenks, William, and Warne, Joseph A., 138.
[Jenner, Thomas,] *The Ages of Sin, or Sinnes Birth & groweth*, 151.
Jerome, 148.
Jewell, John, *An Exposition Vpon the two Epistles of the Apostle Saint Paul to the Thessalonians*, 134.
Joachim, 135.
John, Katherine, 133.
John of Damascus, *Exposition of the Orthodox Faith*, 134.
Johnson, Samuel, 139, 154.
Journal de Trévoux, 141.
Junius, Francis, v, 60, 73; *The Apocalyps, Or Revelation Of S. Iohn*, 131, 141, 144, 146, 149, 159; see Tremellius and Junius.
Kaufmann, U. Milo, 143.
Keightley, Thomas, 139.
Kelley, Maurice, 1, 2, 12, 21, 119, 125, 127, 129, 130, 132, 143, 154.
Kenrick, Edward F., 126.
Kiffen (?), William, *Glimpse Of Sions Glory*, 123.
Kivette, Ruth Montgomery, 127, 133, 141.
Knollys, Hanserd, *The World that Now is*, 147.
Kocher, Paul H., 148.
Korn, Dietrich, 122.
Kranidas, Thomas, 138, 155.
Lactantius, *Divine Institutes*, 135, 139.
La Primaudaye, Peter de, *The French Academie*, 156.
Lawrence, Henry, *Of Our Commvnion And Warre With Angels*, 145, 146.
L'Estrange, Hamon, *Gods Sabbath Before the Law and Under the Gospel*, 158.
Legionensis, Martin, "Expositio Libri Apocalypsis," 137.
Leigh, Edward, *A Treatise of Divinity*, 128; *A Treatise of the Divine Promises*, 129.
Le Journal Littéraire, 126, 133.
Leo, William, *A Sermon Preached At Lambeth*, 128.
Leslie, Charles, 3, 4, 7; *The History Of Sin and Heresie*, 3, 125, 134, 138.
Levine, Philip, 127, 149, 154.
Lewalski, Barbara Kiefer, 155.
Lewis, C. S., 53, 55, 141.
Lilly, William, *Monarchy Or No Monarchy*, 147.
L[odge,] T., *A Learned Summary Upon the famous Poeme of William of Saluste Lord of Bartas*, 145.
Love, Christopher, *Hell's Terror*, 81, 145, 146, 149; *Heavens-Glory*, 147.
Löwith, Karl, 135.
Lubac, Henri de, 137.
Lünemann, Göttlieb, 126.

L[upton], T., *Babylon is Fallen*, 123.

Luther, Martin, 143, 144; *Luther Still Speaking...A Commentary on the first five chapters of the Book of Genesis*, 137.

Lycosthenes, *Prodigiorum Ac Ostentorum Chronicon*, 147.

Lye, Thomas, *The King of Terrors*, 146.

Lyra, Nicholas de, 106, 135.

McClennen, Joshua, 143.

McColley, Grant, 2,125, 129, 134, 136, 137, 145.

McLachlan, H., 126.

Madsen, William G., 125, 143.

Man, John, 142.

Manton, Thomas, 38; *A Practical Commentary...On the Epistle of Jude*, 38, 137, 142, 145.

Marbeck, John, *A Booke Of Notes and Common places*, 83, 143, 150.

Marlorat, Augustin, 73, 119; *A Catholike and Ecclesiasticall exposition of the holy Gospell after S. Iohn*, 82–83, 150; *A Catholike And Ecclesiasticall exposition of the holy Gospell after S. Mathewe*, 160; *A Catholike exposition vpon the Reuelation of Sainct Iohn*, 62, 87, 131, 132, 135, 136, 139, 143, 144, 148, 150, 161.

Marshall, Stephen, *The Song of Moses The Servant Of God, And the Song Of The Lambe*, 136.

Martyr, Justin, *Apology*, 152.

Massey, William, 148.

Mather, Increase, *The Mystery Of Israel's Salvation*, 147.

Mayer, John, 35, 36, 37, 101, 119; *A Commentarie Vpon The New Testament*, 145; *Ecclesiastica Interpretatio*, 12, 36, 93, 128, 131, 134, 136, 137, 139, 141, 142, 144, 145, 146, 153, 154, 159, 160, 161.

Mede, Joseph, 42, 43, 124; *The Apostasy Of The Latter Times*, 139; "Discourse 40," 150; *The Key of the Revelation*, 123, 134, 135, 138, 142; *Works*, 139, 145, 146.

Melanchthon, Phillip, *Loci Commvnes Theologici*, 141.

Michelangelo, "Temptation and Expulsion," 152.

Migne, J. P., 126.

Miller, John C., 128, 139.

Milton, John, *Animadversions Upon The Remonstrants Defence*, 70, 144; *The Christian Doctrine*, 1, 2, 3, 4, 5–10, 16, 20, 30, 40, 41, 50, 65, 70, 71, 96, 125, 127–130, 132, 133, 144, 145, 148, 156, 159; *Considerations Touching The likeliest means to remove Hirelings out of the church*, 149; *The Doctrine And Discipline Of Divorce*, 156; *Eikonoklastes*, 144; *Of Education*, 59; *Of Reformation...In England*, 144, 149; *Of True Religion, Haeresie, Schism, Toleration*, 119; *The Reason Of Church-governement Urg'd against Prelaty*, 63, 136, 144; *Samson Agonistes*, 136; *Tet-*

rachordon, 144; *A Treatise Of Civil power In Ecclesiastical causes*, 149.

Molina, Luis de, 104.

Montanus, 94.

More, Henry, 69, 70; *Synopsis Prophetica*, 147.

More, Richard, 134.

Morland, Samuel, *The Urim of Conscience*, 133.

Mosse, Miles, *Ivstifying And Saving Faith Distingvished from the faith of the Deuils*, 136.

Muir, Kenneth, 1, 125, 141.

Murphey, Arthur, 139, 154.

Murry, John Middleton, 141.

Musculus, Wolfgang, *Common places of Christian Religion*, 142.

Napier, John, 69, 70, 73, 124; *A Plaine Discouery of the whole Reuelation of Saint Iohn*, 123, 142, 143, 145, 146, 147, 148, 159.

Neale, J. M., and Littledale, R.F., 127, 150.

Nemsius, *The Nature Of Man*, 129.

Newton, Thomas, 35, 138, 156.

Nicolai, Philipp, *Chronologia Sacra*, 123.

Nicols, James, 155.

Nicolson, Marjorie, 149, 160.

Noble, John, 119; *The Conception And Birth of Sin*, 102–103, 115, 155, 158, 159.

Norton, Thomas, 128.

Oisander, Andreas, *Coniectures of the ende*, 122.

Origen, 36, 102, 126, 148; "De Principiis," 150.

[Overton, Richard,] *Man wholly Mortel*, 145.

Ovid, 45, 50; *Metamorphoses*, 40, 151.

Owen, John, *A Display Of Arminianisme*, 102, 155.

Pannonius, Coeljus, 135.

Pareus, David, v, 22, 35, 36, 37, 42–44, 60, 61, 71, 119, 136, 147; *A Commentary Upon The Divine Revelation Of The Apostle And Evangelist Iohn*, 23, 36, 37, 41, 71, 73, 88, 94, 131, 132, 134, 135, 136, 137, 138, 142, 144, 145, 146, 148, 150, 153, 159, 160, 161.

Paterson, James, 160.

Patrick, John M., 154.

Patrick, Symon, "Two Sermons On Michaelmas Day, 1672," 134.

Patrides, C. A., 130, 133, 145, 146, 147, 159, 161.

Patterson, Frank Allen, 119, 141, 148.

Pattison, Mark, 134.

Pearson, George, 132.

Pearson, John, *Annotata ad Actus Apostolicos, Epistolas & Apocalypsin*, 135, 138, 143, 144.

Peers, E. Allison, 133.

Pemble, William, 101; "A Short and Sweete Exposition Vpon The First Nine Chapters of Zecharie," 141; "Vindiciae Fidei," 154.

Perkins, William, "An Exposition Vpon The Epistle Of Jude," 146; *A Golden Chaine, Or The Description of Theologie*, 156.

Peter, John, 125, 134, 159.
Peterius, 135.
Peyton, Thomas, *The Glasse Of Time*, 151.
Phillips, Thomas, *The Booke of Lamentations*, 145, 146.
Philo, 71, 126.
Piscator, John, "Apocalypseos Johannis," 128, 131, 142, 154; *Commentarii In Omnes Libros Veteris Testamenti*, 126, 142.
Plato, *Statesman*, 135.
Polanus, Amandus, 15, 16, 128; *The Svbstanec* [sic] *Of Christian Religion*, 15, 129, 142.
Pollok, Robert, 134.
Pont, Robert, *A New Treatise*, 123.
Pope, Alexander, 12.
Powys, John Cowper, 141.
Preston, John, *Life Eternall Or, A Treatise Of the knowledge of the Divine Essence*, 141.
Primasius, 126, 135, 136, 144.
Pseudo-Augustine, "Expositio In Apocalypsim B. Joannis," 31, 135.
Racine, Louis, 24, 133.
Raleigh, Walter, 141.
Rajan, B., 1, 12, 125, 127, 134, 141.
Ramsay, Paul, 155.
Rebells Catechisme, The, 137.
Redwin, Maximillian, 149.
Reesing, John, 157.
Reynolds, Edward, 101; *An Explication Of The Hvndredth And Tenth Psalme*, 129, 142; *A Treatise Of The Passions And Faculties Of the Soule of Man*, 154.
Reynor, William, *Babylons Ruining-Earthquake*, 123.
Ribera, Francisco, 23, 135; *In sacram beati Ioannis Apostoli & Euangelistae Apocalypsin Commentarij*, 23, 132, 159.
Richard, 143.
Ringwalt, Bartholomäus, *Lauter Warheit*, 123.
Rissi, Mathias, 150.
Rivers, J. A., *Devovt Rhapsodies*, 151.
Rivetus, Andraeus, 107, 119; *Opervm Theologicorvm*, 107, 157.
Roberts, Alexander, 150.
Robertson, A. T., 137.
Robinson, Richard, 126.
Rogers, John, 69, 70; *Sagir, Or Doomes-day*, 147.
Rollock, Robert, *A Treatise Of Gods Effectval Calling*, 129, 157.
Rosedale, H. G., 141.
Ross, Alexander, 128; *The New Planet No Planet*, 145.
Ross, Malcolm Mackenzie, 141.
Routh, Bernard, 53, 141.
Rowley, H. H., 122.
Rupert, 143, 144.
Salkeld, John, 104; *A Treatise of Angels*, 128, 142; *A Treatise Of Paradise*, 156, 158.
Sanchez, Gasper, *Sacarum literarum Interpretis In Ezechielem & Danielem*, 141.

Saurat, Denis, 2, 39, 125, 127, 134, 138, 141, 154, 160.
Scherpbier, Herman, 126.
Schmidt, Gerhard, 152.
Schultz, Howard, 141, 142.
Scolari, Filippo, 126.
Scot, Reginald, *The Discovery of Witchcraft*, 128.
Sensabaugh, George, 141.
Sewall, Arthur, 125.
Shawe, John, *A Broken Heart*, 123.
Sibbes, Richard, *Beames of Divine Light*, 149; "The Gloriovs Feast of the Gospel," 89, 150.
Simpson, Evelyn M., and Potter, George R., 142.
Sims, James H., iv, 127.
Smith, Richard, 68; *A Conference of the Catholike and Protestante Doctrine*, 145.
Spencer, Theodore, 151.
Spenser, Edmund, 26, 43, 50; *Faerie Queene*, 39, 151.
Stapleton, Laurence, 127.
Steadman, John M., 139, 148, 150, 153, 156, 160.
Stifler, William H., 134.
Stokes, Margaret, 127.
Strachan, James, 140, 153.
Strigelius, D. Victorinus, *Part Of The Harmony Of King Davids Harp*, 126.
Suárez, Francisco, 119; *Opera Omnia*, 15–16, 128, 129.
Summers, Joseph H., 144.
Svendson, Kester, 127, 157.
Swan, John, *Speculum Mundi*, 147, 158.
Swete, Henry Barclay, 144.
Swinden, Tobias, *An Enquiry Into The Nature and Place Of Hell*, 146.
Sydenham, Humphrey, *Sermons vpon Solemne Occasions*, 150, 153, 156.
Symonds, William, *Pisgah Evangelica*, 159, 161.
Sypher, Wylie, 141.
Tarnov, Paul, *S. Johannis Evangelium Commentarius*, 126, 129.
Tasso, Torquato, 26.
Taylor, Alexander, 134.
Taylor, Jeremy, *A Course of Sermons*, 57, 142, 143, 160.
Taylor, Thomas, *Christs Victorie Over The Dragon*, 38, 46, 134, 135, 136, 138, 139, 142, 143, 144, 146.
Telleen, John Martin, 133, 141.
Temple, Thomas, *Christs Government In and over his People*, 160.
Tertullian, Quintus, 130, 148; "Apologeticus Adversus Gentes Pro Christianis," 136; *On the Resurrection of the Flesh*, 160.
Theophilus, 130.
"Theophilus," 27, 53, 126, 141.
Thorndyke, Lynn, 135.
Thorpe, James, 53, 141.
Tillinghast, J., *Generation-Worke*, 147.

Tillyard, E. M. W., 141, 149, 154, 160.
Todd, H. J., 35, 151, 159.
Tomson, L., 144.
Tong, William, 138.
Toon, Peter, 122, 124.
Trapp, John, 42; *A Commentary or Exposition upon all the books of the New Testament*, 132, 138, 146.
Tremellius, Immanuel, v, 54, 60, 73; *Iesv Christi Domini Nostri Novvm Testamentvm*, 148.
——, and Junius, Francis, 128; *Testamenti Veteris Biblia Sacra*, 126, 139, 142, 149.
Tuitiensis, Rupert, *Commentariorvm In Apocalypsin, Libri XII*, 137.
Turmel, Joseph, 128, 139.
Turnbull, Richard, 104; *An Exposition Vpon the Canonicall Epistle Of Saint Iames*, 156.
Tuveson, Ernest Lee, 124, 138.
Tyconius, 135; "Book of Rules," 136.
Tymme, Thomas, 38, 160; *A Silver Watch-Bell*, 137, 144, 145.
[Tyndale, William,] 119; *The Obedience of a Christen man*, 56, 143.
Valvasone, Erasmo di, 40, 50; *L'Angeleida*, 39.
Van Doren, Mark, 125.
Vatablus, Francis, *Liber Psalmorvm Davidis*, 126.
Verity, A. W., 35.
Vermilius, D. Peter Martir, ... *Commentaries of ... vpon the Epistle of S. Paul*, 154.
Vicars, John, *Decapla in Psalmos*, 90, 149, 153.
Victore, Richard a Saint, "In Apocalypsim Joannis Libri Septem," 137.
Victorinus, 114; "Commentary on the Apocalypse of the Blessed John," 136.
Viegas, Blasius, 135, 136.
Vigenère, Blaise de, *Les Images Ov Tableavx De Platte Peinture Des Devx Philostrates*, 152.
Virgil, 26, 27, 33; *Aeneid*, 33, 151, 160.
Voltaire, 133, 159.
Vorstius, Conrad, "Commentarivs ... In Ephesios," 129.
Waldock, A. J. A., 134, 141, 154.
Walker, D. P., 148, 149, 150.

Walker, George, *The Doctrine Of the Sabbath*, 158.
Warner, Rex, 127.
Webb, Richard, *Christs Kingdome*, 126, 134.
Webster, W., 132.
Werblowsky, R. J. Zwi, 134.
Werdmueller, Otto, *The Hope of the Faythfull*, 132.
Werner, Karl, 129.
Wescott, Brooke Foss, 126.
West, Robert H., 133, 134, 139, 141, 159.
Whitaker, Jeremiah, *The Danger of Greatnesse*, 142.
Whitaker, William, *A Disputation on Holy Scripture*, 57, 143; *Disputatio de Sacra Scriptura*, 143.
White, Charles, 126.
Whiting, George Wesley, 137, 139.
Wiesen, David S., 150.
[Wilcox, Thomas,] *A very godly and learned Exposition, vpon the whole Booke of Psalmes*, 126, 142.
Wilkes, G. A., 161.
Willet, Andrew, *Hexapla In Danielem*, 134; *Hexapla in Genesin*, 158.
Willey, Basil, 108, 157.
Williams, Arnold, 125, 128, 158.
Wilson, Thomas, *A Christian Dictionary*, 51, 132, 141, 143, 144, 145, 151.
Wing, Donald, 126.
Winsor, Gordon C., 150.
Wither, George, 129.
Wolfson, Harry Austryn, 130.
Wollebius, John, v, 15, 16, 101; *The Abridgment Of Christian Divinity*, 14, 101, 102, 128, 143, 145, 154, 155; *Compendium Theologiae Christianae*, 128.
Woodhouse, A. S. P., and Bush, Douglas, 148.
Woodhull, Marianna, 149.
Wright, B. A., 156.
Wright, Thomas, *The Passions of the Minde*, 156.
Wycliffe, John, 143.
Zanchius, Hieronymus, v, 13, 60, 119, 128; *De Operibvs Dei Intra Spacivm Sex Diervm Creatis*, 108, 128, 142, 145, 146, 158, 159.
Zegerus, Nicholas, "Annotationes in Novum Testamentum," 135, 138, 143, 144.

Index of Citations from *Paradise Lost*

I,	36	, 13
	61–68	, 67, 148
	63	, 83
	65–66	, 75
	95	, 90
	107–108	, 82
	111–114	, 79
	116–117	, 88
	143	, 90
	169	, 90
	209–220	, 95

I,	215	, 76
	228–237	, 63
	252–255	, 72
	301–303	, 76
	338–346	, 77, 78
	347–348	, 44, 78
	351–355	, 78
	361–375	, 139
	381–391	, 78
	446–457	, 78
	500–502	, 78

I,   645–647   , 79
      645–649   , 115
      651–656   , 82
      657–658   , 79
      710–730   , 78
      796   , 77

II,   1–4   , 77
      14   , 79
      18–19   , 79
      41–42   , 78
      352–353   , 82
      362–370   , 114
      378–380   , 79
      390–391   , 78
      390–400   , 64
      402–404   , 78
      402–407   , 84
      417–423   , 84
      466–467   , 79
      475–479   , 83
      512   , 63
      514–520   , 159
      557–561   , 53
      648–659   , 86
      666–673   , 86
      744–745   , 90
      747–758   , 98
      747–767   , 92
      749–767   , 92
      845–848   , 90
      890–1009   , 156
      989   , 156
      1024–1030 , 93
      1025   , 94
      1051   , 95

III, 97–117   , 99
      98–111   , 130
      131–132   , 82, 160
      168–175   , 10
      169   , 24
      173–197   , 115
      213–221   , 84
      213–415   , 20
      227–322   , 10
      227–343   , 3
      239   , 24
      241–253   , 10
      250–257   , 75
      279   , 24
      305–308   , 11
      313–316   , 10
      315–317   , 11
      317   , 113
      325–326   , 112
      332–338   , 112
      344–391   , 21
      352   , 21
      390–391   , 130
      474–496   , 78
      510–515   , 95
      588–742   , 161
      636   , 140

IV,   1–10   , 96
      1–12   , 111
      18–23   , 72
      18–26   , 91
      73–79   , 91
      79–80   , 75
      86–92   , 83
      131–408   , 161
      788–819   , 64
      799–809   , 105, 157
      799–856   , 161
      845   , 140
      888–899   , 81
      977–1015   , 64
      990–1004   , 111
      990–1015   , 161
      999–1001   , 115
      1013–1015 , 111, 115

V,   30–93   , 105
      30–121   , 105
      100–113   , 105
      116–119   , 105
      117–119   , 107
      270–277   , 159
      574–575   , 135
      575–576   , 31
      577–583   , 19
      577–615   , 18
      577–627   , 21
      577–802   , 4
      586–599   , 77
      587   , 19
      588   , 19
      596   , 19, 21
      597   , 19, 24
      598   , 19
      600–615   , 10, 29, 78
      603   , 19
      603–605   , 11
      603–608   , 1, 2, 4, 5,
                   6, 21, 133
      605–615   , 19
      606   , 19, 20, 24
      607–608   , 12
      611–615   , 12, 82
      617   , 92, 98
      617–672   , 92
      657–696   , 98
      658–665   , 97
      665   , 13
      679–682   , 19
      718   , 81
      735–737   , 81
      755–766   , 83
      772–777   , 13
      772–871   , 92
      792–793   , 14
      814–818   , 28
      835–841   , 130
      836–837   , 97
      853–861   , 14
      864–866   , 41

VI, 19–21   , 28
     44–55   , 111
     52–53   , 113
     74   , 34
     131   , 13
     156   , 36
     195–197   , 34
     203   , 35, 36
     207–214   , 26
     207–217   , 35
     244–245   , 35
     301–306   , 33
     313–314   , 34
     316–327   , 33
     324   , 36
     327   , 34
     332–333   , 33
     344–347   , 34
     418–422   , 14
     418–445   , 40
     422   , 40
     490–491   , 41
     509–515   , 44
     512   , 42
     589   , 44
     589–594   , 39
     591   , 44
     634–669   , 44
     647–649   , 39
     660–670   , 30
     662–671   , 39
     668–669   , 45
     679   , 52
     680–718   , 112
     684–687   , 46
     689–694   , 41
     699–703   , 46, 52
     742   , 46
     747   , 24
     748–759   , 47
     748–892   , 29
     750   , 51
     757   , 51
     757–759   , 132
     801   , 46
     808–812   , 81
     824–852   , 47
     830   , 51
     838–877   , 139
     849   , 51
     853–866   , 112
     856–868   , 48
     874–875   , 48

VI,   893   , 50
      900–912   , 108

VII, 172–173   , 14, 130
      192–588   , 52

VIII, 491–421   , 14, 130

IX,   58   , 64
      63–64   , 64
      180   , 64
      655–732   , 64
      780–835   , 64
      792   , 65
      856–885   , 64
      954   , 65
      1000–1004 , 64
      1122–1131 , 64

X,   264–281   , 90
      301–305   , 94
      312–313   , 78
      323   , 94
      403–406   , 88
      403–409   , 73
      455–459   , 44
      504–521   , 115
      585–588   , 156
      586   , 156
      588–590   , 65
      635–636   , 95
      990–991   , 90

XI,   1–44   , 10
      14–21   , 116
      14–44   , 111, 115
      25–30   , 158
      67   , 77
      88–89   , 158
      477–493   , 65
      555–627   , 65
      637–711   , 65

XII, 386–410   , 75
      386–455   , 10
      427   , 127
      430–431   , 112
      451–455   , 112
      451–463   , 70
      451–465   , 10
      452–458   , 75
      458–465   , 112
      585–587   , 158